PAUL DLUG

Scott, Foresman and Company
Glenview, Illinois London

Printed in the United States of America.

List of Trademarks

DataEase is a registered trademark of DataEase International, Inc.
IBM is a registered trademark of International Business Machines Corporation.
1-2-3 and Lotus are registered trademarks of Lotus Development Corporation.
DIF is a registered trademark of Software Arts, Inc.
dBase II and dBase III are registered trademarks of Ashton-Tate Inc.
Mailmerge is a registered trademark of Micro-Pro International Corporation.
Multimate is a registered trademark of Multimate Corporation.

Library of Congress Cataloging-in-Publication Data

Dlug, Paul
Understanding DataEase with business applications.

Includes index.
1. Data Ease (Computer program) 2. Business—
Data processing. I. Title.
HF5548.4.D18D58 1988 650'.028'557565 88-4641
ISBN 0-673-18836-1

3 4 5 6 KPF 93 92 91 90 89

Notice of Liability

The information in this book is distributed on an "As Is" basis, without warranty. Neither the author nor Scott, Foresman and Company shall have any liability to customer or any other person or entity with respect to any liability, loss, or damage caused or alleged to be caused directly or indirectly by the programs contained herein. This includes, but is not limited to, interruption of service, loss of data, loss of business or anticipatory profits, or consequential damages from the use of the programs.

Scott, Foresman Professional Publishing Group books are available for bulk sales at quantity discounts. For information, please contact the Marketing Manager, Professional Books, Professional Publishing Group, Scott, Foresman and Company, 1900 East Lake Avenue, Glenview, IL 60025.

To my wife, Rita
and our children: Paul, Laura, and Debra

PREFACE

DataEase is a relational database, produced by DataEase International, Inc., that is easy to use and possesses some extremely powerful features.

This book will enable anyone to use DataEase, even those without a programming background. In order to utilize DataEase's features, you must have a clear grasp of DataEase and its practical applications. DataEase has its own "English-oriented" query language, which is capable of producing both short, or "quick," reports and more detailed full reports. You can create these reports by using the menus in this book.

DataEase can import data from and export data to several popular programs, including dBase II, dBase III, Lotus 1-2-3, Multimate, and others. A user can create customized reports, data-entry, and menus.

This book is a supplement to the reference book and the tutorial manual with disk in the DataEase software package. It is a hands-on tutorial that covers Version 2.5, Release 2 of DataEase. This book is useful to both the novice and intermediate user who would like additional exercises with step-by-step instruction. It introduces these exercises by using a simulated computer store with all its data and reports. All the important features of DataEase are discussed and illustrated through the use of examples related to this simulated computer store.

It is important that you follow the chapters in sequence. Each chapter usually builds on the previous chapter. For example, the first seven chapters explain how to create and enter data into files and also how to generate and print reports from information contained in one or more files. Chapter 5 discusses how to create mailing labels and form letters. Chapter 8 explains how to use DataEase's procedural language to generate and print reports. Chapter 9 discusses how to create customized menus. Chapter 10 discusses database maintenance, while Chapter 11 shows how data can be exported from and imported into DataEase. Chapter 12 demonstrates how to create and access a template, while Chapter 13 discusses other software products that can be used with DataEase.

Since this book is oriented toward the novice or intermediate user, it is not capable of covering every command or application that DataEase possesses. For more advanced users, the reference manual presents all the commands of DataEase. Also, many user groups, such as the New York DataEase Users Group, can answer specific questions. They often have guest lecturers who present and discuss more specific topics.

TABLE OF CONTENTS

INTRODUCTION

In this chapter you will learn what a database is, what DataEase is, and what hardware you need to run DataEase. You will also learn how to install and run DataEase, name a database, install passwords, and select security levels for different users.

WHAT IS A DATABASE?

A database is a collection of data, or information, that is organized and maintained in a logical way. A simple mailing list, personal phone directory, stamp or coin collection, or book inventory are examples of databases.

After a database is created, you may add data to it, retrieve information, change information, sort the information, and print the information out as meaningful reports. A database management system (DBMS) is a software package, such as DataEase, that performs the above operations. DataEase, by DataEase International, Inc., is a user-friendly, flexible, software package that is perfect for complex business applications. For example, it can help businesses keep track of customers, vendors, suppliers, and employee records.

You can use DataEase even if you have little or no computer experience. Unlike most database packages, it requires no programming and uses a simple query language, similar to English, to produce complex reports.

HARDWARE REQUIREMENTS

DataEase can run on a 16-bit microcomputer, such as the IBM PC, IBM PC/XT, or a highly compatible microcomputer that runs PC-DOS/MS-DOS version 2.0 or higher. It needs at least 384 kilobytes RAM, two double-sided disk drives, an 80-character display, and a printer. A hard disk and 640K are recommended.

INSTALLING DATAEASE

DataEase can be installed on either a floppy disk system or a hard disk system. The installation for each is described below.

Floppy Disk System

Insert your copy of DOS (Disk Operating System) 2.0 or higher in drive A and close the door. Turn the machine on. If the power is already on, reset the system for the IBM PC/XT by holding the CTRL and ALT keys, then pressing the DEL key. DOS is now loaded. Enter the data and time when you're prompted. If you press the RETURN key twice, the date and time will be bypassed. However, when you operate DataEase, it's a good idea to enter the correct date and time. DataEase uses this information to insert the system date into letters, invoices, and other reports you create.

The system will now respond with the DOS prompt:

```
A>
```

DataEase comes on two disks: the System and Utilities disk. Since DataEase disks are not copy protected, you should always make working copies using your DOS copy or diskcopy commands. Then label the originals and store them in a safe place. Label the copies "DataEase System Working Disk" and "DataEase Utilities Working Disk." Format another disk and label it "Data Disk." All your databases and report formats will be saved on the Data disk.

If you want to place the DOS start-up files on your DataEase System disk, use the DOS command "Format B:/S" to format a blank disk with DOS start-up files on it. Remove the DOS disk from drive A and replace it with the DataEase System disk. At the A> prompt, type:

```
Copy a:*.* B:
```

Press the RETURN key. As each file is being copied, its name will appear on the screen. If you see the message

```
Insufficient disk space
```

copy the file DEMAINTC.OVL from the System disk to the Utilities working disk. This will have no effect on your use of DataEase.

Place your copy of the DataEase System disk in drive A and formatted Data disk in drive B. To start DataEase, type:

```
DEASE
```

then press the RETURN key. It does not matter if you type in upper or lower case.

On a floppy disk system, DataEase will prompt you when to insert the Utilities disk.

Hard Disk System

Follow the previous instructions for installing DataEase on a floppy disk system. Again, it is best to enter the date and time, but if you press the RETURN key twice, the two entries will be bypassed. The system will respond with the DOS prompt:

```
C>
```

To make a directory for DataEase on your hard disk, at the C> prompt, type:

```
mkdir c:\DEASE
```

and press the RETURN key.

Type at the C> prompt:

```
DEASE
```

then press the RETURN key.

Place your DataEase System disk in the floppy disk drive A. Type:

```
COPY A:*.* C:
```

and press the RETURN key.

The copy process is completed when the C> prompt is on the screen. Remove the DataEase System disk from the floppy disk drive A. Place the DataEase Utilities disk in the floppy disk drive A. To copy it to the hard disk, type:

```
COPY A:*.* C:
```

and press the RETURN key. To start DataEase, type:

```
cd\DEASE
```

then press the RETURN key. It does not matter if you type in upper or lower case.

```
DATAEASE 2.5 Release 2
Copyright Software Solutions Inc, USA. 1986
                                          Serial Number

          D A T A E A S E  - S I G N   O N

        Data base Name ( A to Z ) :

Alt-F1HELP F4EXIT DATABASE   PROG.A: DATA B: DATE        TIME
```

FIGURE 1.1

SIGN-ON SCREEN

When you type DEASE, the SIGN-ON screen appears as shown in Figure 1.1

At the top left of the screen is the version and release number of DataEase. At the top right is the serial number of your particular program. At the bottom of the screen, DataEase lists the keys you may press to proceed. You will notice that at the bottom left of the screen it instructs you to depress the ALT and F1 keys simultaneously if you need help. You can depress these two keys anytime you're using DataEase if you are not sure of what to do or need an explanation of a command. If you press the ALT and F1 keys at this time, the screen will look like Figure 1.2. A window at the bottom of the screen lists the page numbers in the reference manual where you can look up more information. It also gives you some help statements. If you need more help, press the F1 key. DataEase tells you to press the SHIFT and F1 keys simultaneously for auto help. In the auto help mode, the help screens will automatically appear every time you go to a new screen. This feature is very useful when you are beginning to learn DataEase. If the help statements

```
DATAEASE 2.5 Release 2
Copyright Software Solutions Inc, USA. 1986

          D A T A E A S E  - S I G N  O N

         Data Base Name ( A to Z ) :

                                              Page 2-3
          Type the Data Base Name (A through Z) and Press Return.
          Alt-F1 Exit — F1 More Help — Sh-F1 On  Auto Help
Alt-F1HELP F4EXIT DATABASE    PROG.A: DATA B: DATE          TIME
```

FIGURE1.2

in the window are not clear, you can refer to the page numbers in the reference manual that are indicated at the top of the window. If you want to turn on the auto help screens, press the SHIFT F1 AUTO HELP keys. To exit the regular help screen, press the ALT F1 EXIT keys.

DataEase asks you to name your database with the message:

```
Data Base Name (A to Z):
```

As you can see, DataEase allows you to create up to 26 different databases—one for each letter of the alphabet. Each database is separate from the others and is used for a different application. Each can consist of many different files. Beginning in the next chapter, you will develop a database that simulates a computer store and has four files: **EMPLOYEE**, **CUSTOMER**, **ORDERS**, and **PRODUCTS**. These are four different files, in one database, that are related to each other. Separate databases are used for completely different applications. You cannot relate data from separate databases, but you can relate data from different files in one database. In the above example, the data from the four files you will create will be related by a certain piece of data.

The name of a database can be any single letter from A through Z. There is no distinction made between upper and lower case. Thus, you can create 26 separate databases in one subdirectory or on one disk. To create a database, type:

```
A
```

and press the RETURN key. The screen will inform you that a database does not exist on drive B (the drive with your Data disk in it) by printing the following message (the drive name may be different for a hard disk system):

```
Data Base does not exist on drive B:

Create a new data base (y/n) ?:
```

Since your new database, named "A," is created, type:

```
Y
```

The system will now ask for your name. Type your name (up to 15 characters) and press the RETURN key. The screen will now look like Figure 1.3.

The system now asks for your password, which can be up to 8 characters long. Type your password and press the RETURN key. **Do not forget the password and name you have typed into the computer.** If you do not want a password, press the RETURN key without entering a password. A new database will be created. After the database is created, the Main Menu appears.

If a database with the same name already exists, the computer will ask for your name and password. If the computer does not recognize your name and password after three attempts to enter them, it will exit to DOS. All names and passwords are checked against a User file for that particular database. It is imperative that you remember the name and password you have entered.

```
DATAEASE 2.5 Release 2
Copyright Software Solutions Inc, USA. 1986
                                                  Serial Number

            D A T A E A S E  - S I G N  O N

        Data base Name ( A to Z ) : A
        Data Base does not exist on drive B:
        Create a new data base (y/n) ?:  Y
        New data base will be created on drive B:

        What is your name              :  Paul

        What is your security password:

Alt-F1HELP F4EXIT DATABASE   PROG.A: DATA B: DATE          TIME
```

FIGURE 1.3

DATAEASE MAIN MENU

After you have signed on to the system, the Main Menu appears. Each menu selection in the Main Menu will lead you to other menus. See Figure 1.4.

SYSTEM ADMINISTRATION

Since you are creating a database, you will be the one who has the highest security in admitting users to the database, changing and updating files, etc. No one can access a database unless you authorize them to do so by giving them a name and password. To do this you must enter System Administration, the 7th item in the menu. Type:

7

for System Administration. The System Administration Menu now appears as shown in Figure 1.5. You can now tell DataEase which users have access to the database, how your computer is configured, what printer you are using, and how to customize the colors or shading of the screen.

```
DATAEASE

          D A T A E A S E - M A I N   M E N U

          1. Form Definition and Changes

          2. Record Entry and Quick Reports

          3. Full Reports

          4. Data Base Maintenance

          5. Data Base Utilities

          6. Menus and Relationships

          7. System Administration

   1 to 7 — UP — DOWN — RETURN — END

      F4 EXIT    DATABASE A PROG.A: DATA B: DATE        TIME
```

FIGURE 1.4

```
DATAEASE

          S Y S T E M   A D M I N I S T R A T I O N

          1. Define Users

          2. Define Configuration

          3. Define Printers

          4. Define Screen Styles

   1 to 4 — UP — DOWN — RETURN — END

      F4 EXIT    DATABASE A PROG.A: DATA B: DATE        TIME
```

FIGURE 1.5

Defining Users

As mentioned above, you are the person who will create the database and keep a list of all users who may access that database. In this part of the System Administration Menu, users are added and maintained through the user form. Type:

```
1
```

to access the user form. If you are using a dual floppy disk system, DataEase prompts you to insert the Utilities disk in drive A as shown in Figure 1.6. DataEase will always prompt you whenever you need to insert or change disks.

The user form now appears. See Figure 1.7.

Press F3 to view your own sign-on screen. Every field except the name field may be left blank. You can choose a name as short as one character or as long as fifteen characters. You can make the password, which is optional, up to eight characters long. Type in a name and password. **Do not forget the name and password you have entered.**

Security Levels

The security number determines what information the user can access. As shown in the top of Figure 1.7, there are seven security levels divided into three groups. There are three low security levels. A user with one of these three security levels can look at records, run reports, and do database backup functions.

The next three levels are medium security levels, which enable a user to enter, change, or delete records, use the Data Import Facility, and perform the low security functions listed above.

The remaining level is the high security level, which enables the user to define or change forms or reports, perform system administration functions, use maintenance and utilities functions, define menus and relationships, and perform the low and medium security functions listed above. You, as the creator of the database, automatically possess a high security level.

You can restrict the user from certain fields by using field level security. For example, you might want to put a security level on a field called Salary so that only certain people would be allowed to view or change it.

```
DATAEASE
Insert Utilities disk in drive A and hit any key

              S Y S T E M   A D M I N I S T R A T I O N

              1. Define Users

              2. Define Configuration

              3. Define Printers

              4. Define Screen Styles

         ---- 1 to 4 — UP — DOWN — RETURN — END ----

    F4 EXIT     DATABASE A PROG.A: DATA B: DATE        TIME
```

FIGURE 1.6

```
users
1: high 2: medium1 3: Medium2 4: Medium3 5: Low1 6: Low2 7: Low3

                         USER INFORMATION
                         ----------------

          Name          : Rita

          Password      : Kaye

          Level         :

          Screen Style  :
                           Leave blank for system provided default styles.

          Start-up Menu :
                           Leave blank to use system provided menus.

          Help Level    :
                           Leave blank to provide help on demand.


F2ENTER F3VIEW F4EXIT F5FORM CLR F6FLD CLR F7DELETE F8MODIFY F9REPORT F10MULTI
```

FIGURE 1.7

To select a security level, press the number that corresponds to the security level you want. As shown in the top of Figure 1.7, if you press 1 you will get a high security level. If you press 7, you will obtain a low security level.

Help Level

If this field is left blank, help will be provided only on demand (when the user presses ALT-F1 HELP). If you enter

```
Automatically
```

into the field, it allows the user to receive all help messages automatically without pressing the ALT-F1 HELP keys.

Saving the Changes

For each new user, fill in the form and press the F2 ENTER key.

To view an existing user, type the user name in the blank form and press the F3 VIEW key. To change the characteristics, type the changes and press the F8 MODIFY key. To delete a user record, press the F7 DELETE key after you obtain that particular record.

Define Configuration

By default the standard configuration supplied with the system, as shown in Figure 1.8, is:

- Monochrome card with the monochrome monitor, or color card with the color monitor
- Program Drive A and Data Drive B
- EPSON MX-80 printer (or the IBM-PC dot-matrix printer) on parallel printer port 1

If your computer system matches that configuration, you can **omit** the rest of this section.

If you want to change the configuration, press 2 on the System Administration Menu.

```
configuration
1: Color 2: Monochrome 3: Color card - - Mono screen

                    SYSTEM CONFIGURATION

 SCREEN STYLE                        (Leave blank for system default)

 DISK DRIVES                    NAME         CAPACITY (K bytes)
     Default Program Drive       A:               320
     Default System Data Drive   B:               320
     Additional Data Drive
     Additional Data Drive

 PRINTERS          PORT TYPE     PORT NUMBER     PRINTER NAME

     Printer 1 :     parallel         1            Epson MX-80
     Printer 2 :

  Default Printer : Printer 1

  If a printer with SERIAL PORT is used, specify the following:

  Baud rate :  1200  Parity : None   Stop Bits :  1 bit   Word length :  8 bits
  Protocol   : XON/XOFF
F2ENTER F3VIEW F4EXIT F5FORM CLR F6FLD CLR F7DELETE F8MODIFY F9REPORT F10MULTI
```

FIGURE 1.8

Disk Drives

On a hard disk, the data drive may be the same as the program drive. Otherwise, select both your Default Program Drive and Default Data Drive.

Printers

You may specify up to two printers. For each printer, specify port type, port number, and printer name. Port type is either **1** for parallel or **2** for serial. Port number is either **1** or **2**. Printer name is the name assigned to the type of printer you are using. Many printers are predefined with the system. The printer name in the configuration form should match the name in the Printer Definition file. Figure 1.9 shows the Printer Definition for the IBM Proprinter, which is the 9th printer listed (see the top left of Figure 1.9, which says **Record 9 on screen**). To scroll through the list of printers, press the F3 VIEW key.

Another option lets you specify serial port, country configuration (which includes currency name, date standard, and number of digits to the right of the decimal point). You can also eliminate the beep sound when an error occurs. You may access the information on the second and

```
printers                                       Record found
Record 9 on screen
                      P R I N T E R   D E F I N I T I O N

                      Name                    IBM Proprinter
                      Default Paper Width  8.5   inches (normally 8.5)
                      Default Paper Length 11    inches (normally 11)
                      Line Advance String  ØDØA         (normally ØDOA
                      Form Advance String  Ø            (normally ØC)

                                 CHARACTERS PER INCH (Define upto 4 sets)
  1 : 1Ø     turn-on string 12             2 : 12    turn-on string 1B3A
  3 : 17     turn-on string 1BØF           4 : 5     turn-on string 1B57Ø1
                                   LINES PER INCH   (Define upto 4 sets)
  1 : 6      turn-on string 1B4A24         2 : 8     turn-on string 1B3Ø
  3 : 10.28 turn-on string 1B31            4:        turn-on string

                                 SPECIAL EFFECTS    (Define all applicable
                   EFFECT        TURN-ON STRING       TURN-OFF STRING
                   Boldface      1B34                 1B46
                   Underline     1B2DØ1               1B2DØØ
                   Italicise     1B45                 1B46
                   Special 1     1B'G                 1B'H
                   Special 2
F2ENTER F3VIEW F4EXIT F5FORM CLR F6FLD CLR F7DELETE F8MODIFY F9REPORT F10MULTI
```

FIGURE 1.9

third pages of the form by pressing the PGDN key. After you've made all the changes, press the F2 ENTER key to record them.

Define Printers

Most popular printers are predefined in the Printers file when the system is defined. View the file to see if your printer is already defined. The printer definition form must be used if your printer is not defined. To enter the printers form, select 3 in the System Administration Menu. The printers form appears on the screen. You should check your printer manual to enter fields as printer name (up to 15 characters), default paper width (8.5 for letter size paper and 11 for legal size), default paper length (11 inches for letter size paper and 14 inches for legal size), line advance string (for most printers it is 0D0A), form feed string (for most printers it is 0C), characters per inch (one-mode printers normally print at 10 characters per inch), lines per inch (most print at 6 lines per inch), and special effects (BOLDFACE, UNDERLINE, ITALICS, and SPECIAL EFFECTS 1 and 2, which allow you to switch between correspondence and draft quality modes). You will find most of these codes in your printer's manual.

To save the new printer form, fill in the new form, and press F2 ENTER. To view an existing printer, type in the printer name and press the F3 VIEW key. You may then retype the fields you want, then press the F8 MODIFY key. To delete the printer definition, press the F7 DELETE key.

Define Screen Styles

In most computers, you do not have to use this option. The screen styles form is available only for the IBM-PC. It allows you to customize your screen to use monochrome, color, and color-mono, as shown in Figure 1.10.

To enter the screen styles form, select 4 from the System Administration Menu. Fill in the form's screen style name (can be up to 20 characters), screen style table, foreground and background colors, and intensify and blink, which allows you to highlight the yes or no field.

```
screen styles                              Record found
Record 1 on screen
                SCREEN  STYLE  NAME : color

                     FOREGROUND    BACKGROUND   INTENSIFY?   BLINK ?
  Title Area         Brown         Black          yes          no

  Cursor/Mode Area   Cyan          Black          yes          no

  Message Area       Red           Black          yes          no

  Prompt Line        Black         Green          no           no

  Fields:  Regular   Brown         Blue           yes          no
       Highlight 1   Light Gray    Red            yes          no
       Highlight 2   Brown         Black          yes          no
       Highlight 3   Black         Black          no           no
  Menu Highlighting  Light Gray    Blue           yes          no

  Key Names          Light Gray    Red            yes          no

  All Other          Brown         Black          yes          no
F2ENTER F3VIEW F4EXIT F5FORM CLR F6FLD CLR F7DELETE F8MODIFY F9REPORT F10MULTI
```

FIGURE 1.10

To save the screen style definition, fill in the form and press the F2 ENTER key. To view an existing screen style, type the screen style name and press F3 VIEW. You may then retype the fields you want, then press the F8 MODIFY key. To delete the screen style definition, press the F7 DELETE key. It is strongly advised that you do not change the default screen styles records already in the system.

CREATING A FORM

In this chapter you will learn how to design a form for a database that simulates the operations of a computer store. To learn how to design a simple form, you will create several forms called **EMPLOYEE**, **CUSTOMER**, **ORDERS**, and **PRODUCTS**, as shown in Figure 2.1. You will learn how to create forms with their respective fields. You will learn the different types of fields, such as text, numeric string, number, date, time, choice, and yes/no. You will also learn how to view, add, and delete a field. You will learn how to print the form definition, which includes a description of a form and all its fields. You will create derived fields, sequenced fields, and lookup formulas.

```
Files Used in Data Base for Simulation of Computer Store


EMPLOYEE                          CUSTOMER
  Employee #                        Cust ID
  Position                          Last Name
  Last Name                         First Name
  First Name                        Street
  Address                           City
  City                              State
  State                             Zip
  Zip                               Phone #
  Date of Birth
  Date Hired
  Phone #
  Social Security Number
  Salary
  Marital Status



PRODUCTS                          ORDERS
  Stock #                         Order #
  Description                     Cust ID
  Quantity                        Stock #
  Price                           Quantity Ordered
                                  Total Order
                                  Date
                                  Emp #
```

FIGURE 2.1

BACKGROUND INFORMATION

Before you start creating these forms and entering information into them, you should learn some basic definitions that are used throughout this book. A ***field*** is the smallest unit of data that has meaning in a database. For example, in Figure 2.1, **Employee #**, **Last Name**, **Position**, **Salary**, etc. are field names. A field may contain up to 255 characters. A ***form***, in DataEase, is a group of fields that appear on the screen and are designed to enter information. Each form may contain up to 255 fields. A form can be up to 16 screens long. DataEase allows up to 255 forms per database. A form that has its fields filled with data is called a ***record***. For example, all the information about one particular product in the **PRODUCTS** file is a record. The group of fields shown in Figure 2.1 —**Stock #**, **Description**, **Quantity**, **Price**—is a Products record. DataEase allows up to 65,535 records per form. The database you will create will have four separate forms: **EMPLOYEE**, **CUSTOMER**, **ORDERS**, and **PRODUCTS**. After data is entered into these forms, they become a collection of records, or a ***file***. A file is a collection of records that contain data. The computer store application you will be creating is a collection of files, called a ***database***. A DataEase database is a collection of forms, records, and reports. A ***report*** in its simplest form is a display of the data contained in a file. A report can involve the sorting of data according to certain criteria that uses records that meet specific criteria. Reports are displayed in a format designed by you.

The four files in the computer store simulation are related by some fields. The field **Cust ID** is located in both the **CUSTOMER** and **ORDERS** files. The **Stock #** field is located in both the **PRODUCTS** and **ORDERS** file. You will notice that the field **Employee #** is located in the **EMPLOYEE** file, and **Emp #** is located in the **ORDERS** file. Even though they have different names, they represent the same information. By having a field that is common to two or more files, information in these files can be extracted in a fairly simple way. This will be demonstrated in Chapter 3.

In the computer store application, information is the key to success. Information is needed on employees, customers, products, and orders. You will be able to answer such questions as: Who is the employee with the greatest sales volume? What is the product that is most frequently ordered? What is the total inventory of the company? What will be the total cost if you give each employee a 6% raise? What employee waited on what customer? The list of questions is limited only by your imagination and the data that is in the database.

To answer these questions, you must be able to analyze what data is needed. As you consider these questions, you will realize that they can be grouped into categories, as shown in Figure 2.1. Some of the data can probably fit into more than one category. For example, the customer name could probably be placed in both the Customer and Orders file. You must decide which data belongs in what file before you start creating the files. It is possible to spend as much time designing the structure of the database as it is to create the database using DataEase.

DataEase communicates with the user through a series of menus, which contain prompts at the top and bottom of the screen. You choose a function by selecting an option or a number. For example, DataEase may prompt you to create a form, modify a form, enter data, print a report, etc.

INSERTING, CORRECTING, DELETING, COPYING, AND PASTING TEXT

It is always a good idea to learn how you can correct text before you start typing. To change existing text, position the cursor on the existing text and type over it. If you want to insert characters into text, enter the insert mode by pressing the INS key. The word INSERT appears in the mode area. The mode area of the screen is the center portion of the top line. Place the cursor in the position that you would like to insert text and type the new text. If you want the text mode to go back to normal, press the INS key again. To insert a blank line in the form, place the cursor anywhere on the line and press the F8 INSERT LINE key. The cursor stays on the newly created blank line, and all the following lines are shifted down by one line.

To delete a character, place the cursor on the character to be deleted and press the DEL key. The character under the cursor is deleted. Press the DEL key as many times as the number of characters you want to delete. If you want to delete a line, place the cursor on the line to be deleted and press the F7 DELETE LINE key.

If you want to delete a block of text, place the cursor at the start of the block of text to be deleted. Press the F3 CUT key. Move the cursor to the end of the block that you wish to delete and again press the F3 CUT key. The block is now deleted. On the status line, you will notice that the F6 PASTE key is highlighted. If you want to paste, or move, the block somewhere else, position the cursor where you want the block pasted and press the F6 PASTE key. The block is now pasted at that location. Even though the PASTE indicator is no longer on the status line, the block is still available for pasting in other locations. If you want to remove the PASTE highlighting without pasting the block, press the ESC key to remove the highlighting.

If you want to copy text or fields, place the cursor at the starting position of the text you want copied, press the F5 COPY key, and select 1: Copy Block . Position the cursor at the end of the block you want copied and press the F5 COPY key again. The F6 PASTE key on the status line is now highlighted, and the block is available for pasting anywhere on the form.

CREATING A FORM WITH ITS FIELDS

Example of Text Field, Numeric String Field, Number Field, Date Field, Choice Field

You will now construct a form that will consist of the fields in the **EMPLOYEE** file. The form itself has no data in it but contains the structure for the types of information that will be entered into the form. The structure of the form defines what fields will appear and where they will appear in the record. For example, the **EMPLOYEE** form will contain fields such as **Employee #**, **Last Name**, **First Name**, **Position**, **Social Security Number**, **Salary,** and **Date of Birth**. The structure of the form also defines the characteristics of those fields. The field characteristics tell you if the field will be made up of words, numbers, both words and numbers, or dates. They also indicate whether the field will have a special format, such as a telephone number or social security number.

From the Main Menu of DataEase, press **1** to select the **Form Definition and Changes** option. To define a form, select **1: Define a form**. DataEase now asks you for the name of the form. The screen appears as in Figure 2.2.

The form name can be up to 20 characters long, and it should start with a letter. Any other characters, including letters, spaces, digits, or punctuation marks, can follow the initial letter. **Do not use the asterisk (*) or the question mark (?) or quotes ('') in any form name or field name, since these characters have special significance in DataEase.** If you make a mistake, press either the BACKSPACE key or the LEFT arrow key.

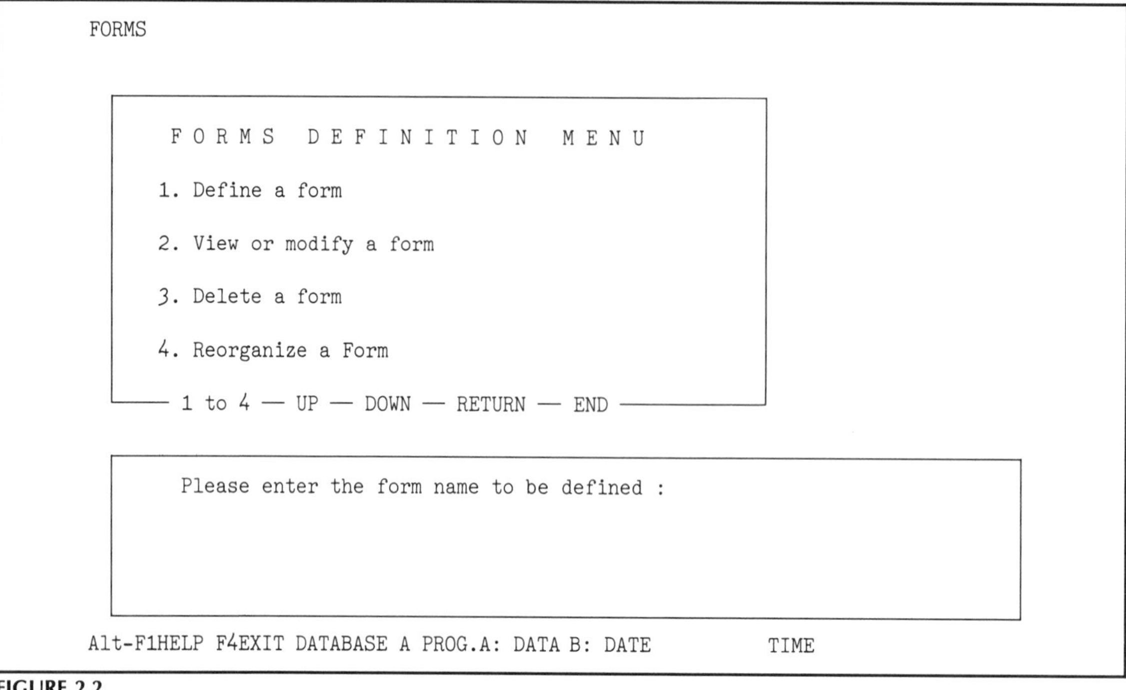
FORMS

F O R M S   D E F I N I T I O N   M E N U

1. Define a form

2. View or modify a form

3. Delete a form

4. Reorganize a Form

1 to 4 — UP — DOWN — RETURN — END

Please enter the form name to be defined :

Alt-F1HELP F4EXIT DATABASE A PROG.A: DATA B: DATE TIME

FIGURE 2.2

Type:

```
Employee
```

as the name of the form and press the RETURN key.

NOTE: If you are using a dual-drive floppy system, DataEase will ask you to insert the Utilities disk in drive A and hit any key.

The Form Definition screen appears. The status line, in the top left corner of the screen, shows the form's name, which in this case is **Employee**. On the top center of the screen is the cursor position indicator. It shows the location of the cursor by row and column coordinates. Initially it is R 1 C 1, which means row 1 column 1. As you move the cursor around the keyboard (by using the arrow keys on the numeric keypad), you can see the coordinates change in the cursor position indicator.

Move the cursor to R 2 C 4 and type:

```
Employee #:
```

This will be the name of your first field. A field name can be up to 20 characters long and should start with a letter. If the name on the form is more than 20 characters, only the first 20 are used. You should always choose meaningful names and, if possible, avoid abbreviations. Make sure the cursor is now at R 2 C 17 and press the F10 FIELD key. The F10 key indicates that you want to define the characteristics for that field and that you want the data entry to begin precisely where the cursor is located. You should allow two spaces after the colon to make the form less crowded when you are entering data. The next chapter will show you how to enter data into the database.

By pressing the F10 FIELD key, you enter the field definition mode. DataEase will always prompt you for the characteristics of the field by showing a series of questions that are pertinent to that field. DataEase will prevent you from entering answers that do not make sense. The first prompt on the left side of the screen asks for

```
Field name:
```

On the right-hand side of the screen, you will notice that DataEase has already placed the field name **Employee #**. DataEase picks up the name starting with a letter, removes any extra spaces, and removes any question mark (?) or colon (:) at the end of the name. In your case, the colon is removed. Press the RETURN key to accept **Employee #** as the field name. If you would like to change the name, use the cursor keys to type over it or change it. This changes the name only in definition—not on the entry screen. You can use the INS and DEL keys or the F6 CLEAR FIELD key.

Now DataEase would like to know the field type. At the top of the screen, you will notice several choices that are listed. If you press the F1 MORE key, you will see a complete listing of all the field types. See Figure 2.3.

Remember from the first chapter you can press the ALT F1 keys any time you need help. If you press the ALT F1 keys here, the screen appears as in Figure 2.4. Notice the window at the bottom of the screen. It gives you the pages you can refer to in the DataEase reference manual

```
FORM Employee

     Field name :                          Em
     Field type :                           1: Text
                                            2: Numeric Setting
                                            3: Number
                                            4: Date
                                            5: Time
                                            6: Dollar
                                            7: Yes or No
                                            8: Choice

                                            1 to 8 UP DOWN RETURN
F6 CLEAR FIELD
```

FIGURE 2.3

```
FORM Employee
     Field name :                          Em
     Field type :                           1: Text
                                            2: Numeric String
                                            3: Number
                                            4: Date
                                            5: Time
                                            6: Dollar
                                            7: Yes or No
                                            Pages 4-1Ø, 11, 12, 13, 15
                      FIELD TYPES
 Type             Characters Allowed          Max. Length

 Text             All                         255 Max.
 Numeric String   Digits, Punctuation         255 Max.
 Number           Integer, Fixed or Floating  14
 Date             Ø1/Ø1/Ø1 to 12/31/99
 Time             ØØ:ØØ:ØØ to 23:59:59
 Dollar           Digits (automatic Commas)   14
 Yes or No        -
 Choice           All                         99 choices, each up to 6Ø long.
 Alt-F1 Exit — F1 More Help — Sh-F1 On Auto Help
                                              1 to 8 UP DOWN RETURN
F6 CLEAR FIELD
```

FIGURE 2.4

```
FORM Employee
1: no 2: soc.sec.no. 3: phone no. 4: other format
     Field name :                              Employee #
     Field type :                              Numeric String
     Is it a formatted string ?



                                                      Page 4-1Ø
      Select No for a numeric string without any formatting characters,
             Phone No. or Soc.Sec.No. predefined formats,
             Other to define a format for the field.
      Alt-F1 Exit — F1 More Help — Sh-F1 On  Auto Help

F6 CLEAR FIELD
```

FIGURE 2.5

if you need more help. To exit the help screen, press the ALT F1 EXIT keys.

Since **Employee #** is a numeric string, press **2** for **Numeric String**, then press the RETURN key. The screen now appears as in Figure 2.5. The corresponding help window also appears.

Numeric string fields are used to enter a sequence of digits. The number will be automatically padded with leading zeroes. For example, Employee # 5 would be entered as ØØØØ5.

NOTE: If you press the wrong number key by mistake, keep pressing **1** followed by the RETURN key until you see the following function line key.

```
F2 ENTER  F7 DELETE  F8 MODIFY
```

Press F7 DELETE to remove the field and press F10 FIELD to begin again. If you press F8 MODIFY, the sequence of questions will begin again and let you change the answer, if needed.

DataEase will now ask:

```
Is it a formatted string?
```

Type:

```
1
```

to answer "no." Examples of a formatted string are a social security number, a telephone number, or any other number, such as an ID number, that you would format yourself.

DataEase will now respond:

```
Maximum length of field:
```

Type:

```
5
```

then press the RETURN key. Since this is an important or significant field, when DataEase asks:

```
Is this field REQUIRED to be entered?:
```

Type:

```
2
```

to answer "yes." The field must be filled before a record can be entered into the system.

DataEase asks:

```
Does this field require fast (INDEXED) access?:
```

Type:

```
2
```

to answer "yes." An indexed field provides faster access when you search this field to select records, sort records, or create relationships. (These functions will be discussed later.) One disadvantage of an indexed field is that it takes up extra space on the disk. It also is very slow in updating the index when you add, modify, or delete a record. The speed is affected when you have many indexed fields and thousands of records. Indices may be added or deleted at any time. There are no restrictions on how many fields may be indexed, but you should try to limit the number to no more than four.

DataEase will now ask:

```
Is it one of the UNIQUE fields? :
```

Type:

```
2
```

to answer "yes." A unique field is one that has no duplicate numbers, such as social security number or employee number. If you try entering a new record that has a duplicate number, DataEase will ask you if you want to update the record. The first unique field should be indexed, as it is in this case. This will help speed up searching the file for duplicate records.

Some numbers entered into the record may have an upper or lower bound. For example, if you are doing computations with salaries, there is normally an upper or lower bound so that these numbers fall in the proper range when they are entered. Since in your application, or definition, a range check isn't necessary, press the RETURN key. Type **1** to answer "no" to the next two questions. It is not a derived field, and you do not wish to prevent data entry in the field. A derived field is a field that is computed from information that is found in another field. For example, if all or several salaries are increased by 6%, these raises would be derived fields. They are not read in as data, but are computed.

Since you do not care who views the field, select the minimum security level on the form by pressing **7** for **Low3** security. If you press the RETURN key, DataEase automatically chooses the lowest security level. Since you do not want everyone to write to this field, press **1** for a high security level to write to this field. DataEase provides seven security levels. Defining and modifying forms should be available only to high level users. Each field in a form may be secured by specifying a field level security. If the security level is left blank, any user will be able to view the field—the system defaults to the lowest security level.

You are now finished with this field, which should now look like Figure 2.6. Press F2 ENTER to save the field characteristics.

The next field you will create is **Last Name**. Place the cursor on R 4 C 4 and type:

```
Last Name:
```

```
FORM Employee
Please hit Enter, Delete or Modify key
     Field name :                                 Employee #
     Field type :                                 Numeric String
     Is it a formatted string                     no
     Maximum length of field :                      5
     Press ENTER, MODIFY or DELETE any time to skip the remaining questions
     Is this field REQUIRED to be entered? :                     yes
     Does this field require fast (INDEXED) access ?:            yes
     Is it one of the UNIQUE fields? :                           yes
     Does the field require a RANGE CHECK? :                     no
     Is the field DEFINED (calculate/lookup/sequence/default)? :no
     PREVENT data-entry in the field? :           no
     Minimum Security Level to View the Field:    Low3
     Minimum Security Level to Write the Field:   High
     Field Help


     Field display attribute:



F2 ENTER F7 DELETE F8 MODIFY
```

FIGURE 2.6

Press the SPACEBAR twice (it's not necessary, but it's useful in formatting) and press the F10 FIELD key. Press RETURN to accept **Last Name** as the field name and press **1** for text field type. Text field type allows you to enter any type of character, including letters and numbers, into the field. You can assume that no one has a last name longer than 15 characters so type **15** for maximum length of field, then press the RETURN key. Type **2** (for "yes") to indicate that is is a required field, as shown in Figure 2.7. Press F2 ENTER to save this field's characteristics. You do not have to answer the rest of the questions. Since F2 ENTER was pressed, answers to all the other questions default to a value of "no."

Place the cursor at R 4 C 37. Type:

```
First Name:
```

as a field name, then press the SPACEBAR twice. Press the F10 FIELD key. Again, make this a text field, 15 characters in length, and required. Press F2 ENTER to save this field's characteristics.

```
FORM Employee
1: no 2: yes
     Field name :                                  Last name
     Field type :                                  Text
     Maximum length of field :                     15
     Press ENTER, MODIFY or DELETE any time to skip the remaining questions
     Is this field REQUIRED to be entered? :                      yes
     Does this field require fast (INDEXED) access ?:

 F2 ENTER F7 DELETE F8 MODIFY
```

FIGURE 2.7

Place the cursor at R 6 C 4. Type:

```
Address:
```

as a field name, press the SPACEBAR twice, then press the F10 FIELD key. Make this a text field, 20 characters in length, and required. Press F2 ENTER to save this field's characteristics.

Place the cursor at R 6 C 37. Type:

```
City:
```

as a field name, press the SPACEBAR twice, then press the F10 FIELD key. Make this a text field, 20 characters in length, and required. Press F2 ENTER to save this field's characteristics.

Place the cursor at R 8 C 4. Type:

```
State:
```

as a field name, press the SPACEBAR twice, then press the F10 FIELD key. Make this a text field, 2 characters long, and required. Press F2 ENTER to save this field's characteristics.

Place the cursor at R 8 C 37. Type:

```
Zip:
```

as a field name, press the SPACEBAR twice, then press the F10 FIELD key. Make this a numeric string by pressing **2**, pressing **1** to indicate no format, and pressing **5** to make it 5 characters in length. Press F2 ENTER to save this field's characteristics.

Place the cursor at R 10 C 4. Type:

```
Date of Birth:
```

as a field name, press the SPACEBAR twice, then press the F10 FIELD key. Make this a date field by pressing **4**. Press F2 ENTER to save this field's characteristics. Date fields are automatically formatted as MM/DD/YY. They can be changed to the international standard of

DD/MM/YY through system configuration. You can do this by pressing **7** from the DataEase Main Menu to enter the System Administration Menu. Press **2** for **Define Configuration** and press PGDN to enter country customization. Choose **2** for **International Customization** as your date format and press F2 to save the new configuration.

Place the cursor at R 10 C 37. Type:

```
Date Hired:
```

as a field name, press the SPACEBAR twice, then press the F10 FIELD key. Make this a date field by pressing **4**. Press F2 ENTER to save this field's characteristics.

Place the cursor at R 12 C 4. Type:

```
Phone #:
```

as a field name, press the SPACEBAR twice, then press the F10 FIELD key. Make this a numeric string by pressing **2**. When DataEase asks if it is a formatted string, type **3** to indicate that is is a phone number. Press F2 ENTER to save this field's characteristics.

Place the cursor at R 12 C 37. Type:

```
Social Security Number:
```

as a field name, press the SPACEBAR twice, then press the F10 FIELD key. You will notice in Figure 2.8 that the field name is shortened to **Social Security #**, because DataEase takes only the first 20 letters. Make this a numeric string field by pressing **2**. If you wanted to, you could change **Social Security Numb** to **Social Security #** to make the field name more understandable when generating reports. When DataEase asks if it is a formatted string, press **2** to indicate that it is a social security number. Answer **2** (for ''yes'') to the questions that make it required, indexed, and unique. Press F2 ENTER to save this field's characteristics.

```
FORM Employee
Please hit Enter, Delete or Modify key
     Field name :                                  Social Security  #
     Field type :                                  Numeric String
     Is it a formatted string ?                    soc.sec.no.
     Press ENTER, MODIFY or DELETE any time to skip the remaining questions
     Is this field REQUIRED to be entered? :                      yes
     Does this field require fast (INDEXED) access ?:             yes
     Is it one of the UNIQUE fields? :                            yes
     Does the field require a RANGE CHECK? :                      no
     Is the field DERIVED (calculate/lookup/sequence/default)? :no
     PREVENT data-entry in the field? :            no
     Minimum Security Level to View the Field:
     Minimum Security Level to Write the Field:
     Field Help


     Field display attribute:




F2 ENTER F7 DELETE F8 MODIFY
```

FIGURE 2.8

Place the cursor at R 14 C 4. Type:

```
Salary:
```

as a field name, press the SPACEBAR twice, then press the F10 FIELD key. Make this a number field by pressing **3**, or choose the **Dollar** option. When DataEase asks for number type, select **2** to indicate **fixed point**. A fixed point field has a fixed number of decimal positions after the decimal point. If a number is classified as a fixed point field, commas will automatically be inserted after every third digit.

DataEase asks:

```
Maximum digits to the left of decimal?
```

Type:

```
10
```

and press the RETURN key. DataEase then responds:

```
Digits to the right of decimal:
```

Type:

```
2
```

then press the RETURN key. Answer "no" to all the other questions except the minimum security level to view and write the field. Press **1**, which is the highest security level. You do not want anybody to look at or change the field, unless they have a high security clearance. The completed field characteristic is shown in Figure 2.9. Press F2 ENTER to save this field's characteristics.

```
FORM Employee

     Field name :                                   Salary
     Field type :                                   Number
     Number Type :                                  Fixed point
     Maximum digits to the left of decimal? :       1Ø
     Digits to the right of decimal :                2
     Press ENTER, MODIFY or DELETE any time to skip the remaining questions
     Is this field REQUIRED to be entered? :                       no
     Does this field require fast (INDEXED) access ?:              no
     Is it one of the UNIQUE fields? :                             no
     Does the field require a RANGE CHECK? :                       no
     Is the field DERIVED (calculate/lookup/sequence/default)? :no
     PREVENT data-entry in the field? :             no
     Minimum Security Level to View the Field:      High
     Minimum Security Level to Write the Field:     High
     Field Help




F2 ENTER F7 DELETE F8 MODIFY
```

FIGURE 2.9

The last field you wish to enter at this time is **Marital Status.** Place the cursor on R 16 C 4. Type:

```
Marital Status:
```

as a field name, press the SPACEBAR twice, then press the F10 FIELD key. To see the rest of the field types, press the F1 MORE key at the Field Type Menu, then press **8** for **Choice**. A choice field allows you to specify the possible options allowed in the field. A choice field results in faster and more accurate data entry. It also results in a significant saving of disk space. You are allowed up to 99 choices, each of which can be up to 60 characters in length. Press the RETURN key to avoid the **Optional choice field type name:**. The **Optional choice field type name** is used if the set of choices for this field will be used in other fields of the current form. Enter the four choices as shown in Figure 2.10. To exit and save the field description, press RETURN to leave **Choice 5** blank, then press F2 ENTER.

```
FORM Employee

     Field name :                                 Marital Status
     Field type :                                 Choice
     Optional choice field type name :
     Choice 1 : Married
     Choice 2 : Single
     Choice 3 : Divorced
     Choice 4 : Separated
     Choice 5 :









F6 CLEAR FIELD
```

FIGURE 2.10

The final **EMPLOYEE** form is shown in Figure 2.11. The underlines or shaded areas that denote field length are shown on the screen, but they are not printed out unless you print the form definition or print a record. The underline is shown on a monochrome monitor, while the shaded area (usually blue) is shown on a color monitor. They can be printed out by printing the form definition, as discussed below. Be sure to print them out only when your printer is connected to the microcomputer.

PRINTING THE FORM DEFINITION

If you are in the Form Editing mode, you can press the F9 PRINT key to get a printed copy of the form definition. The form definition shows the name of the form followed by a ruled line to help you see the positioning of the fields. The form that appears on the screen with the field lengths is printed below the ruled line. Another ruled line follows the form.

The field descriptions for each of the fields are printed out in columns. The field name, type, and all the other characteristics are printed.

```
FORM Employee                R 16 C  21

   Employee #:

   Last Name:                         First Name:

   Address:                           City:

   State:                             Zip:

   Date of Birth:                     Date Hired:

   Phone #:                           Social Security Number:

   Salary:

   Marital Status:




F2ENTER F3CUT F4EXIT F5COPY F6PASTE F7DEL LINE F8INS LINE F9PRINT F1ØFIELD
```

FIGURE 2.11

DataEase also indicates which fields are required, indexed, unique, etc. It is highly recommended that you print out the form definition after each form is created. The form definition gives a quick summary of all the information about a form and should be used for later reference. The form definition for the **EMPLOYEE** form you just created is shown in Figure 2.12.

VIEWING, CHANGING, OR DELETING A FIELD

If you want to view a brief summary of the characteristics of a field, place the cursor anywhere on the field (where the underline on the screen is shown) and press the SPACEBAR. Figure 2.13 shows the abbreviated definition when the cursor is placed on the field **Employee #**. The field information is shown at the top of the screen.

If you want to view the complete definition of a field, place the cursor on the field (where the underline or highlight on the screen is shown) and press the F10 FIELD key. The complete field definition is now shown. If you press the F2 ENTER key, no changes are made to the form. By looking at the field definition, you can determine whether any changes need to be made to the field. If you press the F8 MODIFY key, you can change any answers to the field definition questions. Hit the RETURN key until you reach the questions about characteristics you wish to change. If you press the F7 DELETE key, the field is deleted. The form is then displayed without that field. When you have made all the necessary changes, hit the F2 ENTER key to save the field definition with the modified form.

SAVING THE FORM DEFINITION

The definition of the form is now saved on the Data disk. The message

```
Form definition saved
```

is displayed, and you are returned to the Forms Definition Menu. When you save the form definition, two or more files are saved on the disk. The Form Definition file, the Record file, and an Index file for each indexed field are saved on the data disk.

CANCELLING THE FORM DEFINITION

If you want to cancel the form definition without saving the form, press the F4 EXIT key to exit the Form Editing mode. DataEase will allow you to change your mind by responding:

```
      FORM   Employee
      ---------------------------

1       10        20        30        40        50        60        70        80
----+----+----+----+----+----+----+----+----+----+----+----+----+----+----+----+

   Employee #:  _____

   Last Name:   _______________   First Name:  _______________

   Address:  ____________________   City:  ____________________

   State:  __                     Zip:  _____

   Date of Birth:  ________       Date Hired:  ________

   Phone #:  ______________       Social Security Number:  ___________

   Salary:  ________________

   Marital Status:  _________

----+----+----+----+----+----+----+----+----+----+----+----+----+----+----+----+
1       10        20        30        40        50        60        70        80

      FIELD DESCRIPTIONS
      ------------------

No. Name                 Type       Long Reqd In- Uni- Der- Rng Pre-  Record
                                              dex que  ived Chk vent size offset
--- -------------------- ---------- ---- ---- --- ---- ---- --- ---- ---- ------
  1 Employee #           Num.String    5 Yes  Yes Yes  No   No  No      5      4
      View Security Required: Low1,  Write Security Required: High
  2 Last Name            Text         15 Yes  No  No   No   No  No     15      9
  3 First Name           Text         15 Yes  No  No   No   No  No     15     24
  4 Address              Text         20 Yes  No  No   No   No  No     20     39
  5 City                 Text         20 Yes  No  No   No   No  No     20     59
  6 State                Text          2 Yes  No  No   No   No  No      2     79
  7 Zip                  Num.String    5 No   No  No   No   No  No      5     81
  8 Date of Birth        Date          8 No   No  No   No   No  No      6     86
  9 Date Hired           Date          8 No   No  No   No   No  No      6     92
 10 Phone #              Num.String   14 No   No  No   No   No  No     10     98
 11 Social Security Numb Num.String   11 Yes  Yes Yes  No   No  No      9    108
 12 Salary               Number       16 No   No  No   No   No  No      8    117
      Number Type : Fixed point
      Digits to left of decimal  =  13
      View Security Required: High,  Write Security Required: High
 13 Marital Status       Choice        9 No   No  No   No   No  No      1    125
      Choice 1: Married
      Choice 2: Single
      Choice 3: Divorced
      Choice 4: Separated
--- -------------------- ---------- ---- ---- --- ---- ---- --- ---- ---- ------

Record size 126

Memory required for form: Text  385, Fields 398, Total 783 bytes.
```

FIGURE 2.12

```
FORM Employee                R  2 C  21
FIELD: Employee #,Num.String,5,Required,Indexed,Unique

   Employee #:

   Last Name:                        First Name:

   Address:                          City:

   State:                            Zip:

   Date of Birth:                    Date Hired:

   Phone #:                          Social Security Number:

   Salary:

   Marital Status:



F2ENTER F3CUT F4EXIT F5COPY F6PASTE F7DEL LINE F8INS LINE F9PRINT F10FIELD
```

FIGURE 2.13

```
Do you want to abandon modified form data (y or n)?
```

If you want to cancel the form definition, press **y**. The changes are cancelled, and you are returned to the Forms Definition Menu. If you are cancelling the form definition of a new form, the whole form disappears.

If you change your mind, press **n**. You will now return to the Form Editing mode.

MODIFYING A FORM—CHANGING, ADDING, AND DELETING FIELDS

You just realized that you left off a field named **Position** and would now like to add it to the existing form. You would also like to rename the form **Employees**. To modify or view a form, select **2** on the Forms Definition Menu. The names of the existing forms are displayed in a window on the right side of the screen. Move the cursor to the form named **Employee** (or press **2**), then press the RETURN key. Move the cursor to R 2C 37. Type:

```
Position:
```

```
FORM Employee              R  2 C  48

   Employee #:                       Position:

   Last Name:                        First Name:

   Address:                          City:

   State:                            Zip:

   Date of Birth:                    Date Hired:

   Phone #:                          Social Security Number:

   Salary:

   Marital Status:



F2ENTER F3CUT F4EXIT F5COPY F6PASTE F7DEL LINE F8INS LINE F9PRINT F10FIELD
```

FIGURE 2.14

and press the F10 Field key. Make it a text field type of 20 characters in length, and a required field. Press the F2 ENTER key to save field. The new form looks like Figure 2.14.

Using the same procedure, you can change or delete any field. You must be very careful when you're changing or deleting fields, especially if data has already been entered into the database. Data can be lost or altered if a field is deleted or changed.

When you press F2 ENTER to save the form, DataEase asks you if you wish to save it under another name, as shown in Figure 2.15. If you save the form using the same name, DataEase will give you a warning that the original form will be overwritten or erased.

Answer "yes." Type:

```
Employees
```

for the name of the new form, then press the RETURN key.

```
FORM Employee                R  2 C  48

Do you want to save modified form under another name(y/n) :yes

Please enter the new form name :Employees

Phone #:                          Social Security Number:

Salary:

Marital Status:
```

FIGURE 2.15

There are now two forms on the disk, **Employee** and **Employees.** They are exactly the same except for the fact that **Employees** has one more field—**Position**.

You can always obtain a new printout of the Form Definition of **Employees** by pressing the F9 PRINT key while in the Form Editing mode.

CREATING SEVERAL DATA FILES

Derived Fields, Sequenced Fields, Lookup Formulas

To continue with our database of the computer store, you will now create the three other files and their fields, which are shown in Figure 2.1. In the Forms Definition Menu, press **1** for **Define a Form**. Type:

```
Customer
```

as the form name. You will first create the file named **Customer**, whose form is shown in Figure 2.16.

```
FORM Customer                 R 1Ø C  11

Cust ID:

Last Name:                          First Name:

Street:

City:                        State:        Zip:

Phone #:




F2ENTER F3CUT F4EXIT F5COPY F6PASTE F7DEL LINE F8INS LINE F9PRINT F1ØFIELD
```

FIGURE 2.16

Before you do this, look at the field characteristics for Cust ID. You notice that in Figure 2.17, this is a derived field.

The field derivation formula is:

```
sequence from "C-ØØØ1"
```

The double quotes are required to indicate the starting value for all text fields. In Record Entry mode (which will be discussed in the next chapter), you will have no reason to enter data in the **Cust ID** field. DataEase will do it automatically, increasing the count by one every time a new record is entered. The first customer ID will be C-ØØØ1, the second customer ID will be C-ØØØ2, etc.

The form definition for the **Customer** file is shown in Figure 2.18. Using the same procedure you used to create the **Employees** file, create the **Customer** file with the fields and field descriptions, as shown

```
FORM Customer
Please hit Enter, Delete or Modify key
     Field name :                                 Cust ID
     Field type :                                 Text
     Maximum length of field :                      7
     Press ENTER, MODIFY or DELETE any time to skip the remaining questions
     Is this field REQUIRED to be entered? :                     yes
     Does this field require fast (INDEXED) access ?:            no
     Is it one of the UNIQUE fields? :                           yes
     Does the field require a RANGE CHECK? :                     no
     Is the field DERIVED (calculate/lookup/sequence/default)? :yes
     Field derivation formula :                   sequence from "C-ØØØØ1"


     PREVENT data-entry in the field? :           yes
     Minimum Security Level to View the Field:
     Minimum Security Level to Write the Field:
     Field Help


     Field display attribute:


F2 ENTER F7 DELETE F8 MODIFY
```

FIGURE 2.17

in Figure 2.18. Do not worry about what columns should contain **First Name**, **State**, and **Zip**.

After you have created the **Customer** file, you will then create the **Products** file, whose form is shown in Figure 2.19. In the Forms Definition Menu, press **1** for **Define a Form** and type:

```
Products
```

as the form name.

Before you do this, let's look at the field characteristics for **Stock #**. Notice that in Figure 2.20, this is a derived field.

The field derivation formula is:

```
sequence from 1
```

```
FORM   Customer
---------------------------

1       10        20        30        40        50        60        70        80
----+----+----+----+----+----+----+----+----+----+----+----+----+----+----+----+

Cust ID: ______

Last Name: _______________        First Name: _______________

Street: ____________________

City: ____________________  State: _____  Zip: _____

Phone #: _______________

----+----+----+----+----+----+----+----+----+----+----+----+----+----+----+----+
1       10        20        30        40        50        60        70        80
```

FIELD DESCRIPTIONS

No.	Name	Type	Long	Reqd	In-dex	Uni-que	Der-ived	Rng Chk	Pre-vent	Record size	Record offset
1	Cust ID #	Text	6	Yes	No	Yes	Yes	No	No	6	3
	Field calculation formula : sequence from "C-00001"										
2	Last Name	Text	15	Yes	No	No	No	No	No	15	9
3	First Name	Text	15	Yes	No	No	No	No	No	15	24
4	Street	Text	20	No	No	No	No	No	No	20	39
5	City	Text	20	No	No	No	No	No	No	20	59
6	State	Text	2	No	No	No	No	No	No	2	79
7	Zip	Num.String	5	No	No	No	No	No	No	5	81
8	Phone #	Num.String	14	No	No	No	No	No	No	10	86

Record size 96

Memory required for form: Text 122, Fields 249, Total 371 bytes.

FIGURE 2.18

```
FORM Products                R  9 C   9

Stock #:

Description:

Quantity:

Price:












F2ENTER F3CUT F4EXIT F5COPY F6PASTE F7DEL LINE F8INS LINE F9PRINT F1ØFIELD
```

FIGURE 2.19

```
FORM Products
Please hit Enter, Delete or Modify key
     Field name :                           Stock #
     Field type :                           Numeric String
     Is it a formatted string ?             no
     Maximum length of field :                6
     Press ENTER, MODIFY or DELETE any time to skip the remaining questions
     Is this field REQUIRED to be entered? :                yes
     Does this field require fast (INDEXED) access ?:       yes
     Is it one of the UNIQUE fields? :                      yes
     Does the field require a RANGE CHECK? :                no
     Is the field DERIVED (calculate/lookup/sequence/default)? :yes
     Field derivation formula:              sequence from 1


     PREVENT data-entry in the field? :     yes
     Minimum Security Level to View the Field:
     Minimum Security Level to Write the Field:
     Field Help


     Field display attribute:

F2 ENTER F7 DELETE F8 MODIFY
```

FIGURE 2.20

In Record Entry mode, there will be no reason to enter data in the **Stock #** field. DataEase will do it automatically, increasing the count by one every time a new record is entered. You may skip leading zeros. The system automatically provides them. The form definition of the **Products** file is shown in Figure 2.21.

The last file to be created is the **Orders** file, whose form is shown in Figure 2.22.

Three new field types appear in this file. In Figure 2.23, you can see that the field **Quantity Ordered** is of type Integer.

Integers do not allow decimal points. If you specify **Integer**, the computer will ask you for the maximum digits in the field. The largest number of digits you can specify is 14. DataEase will automatically place commas after every third digit.

The second new field type discussed in this section is **Date**. The system date is the date on which you are using the database. To automatically enter the system date in a date field, the formula is specified as ??/??/??, as shown in Figure 2.24. Similarly, the time may be obtained in a time field by typing the formula ??:??:??.

The third new field type discussed is one that contains a lookup formula. You will notice in Figure 2.25 that the field **Total Order** has the field derivation formula:

```
Quantity Ordered * lookup Products Price
```

This statement tells DataEase to multiply the field **Quantity Ordered**, which is in the current file **Orders**, by the field **Price**, which is located in the file **Products**. The lookup is based on the relationship of the two files, which will be discussed in the beginning of the next chapter. You do not have to define the relationship before you specify the lookup function. However, it must be defined before you enter data into the forms.

The form definition of the **Orders** file is shown in Figure 2.26. Finish entering the fields and field characteristics of the **Orders** file and save it to disk by pressing the F2 ENTER key.

```
      FORM   Products
      ---------------------------


1        10        20        30        40        50        60        70        80
----+----+----+----+----+----+----+----+----+----+----+----+----+----+----+----+


Stock #:  ______

Description:  __________________________________________

Quantity:  ___

Price:  _____________

----+----+----+----+----+----+----+----+----+----+----+----+----+----+----+----+
1        10        20        30        40        50        60        70        80


        FIELD DESCRIPTIONS
        ------------------


No. Name                 Type       Long Reqd In- Uni- Der- Rng Pre-  Record
                                              dex que  ived Chk vent size offset
--- -------------------- ---------- ---- ---- --- ---- ---- --- ---- ---- ------
  1 Stock #              Num.String    6 Yes  Yes Yes  Yes  No  Yes     6      3
      Field calculation formula : sequence from 1
  2 Description          Text         40 Yes  No  No   No   No  No     40      9
  3 Quantity             Number        3 Yes  No  No   No   No  No      2     49
      Number Type : Integer
  4 Price                Number       13 Yes  No  No   No   No  No      8     51
      Number Type : Fixed point
      Digits to left of decimal  = 10
--- -------------------- ---------- ---- ---- --- ---- ---- --- ---- ---- ------

Record size 59

Memory required for form: Text   63, Fields 147, Total 210 bytes.
```

FIGURE 2.21

```
FORM Orders                    R  9 C  43

Order #:                            Cust ID:

Stock #:                            Quantity Ordered:

Total Order:

Date:                               Emp #:













F2ENTER F3CUT F4EXIT F5COPY F6PASTE F7DEL LINE F8INS LINE F9PRINT F10FIELD
```

FIGURE 2.22

```
FORM Orders
Please hit Enter, Delete or Modify key
     Field name :                                Quantity Ordered
     Field type :                                Number
     Number Type :                               Integer
     Maximum digits in the field :                4
     Press ENTER, MODIFY or DELETE any time to skip the remaining questions
     Is this field REQUIRED to be entered? :                    yes
     Does this field require fast (INDEXED) access ?:           no
     Is it one of the UNIQUE fields? :                          no
     Does the field require a RANGE CHECK? :                    no
     Is the field DERIVED (calculate/lookup/sequence/default)? :no
     PREVENT data-entry in the field? :          no
     Minimum Security Level to View the Field:
     Minimum Security Level to Write the Field:
     Field Help


     Field display attribute:




F2 ENTER F7 DELETE F8 MODIFY
```

FIGURE 2.23

```
FORM Orders
1: Normal 2: Highlight 1 3: Highlight 2 4: Highlight 3
     Field name :                                Date
     Field type :                                Date
     Press ENTER, MODIFY or DELETE any time to skip the remaining questions
     Is this field REQUIRED to be entered? :                    no
     Does this field require fast (INDEXED) access ?:           no
     Is it one of the UNIQUE fields? :                          no
     Does the field require a RANGE CHECK? :                    no
     Is the field DERIVED (calculate/lookup/sequence/default)? :yes
     Field derivation formula :                  ??/??/??


     PREVENT data-entry in the field? :          no
     Minimum Security Level to View the Field:
     Minimum Security Level to Write the Field:
     Field Help


     Field display attribute:


F2 ENTER F7 DELETE F8 MODIFY
```

FIGURE 2.24

```
FORM Orders

     Field name :                                Total Order
     Field type :                                Number
     Maximum digits to the left of decimal? :     7
     Digits to the right of decimal :             2
     Press ENTER, MODIFY or DELETE any time to skip the remaining questions
     Is this field REQUIRED to be entered? :                    yes
     Does this field require fast (INDEXED) access ?:           no
     Is it one of the UNIQUE fields? :                          no
     Does the field require a RANGE CHECK? :                    no
     Is the field DERIVED (calculate/lookup/sequence/default)? :yes
     Field derivation formula:
       Quantity Ordered * lookup Products Price

     PREVENT data-entry in the field? :          yes, and do not save (virtual)
     Minimum Security Level to View the Field:
     Minimum Security Level to Write the Field:
     Field Help



F2 ENTER F7 DELETE F8 MODIFY
```

FIGURE 2.25

```
FORM   Orders
---------------------------


1       10        20        30        40        50        60        70        80
----+----+----+----+----+----+----+----+----+----+----+----+----+----+----+----+

Order #: _______                  Cust ID: ______

Stock #: _______                  Quantity Ordered: _____

Total Order: ____________

Date: ________                    Emp #: _____

----+----+----+----+----+----+----+----+----+----+----+----+----+----+----+----+
1       10        20        30        40        50        60        70        80
```

FIELD DESCRIPTIONS

No.	Name	Type	Long	Reqd	In-dex	Uni-que	Der-ived	Rng Chk	Pre-vent	Record size	offset
1	Order #	Text	6	Yes	No	Yes	No	No	No	6	3
2	Cust ID	Text	6	Yes	No	No	No	No	No	6	9
3	Stock #	Num.String	6	Yes	No	No	No	No	No	6	15
4	Quantity Ordered Number Type : Integer	Number	5	Yes	No	No	No	No	No	2	21
5	Total Order Number Type : Fixed point Digits to left of decimal = 9 Field calculation formula : Quantity Ordered * lookup Products Price	Number	12	Yes	No	No	Yes	No	Virt	8	34
6	Date Field calculation formula : ??/??/??	Date	8	No	No	No	Yes	No	No	6	23
7	Emp #	Num.String	5	No	No	No	No	No	No	5	29

Record size 34

Memory required for form: Text 162, Fields 336, Total 498 bytes.

FIGURE 2.26

SUMMARY OF FIELD TYPES AND CHARACTERISTICS

FIELD TYPE	CHARACTERISTICS
Text	Allows any type of data to be entered Maximum length is 255 characters
Numeric String	Series of digits not used for calculations; leading zeroes MUST be entered
Unformatted	Maximum length is 255 digits
Soc. Sec. No.	Format: ØØØ-ØØ-ØØØØ
Phone No.	Format: (ØØØ)-ØØØ-ØØØØ
Formatted	Maximum length is 4Ø characters
Number	Contains numeric data Up to 14 digits allowed
Integer	No decimal point allowed Commas automatically entered, if needed
Fixed Point/ Dollar	Fixed number of decimal places after the decimal point Commas automatically entered, if needed
Floating Point	Decimal point may be placed anywhere No provision for commas
Date	Automatically formatted as MM/DD/YY Can be changed to international standard Calculations are allowed
Time	Automatically formatted as HH:MM:SS Follows the 24 hour time clock Calculations are allowed
Choice	Allows set of choices to be defined for field Can specify up to 99 choices Each choice can be up to 6Ø characters long
Yes or No	Special type of Choice field Choices are predefined: ''1: no, 2: yes''

FIGURE 2.27

Setting Up File Relationships
Adding Data to a Form

In this chapter you will learn how to set up the relationships between the four files in your simulated computer store. You will learn how to enter and edit data in the four files, and how to search the files to find required records. Finally, you will be able to search for data that is located in several files.

RELATED FILES

If you look at the four files in Figure 3.1, you see that the files have relationships between them. The field **Employee #** in the **EMPLOYEES** file is the same as the **Emp #** of the **ORDERS** file. Even though they have different field names, they represent the same data. These two fields are related. By looking at the field **Emp #** in the **ORDERS** file, DataEase can look up the corresponding information in the **EMPLOYEES** file, such as the last name, first name, address, city, state, zip, and phone number of the employee who made that order. The two files are linked, or related, by those two fields. By searching for information in one of the files, you can obtain information in the corresponding, or related, file.

In a similar manner, the field **Cust ID** is located in two files—**CUSTOMER** and **ORDERS**. These two forms are related by that common field. In this case, the field names are the same. Likewise, **Stock #** is the field that is common between the **PRODUCTS** and **ORDERS** files.

By accessing the **ORDERS** file, you can access the information in the other three files once these relationships have been created. This is shown in Figure 3.1.

Relationships are created by using the relationship form accessed through choice **6**, **Menus & Relationships**, from the Main Menu. You must specify all relationships during record entry before a lookup function can be performed. In the computer store simulation, the derivation field **Total Order** of the **ORDERS** file contains a lookup formula. DataEase looks up the price in the **PRODUCTS** file (see Figure 2.19). During data entry, the computer will calculate the total price by multiplying the quantity ordered by the price of each product. Therefore, the relationship between the two files must exist before the computer can look up the price.

```
Files Used in Data Base for Simulation of Computer Store


EMPLOYEES                          CUSTOMER
  Employee #                         Cust ID
  Position                           Last Name
  Last Name                          First Name
  First Name                         Street
  Address                            City
  City                               State
  State                              Zip
  Zip                                Phone #
  Date of Birth
  Date Hired
  Phone #
  Social Security Number
  Salary
  Marital Status


PRODUCTS                           ORDERS
  Stock #                            Order #
  Description                        Cust ID
  Quantity                           Stock #
  Price                              Quantity Ordered
                                     Total Order
                                     Date
                                     Emp #
```

FIGURE 3.1

THE RELATIONSHIPS FORM

To define relationships, select **6, Menus and Relationships**, from the Main Menu. Then select **2** for the **Relationships Form** (see Figure 3.2).

A blank relationship form appears on the screen. As shown in Figure 3.3, you can enter the two form names—**Employees**, by pressing **6**, and **orders**, by pressing **3**—in the two fields at the top. NOTE: these numbers will be correct if you have created the database exactly as detailed in this book, and if no other forms exist in the directory.

Rather than specifying the form's numbers, you can type the form's names in, using either upper or lower case. On each side of the form, you specify the names of the matching fields. Select **Employee #**, by

```
DATAEASE


          M E N U S   A N D   R E L A T I O N S H I P S

          1. Define Menus

          2. Define Relationships

            1 to 2 — UP — DOWN — RETURN — END


     F4EXIT      DATABASE A PROG.A: DATA B: DATE          TIME
```

FIGURE 3.2

```
relationships                          To skip the menu, press Esc
1: System 2: Employee 3: orders 4: Customer 5: Products 6: Employees

                              FORM RELATIONSHIP
                              -----------------

BETWEEN:
        Form  1:Employees              And 2:orders

BASED ON
        THE FOLLOWING FIELDS BEING EQUAL: (Define at least one set of fields.)

        Field   Employee #               =    Emp #

    And Field                            =

    And Field                            =

OPTIONAL RELATIONSHIP NAMES:
        (Form names are used as a default.)

     for form 1:                      form 2:

F2ENTER F3VIEW F4EXIT F5FORM CLR F6FLD CLR F7DELETE F8MODIFY F9REPORT F1ØMULTI
```

FIGURE 3.3

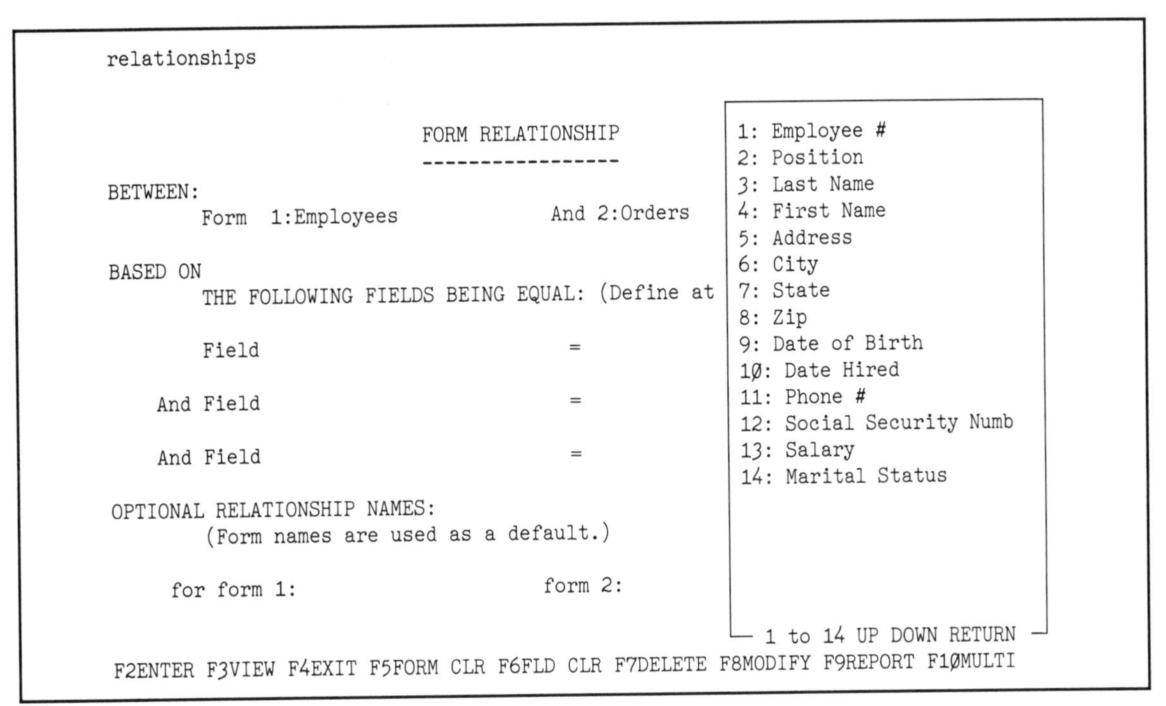

```
relationships

                        FORM RELATIONSHIP            1: Employee #
                        -----------------            2: Position
BETWEEN:                                             3: Last Name
     Form  1:Employees            And 2:Orders       4: First Name
                                                     5: Address
BASED ON                                             6: City
     THE FOLLOWING FIELDS BEING EQUAL: (Define at    7: State
                                                     8: Zip
     Field                      =                    9: Date of Birth
                                                     1Ø: Date Hired
   And Field                    =                    11: Phone #
                                                     12: Social Security Numb
   And Field                    =                    13: Salary
                                                     14: Marital Status
OPTIONAL RELATIONSHIP NAMES:
     (Form names are used as a default.)

    for form 1:                form 2:

                                                     1 to 14 UP DOWN RETURN
F2ENTER F3VIEW F4EXIT F5FORM CLR F6FLD CLR F7DELETE F8MODIFY F9REPORT F1ØMULTI
```

FIGURE 3.4

pressing **1** as shown in Figure 3.4. The window box, as shown on the right side of Figure 3.4, is obtained by pressing the F1 key. It shows a list of all the fields you can enter. To select the field, use the up and down arrows to highlight the field you want and press the RETURN key. You may also select the field by typing in the number for that particular field and pressing RETURN.

In a similar manner, select **Emp #** by pressing **7**, as shown in Figure 3.5.

The final relationship form should look like Figure 3.3.

The optional relationship names will be left blank. These names are needed when you have multiple relationships within a form or are setting up multiple relationships between two forms. To save the relationship you have created, press the F2 ENTER key. Press F5 FORM CLR to clear the form in preparation for entering new relationships.

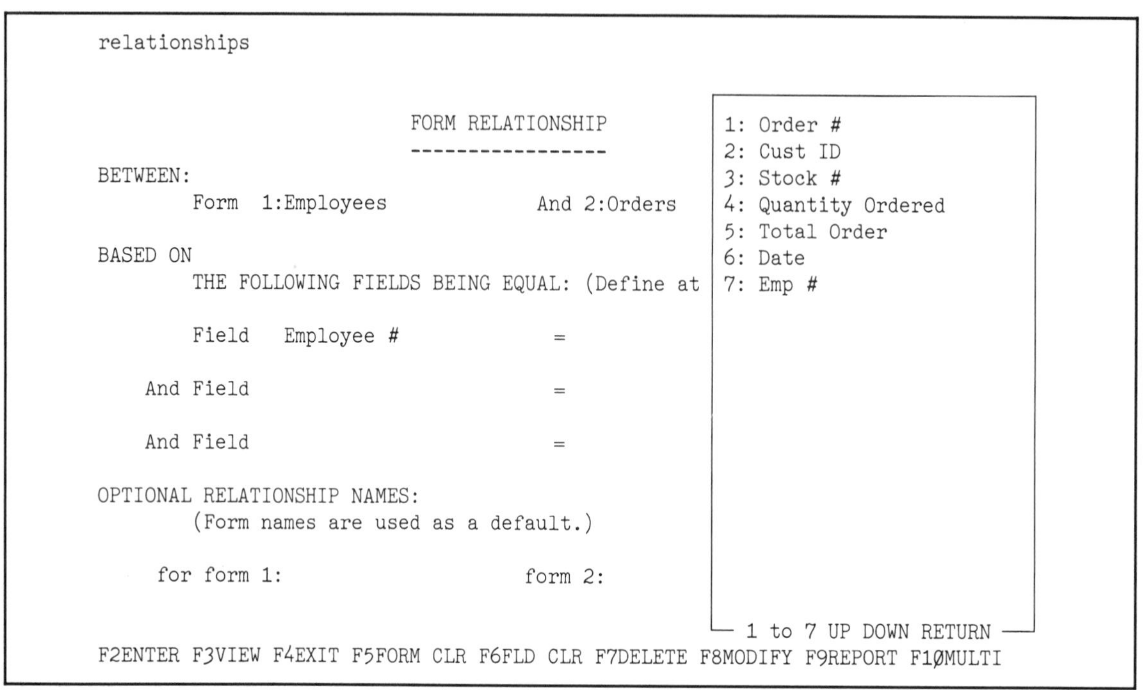

```
relationships

                        FORM RELATIONSHIP          1: Order #
                        -----------------          2: Cust ID
BETWEEN:                                           3: Stock #
     Form  1:Employees          And 2:Orders       4: Quantity Ordered
                                                   5: Total Order
BASED ON                                           6: Date
     THE FOLLOWING FIELDS BEING EQUAL: (Define at  7: Emp #

     Field   Employee #            =

  And Field                        =

  And Field                        =

OPTIONAL RELATIONSHIP NAMES:
     (Form names are used as a default.)

   for form 1:                  form 2:

                                                    1 to 7 UP DOWN RETURN
F2ENTER F3VIEW F4EXIT F5FORM CLR F6FLD CLR F7DELETE F8MODIFY F9REPORT F1ØMULTI
```

FIGURE 3.5

In a similar manner, create two new form relationships, as shown in Figures 3.6 and 3.8. Figure 3.6 shows the field **Cust ID** which is common to the two files **ORDERS** and **CUSTOMER**. **Remember that you must create these relationships before you enter data into the forms.**

Figure 3.7 shows how easy it is to select any field by typing the number or pressing the arrow keys. As shown in the Figure 3.7, all you have to do is press **1** and press the RETURN key to select the field **Cust ID**. To save this relationship, press the F2 ENTER key. Press the F5 FORM CLR key to clear the form in preparation for entering a new relationship.

You will now create one more form relationship. Figure 3.8 shows the field **Stock #**, which is common to the two files **ORDERS** and **PRODUCTS**.

```
relationships                                  To skip the menu, press Esc
1: System 2: Employee 3: orders 4: Customer 5: Products 6: Employees

                                 FORM RELATIONSHIP
                                 -----------------

BETWEEN:
        Form  1:orders                    And 2:Customer

BASED ON
        THE FOLLOWING FIELDS BEING EQUAL: (Define at least one set of fields.)

        Field   Cust ID                  =   Cust ID

    And Field                            =

    And Field                            =

OPTIONAL RELATIONSHIP NAMES:
        (Form names are used as a default.)

     for form 1:                       form 2:

F2ENTER F3VIEW F4EXIT F5FORM CLR F6FLD CLR F7DELETE F8MODIFY F9REPORT F10MULTI
```

FIGURE 3.6

```
relationships
                                                      ┌──────────────────────────┐
                                 FORM RELATIONSHIP    │ 1: Cust ID               │
                                 -----------------    │ 2: Last Name             │
BETWEEN:                                              │ 3: First Name            │
        Form  1:Orders                And 2:Customer  │ 4: Street                │
                                                      │ 5: City                  │
BASED ON                                              │ 6: State                 │
        THE FOLLOWING FIELDS BEING EQUAL: (Define at  │ 7: Zip                   │
                                                      │ 8: Phone #               │
        Field   Cust ID                  =            │                          │
                                                      │                          │
    And Field                            =            │                          │
                                                      │                          │
    And Field                            =            │                          │
                                                      │                          │
OPTIONAL RELATIONSHIP NAMES:                          │                          │
        (Form names are used as a default.)           │                          │
                                                      │                          │
     for form 1:                       form 2:        │                          │
                                                      └─ 1 to 8 UP DOWN RETURN ──┘
F2ENTER F3VIEW F4EXIT F5FORM CLR F6FLD CLR F7DELETE F8MODIFY F9REPORT F10MULTI
```

FIGURE 3.7

```
relationships                          To skip the menu, press Esc
1: System 2: Employee 3: orders 4: Customer 5: Products 6: Employees

                        FORM RELATIONSHIP
                        -----------------

BETWEEN:
        Form  1:orders                And 2:Products

BASED ON
        THE FOLLOWING FIELDS BEING EQUAL: (Define at least one set of fields.)

        Field   Stock #                 =   Stock #

    And Field                           =

    And Field                           =

OPTIONAL RELATIONSHIP NAMES:
        (Form names are used as a default.)

     for form 1:                      form 2:

F2ENTER F3VIEW F4EXIT F5FORM CLR F6FLD CLR F7DELETE F8MODIFY F9REPORT F10MULTI
```

FIGURE 3.8

DATA ENTRY INTO FORMS

Once your forms are defined and relationships between them have been established, you may enter data into the forms. A database is useless without data. Every time you fill in a form with data, a record is created and added to a file. During record entry, you may view, modify, or delete existing records in a file.

You can also enter data in a number of related files at the same time through the use of the Multi-View feature. You can search or update records in any number of files.

During data entry, you will be able to produce quick reports without leaving the data-entry module. This will be discussed in the following three chapters.

RECORDS MENU

To return to the Main Menu press F4 EXIT twice. When you select **2, Record Entry and Quick Reports**, from the Main Menu, the Records

```
RECORDS

    D A T A E A S E   R E C O R D S   M E N U        Ø: NONE
                                                     1: System
Please select a form.                                2: Employee
                                                     3: Employees
Enter a number from Ø to 6 :                         4: Customer
                                                     5: Products
                                                     6: Orders

NOTE:
You must return to this menu after adding or
changing any records, and before turning off
the power or removing any diskettes.
                                                     Ø to 6 UP DOWN RETURN
Alt-F1HELP F4EXIT DATABASE A PROG.A: DATA B: DATE         TIME
```

FIGURE 3.9

Menu will appear. In the Window Menu on the right side of the screen, the names of all existing forms appear. DataEase now asks:

```
Please select a form.

Enter a number from Ø to 6:
```

To select a form, type in the number of the form you wish, or move the cursor key to the form name and press the RETURN key. If you want to exit the Records Menu, press the F4 EXIT key. See Figure 3.9.

To enter data into the **EMPLOYEES** file, select **3**, and the **Employees** form, similiar to Figure 3.10, will appear on the screen.

The top left of the form indicates the name of the selected file: **EMPLOYEES**. The prompt line says

```
No record on screen
```

```
Employees
No record on screen

   Employee #:                     Position:

   Last Name:                      First Name:

   Address:                        City:

   State:                          Zip:

   Date of Birth:    / /           Date Hired:    / /

   Phone #:  (   )-   -            Social Security Number:    - -

   Salary:

   Marital Status:



F2ENTER F3VIEW F4EXIT F5FORM CLR F6FLD CLR F7DELETE F8MODIFY F9REPORT F1ØMULTI
```

FIGURE 3.10

As you fill in each record, and save it by pressing the F2 ENTER key, the prompt line will change and display the record number. If a form has several pages, only the first page will be shown.

During record entry, you may enter new records (press the F2 ENTER key to save each record) or view (press the F3 VIEW key), modify (press the F8 MODIFY key), delete (press the F7 DELETE key), or print existing records (press the SHIFT F9 PRINT keys). While in the Records Entry mode, you can generate quick reports by pressing the F9 REPORTS key. You can also view and enter records in another file by pressing the F10 MULTI key and F2 ENTER key.

CURSOR MOVEMENTS BETWEEN FIELDS

Data is usually entered in the order the fields are displayed. If you fill in the last position of a field, the cursor will automatically go on to the next field. If you do not fill in a field completely, press the RETURN key to advance to the next field.

The following keys will move the cursor from one field to the other. These functions are useful if you make a mistake and want to correct it.

KEY	FUNCTION
RETURN	Next Field
TAB	Next Field
SHIFT TAB	Previous Field
↓	Field Under Cursor
↑	Field Above Cursor
HOME	First Field on the Form
END	Last Field on the Form
PgUp	First Field on Current or Previous Page
PgDn	First Field on Next Page

FILLING A FIELD

The first form with data is shown in Figure 3.11. Data is entered from left to right in most field types. As you type a character, the cursor moves to the right. When the field is filled, the cursor will automatically advance to the next field. If it is not filled, press the RETURN or TAB keys to advance to the next field. Text fields, such as **Last Name**, **First Name**, **Position**, **Address**, **City**, and **State** conform to this set of rules.

Formatted numeric string, date, and time fields appear with format characters that are displayed in fixed positions. On your form, the fields **Date of Birth**, **Date Hired**, **Phone #**, and **Social Security Numb** are examples of formatted numeric strings. Digits are accepted in these fields from left to right (left justified). The cursor automatically skips over all punctuation characters. When the last position of the field is filled, the cursor automatically moves to the next field.

Salary is a fixed point number field that has a decimal point and a fixed number of digits after the decimal point. The cursor starts out on the decimal point and inserts digits to the left of the decimal point. Commas appear automatically after every third digit. Therefore, you do not need to enter commas as you are entering data. When you press the decimal point, digits are entered to the right of the decimal point until the field is filled. If you exit the field without typing in the decimal point, the digits to the right of the decimal point are filled in with

0's. If you fill in the last decimal place, the cursor automatically advances to the next field.

Marital Status is a multiple choice field. As the cursor enters the field, the choices for that field appear in the prompt line. Look at the prompt line at the top of Figure 3.11. Each choice is preceded by a choice number. In our example, if you press **1**, **Married** will be entered in the field. Finish entering the data as shown in Figure 3.11. If you make any mistakes, use the keys mentioned in the last section to edit the field data. The F6 key will clear data out of the field in which the cursor is positioned.

When you have finished entering data in this form, press F2 ENTER to save the record. Continue entering data in records as shown in Figure 3.12. Press the F5 FORM CLEAR key after each record to obtain a blank form. Then enter data in the next record. You may set up a default value for any desired field by pressing the SHIFT F2 ENTER DEFAULT keys to save the Default record. This would be advantageous

```
Employees
1: Married 2: Single 3: Divorced 4: Separated

   Employee #:  12121                Position:  Manager

   Last Name:   DeTrinis             First Name:  Vincent

   Address:  11 Oxford Avenue        City:  Massapequa

   State:  NY                        Zip:  11758

   Date of Birth:  Ø9/14/38          Date Hired:  Ø3/13/66

   Phone #:  (516)-798-5268          Social Security Number:  Ø35-66-5234

   Salary:          56,ØØØ.ØØ

   Marital Status:  Married



F2ENTER F3VIEW F4EXIT F5FORM CLR F6FLD CLR F7DELETE F8MODIFY F9REPORT F1ØMULTI
```

FIGURE 3.11

```
==============================================================================
Employee #                              12121
Position                                Manager
Last Name                               DeTrinis
First Name                              Vincent
Address                                 11 Oxford Avenue
City                                    Massapequa
State                                   NY
Zip                                     11758
Date of Birth                           09/14/38
Date Hired                              03/13/66
Phone #                                 (516)-798-5268
Social Security Numb                    035-66-5234
Salary                                         56,000.00
Marital Status                          Married

Employee #                              21346
Position                                Ass't Manager
Last Name                               DeTrinis
First Name                              Joan
Address                                 11 Oxford Avenue
City                                    Massapequa
State                                   NY
Zip                                     11758
Date of Birth                           09/22/40
Date Hired                              03/13/66
Phone #                                 (516)-798-5268
Social Security Numb                    042-71-7230
Salary                                         45,000.00
Marital Status                          Married

Employee #                              29952
Position                                Salesperson
Last Name                               DiToro
First Name                              Hank
Address                                 4522 Heavenly Court
City                                    Bethpage
State                                   NY
Zip                                     11714
Date of Birth                           04/22/45
Date Hired                              06/23/74
Phone #                                 (516)-565-9812
Social Security Numb                    049-56-7867
Salary                                         39,000.00
Marital Status                          Married
```

FIGURE 3.12

Employee #	34343
Position	Salesperson
Last Name	Duke
First Name	Joan
Address	1313 Golden Wayourt
City	Farmingdale
State	NY
Zip	11735
Date of Birth	11/03/35
Date Hired	04/17/73
Phone #	(516)-324-6645
Social Security Numb	033-21-3761
Salary	28,000.00
Marital Status	Divorced
Employee #	03999
Position	Salesperson
Last Name	Comforto
First Name	Anthony
Address	259 N. Queens Avenue
City	Massapequa
State	NY
Zip	11758
Date of Birth	10/02/39
Date Hired	11/22/71
Phone #	(515)-798-0023
Social Security Numb	022-55-1221
Salary	31,000.00
Marital Status	Married
Employee #	04545
Position	Salesperson
Last Name	Krawiec
First Name	Agnes
Address	288-11th Street
City	Brooklyn
State	NY
Zip	11215
Date of Birth	01/02/44
Date Hired	02/13/75
Phone #	(212)-788-7114
Social Security Numb	112-54-2853
Salary	27,500.00
Marital Status	Married

FIGURE 3.12 (continued)

Employee #	87698
Position	Salesperson
Last Name	Talamo
First Name	Louis
Address	18 Golf Drive
City	Queens
State	NY
Zip	11203
Date of Birth	12/02/48
Date Hired	04/05/71
Phone #	(516)-343-5714
Social Security Numb	125-78-9877
Salary	29,250.00
Marital Status	Married

Employee #	65456
Position	Secretary
Last Name	Caravan
First Name	Peggy
Address	322 Carr Avenue
City	Keansburg
State	NJ
Zip	07734
Date of Birth	11/11/49
Date Hired	05/30/72
Phone #	(201)-265-7979
Social Security Numb	033-22-4111
Salary	27,500.00
Marital Status	Divorced

Employee #	98798
Position	Salesperson
Last Name	Braun
First Name	Sheila
Address	3011 Bluepoint Court
City	Wantagh
State	NY
Zip	11793
Date of Birth	07/22/46
Date Hired	07/01/69
Phone #	(516)-785-1921
Social Security Numb	044-55-2323
Salary	33,000.00
Marital Status	Separated

FIGURE 3.12 (continued)

```
Employee #                          76723
Position                            Salesperson
Last Name                           Wasniewski
First Name                          Joann
Address                             147 Fox Chase Drive
City                                Brooklyn
State                               NY
Zip                                 11215
Date of Birth                       11/23/56
Date Hired                          Ø9/18/77
Phone #                             (212)-461-4365
Social Security Numb                Ø23-45-4242
Salary                                     31,5ØØ.ØØ
Marital Status                      Separated
================================================================================
```

FIGURE 3.12 (continued)

if all the people were from the same town or state. For example, if most of the people lived in the city Miller Place, there would be no need to continually type in this piece of information. You could set the default value of the city to Miller Place. You would need to change or retype the city only if it was different. The SHIFT F5 DEFAULT FORM or SHIFT F6 DEFAULT FIELD keys may be used to retrieve the default value. When you have finished entering and checking the data, press the F4 EXIT key.

In a similar manner, you will enter data for the next three files. You will now enter information in the **CUSTOMER** file. From the Main Menu select **3** to enter the **CUSTOMER** file and press the RETURN key. Figure 3.13 shows the first record with the information already filled.

Leave the information blank for the field **Cust ID**. This is a sequenced number field. Because it is a sequenced field, you should not enter data in this field. DataEase will automatically fill the next sequence number

```
Customer
Record 1 on screen

Cust ID:  C-ØØØ1

Last Name:  Bergen                First Name:  Carol

Street:  37 Wilson Street

City:  Massapequa Park        State:  NY     Zip:  11762

Phone #:  (516)-798-8632








F2ENTER F3VIEW F4EXIT F5FORM CLR F6FLD CLR F7DELETE F8MODIFY F9REPORT F1ØMULTI
```

FIGURE 3.13

when the cursor leaves the field or when you press the F2 ENTER key to save the record. Every time a record is entered, the sequence number is increased by one. Finish entering the rest of the data in the **CUSTOMER** file, as shown in Figure 3.14.

Now enter information into the **PRODUCTS** file. From the Main Menu, select **4** and press the RETURN key. The **Stock #** is a sequenced field, which DataEase will automatically fill in when the cursor leaves the field or when you save the record. Finish typing the data into the first record, as shown in Figure 3.15.

Finish entering the rest of the data in the **PRODUCTS** file, as shown in Figure 3.16.

From the Main Menu, select **5**, then press the RETURN key to enter the **ORDERS** file. Figure 3.17 shows the first record with the information already filled.

```
================================================================================
Cust ID                                   C-0001
Last Name                                 Bergen
First Name                                Carol
Street                                    37 Wilson Street
City                                      Massapequa Park
State                                     NY
Zip                                       11762
Phone #                                   (516)-798-8632

Cust ID                                   C-0002
Last Name                                 Strongly
First Name                                Vincent
Street                                    214-10 24th Avenue
City                                      Bayside
State                                     NY
Zip                                       11360
Phone #                                   (718)-224-5443

Cust ID                                   C-0003
Last Name                                 Willoughby
First Name                                Malcom
Street                                    9876 Molloy Way
City                                      Rockville Center
State                                     NY
Zip                                       11355
Phone #                                   (516)-678-2306

Cust ID                                   C-0004
Last Name                                 Swietnicki
First Name                                Marge
Street                                    290 11th Street
City                                      Brooklyn
State                                     NY
Zip                                       11215
Phone #                                   (718)-213-4299

Cust ID                                   C-0005
Last Name                                 Tabone
First Name                                Toni
Street                                    Rd. 3, Box 124C
City                                      New Berlin
State                                     NY
Zip                                       13411
Phone #                                   (607)-847-4289
```

FIGURE 3.14

Cust ID	C-0006
Last Name	Fitzgerald
First Name	Lisa
Street	9292 Shore Road
City	Brooklyn
State	NY
Zip	11215
Phone #	(718)-680-1026
Cust ID	C-0007
Last Name	Glass
First Name	Jeff
Street	1754 Apple Hollow Rd
City	Hamlin
State	NY
Zip	14464
Phone #	(716)-964-7322
Cust ID	C-0008
Last Name	Herbold
First Name	Mary Ellen
Street	793 Long Island Ave
City	Deer Park
State	NY
Zip	11729
Phone #	(515)-243-2308
Cust ID	C-0009
Last Name	Mena
First Name	Paul
Street	7 Inverary Court
City	Charleston
State	NC
Zip	29407
Phone #	(803)-556-1336
Cust ID	C-0010
Last Name	Swartarm
First Name	Timothy
Street	541 Shoreham Road
City	Massapequa Park
State	NY
Zip	11758
Phone #	(516)-798-8707

FIGURE 3.14 (continued)

```
Cust ID                                 C-0011
Last Name                               Vultaggio
First Name                              Brema
Street                                  33 Bay Drive
City                                    Massapequa
State                                   NY
Zip                                     11758
Phone #                                 (516)-795-7914
================================================================================
```

FIGURE 3.14 (continued)

```
Products                               Record found
Record 1 on screen

Stock # 000001

Description IBM Personal Computer System - Mono

Quantity  30

Price     1,400.00









F2ENTER F3VIEW F4EXIT F5FORM CLR F6FLD CLR F7DELETE F8MODIFY F9REPORT F10MULTI
```

FIGURE 3.15

```
================================================================================
Stock #                                      ØØØØØ1
Description                                  IBM Personal Computer System - Mono
Quantity                                      3Ø
Price                                            1,4ØØ.ØØ

Stock #                                      ØØØØØ2
Description                                  IBM Personal Computer System - Color
Quantity                                      25
Price                                            2,2ØØ.ØØ

Stock #                                      ØØØØØ3
Description                                  2Ø Megabyte Hard Disk Drive
Quantity                                      15
Price                                              725.ØØ

Stock #                                      ØØØØØ4
Description                                  2Ø Megabyte Hard Card
Quantity                                      1Ø
Price                                              95Ø.ØØ

Stock #                                      ØØØØØ5
Description                                  Epson FX-85 Printer
Quantity                                       6
Price                                              45Ø.ØØ

Stock #                                      ØØØØØ6
Description                                  Epson LQ-8ØØ Printer
Quantity                                       3
Price                                              62Ø.ØØ

Stock #                                      ØØØØØ7
Description                                  EGA Monitor
Quantity                                       7
Price                                              52Ø.ØØ

Stock #                                      ØØØØØ8
Description                                  Laser Printer
Quantity                                       2
Price                                            5,432.ØØ

Stock #                                      ØØØØØ9
Description                                  Six Pak Multifunction Board
Quantity                                       7
Price                                              38Ø.ØØ

Stock #                                      ØØØØØ1Ø
Description                                  24ØØ Baud Modem
Quantity                                       3
Price                                              535.ØØ
================================================================================
```

FIGURE 3.16

```
Orders
No record on screen

Order #:  O-ØØ1                     Cust ID:  C-ØØØ3

Stock #:  ØØØØØ1                    Quantity Ordered:      1

Total Order:      1,4ØØ.ØØ

Date:  Ø2/22/87                     Emp #:  98798











F2ENTER F3VIEW F4EXIT F5FORM CLR F6FLD CLR F7DELETE F8MODIFY F9REPORT F1ØMULTI
```

FIGURE 3.17

If your system has a clock, the information in the **Date** field will automatically be entered by the computer when the cursor leaves the field. Do not enter any information in the field **Total Ordered**. The **Stock #** that is entered in the **ORDERS** file is linked to the **Price** field in the **PRODUCTS** file. DataEase will automatically look up the **Price** of the item in the **PRODUCTS** file and multiply it by the **Quantity Ordered** to give the **Total Order**. As soon as the cursor leaves that field, the total amount of money will be entered. This derived field is not saved on the disk. For this reason, it is recorded as a virtual field in the form definition. The value of a virtual field is computed every time it is needed. If the value of an item changes, you need to modify it only in the **PRODUCTS** file. DataEase will always compute the **Total Order** based on the current value. Virtual fields save space on the disk but take more time because they have to be recalculated each time you enter new data. Data entry was not prevented in the **Total Order** field, in case the salesperson wants to give a discount to the customer.

Finish entering the rest of the data in the **ORDERS** file by typing in the data shown in Figure 3.18.

```
================================================================================
Order #                                 O-ØØ1
Cust ID                                 C-ØØØ3
Stock #                                 ØØØØØ1
Quantity Ordered                            1
Total Order                                 1,4ØØ.ØØ
Date                                    1Ø/Ø6/86
Emp #                                   98798

Order #                                 O-ØØ2
Cust ID                                 C-ØØØ8
Stock #                                 ØØØØØ4
Quantity Ordered                            2
Total Order                                 1,9ØØ.ØØ
Date                                    1Ø/Ø6/86
Emp #                                   34343

Order #                                 O-ØØ3
Cust ID                                 C-ØØ11
Stock #                                 ØØØØØ2
Quantity Ordered                            4
Total Order                                 8,8ØØ.ØØ
Date                                    1Ø/Ø6/86
Emp #                                   Ø4545

Order #                                 O-ØØ4
Cust ID                                 C-ØØØ1
Stock #                                 ØØØØØ9
Quantity Ordered                            1
Total Order                                   38Ø.ØØ
Date                                    1Ø/Ø6/86
Emp #                                   65456

Order #                                 O-ØØ5
Cust ID                                 C-ØØ11
Stock #                                 ØØØØØ5
Quantity Ordered                            1
Total Order                                   45Ø.ØØ
Date                                    1Ø/Ø6/86
Emp #                                   98798

Order #                                 O-ØØ6
Cust ID                                 C-ØØØ5
Stock #                                 ØØØØØ7
Quantity Ordered                            1
Total Order                                   52Ø.ØØ
Date                                    1Ø/Ø6/86
Emp #                                   87698
```

FIGURE 3.18

```
Order #                          O-ØØ7
Cust ID                          C-ØØØ9
Stock #                          ØØØØØ8
Quantity Ordered                     1
Total Order                          5,432.ØØ
Date                             1Ø/Ø6/86
Emp #                            Ø3999

Order #                          O-ØØ8
Cust ID                          C-ØØØ8
Stock #                          ØØØØØ1
Quantity Ordered                     2
Total Order                          2,8ØØ.ØØ
Date                             1Ø/Ø6/86
Emp #                            87698

Order #                          O-ØØ9
Cust ID                          C-ØØØ3
Stock #                          ØØØØØ2
Quantity Ordered                     1
Total Order                          2,2ØØ.ØØ
Date                             1Ø/Ø6/86
Emp #                            34343

Order #                          O-Ø1Ø
Cust ID                          C-ØØ11
Stock #                          ØØØØØ5
Quantity Ordered                     1
Total Order                            45Ø.ØØ
Date                             1Ø/Ø6/86
Emp #                            98798
================================================================================
```

FIGURE 3.18 (continued)

CORRECTING FIELD DATA

The following keys can be used to edit your data. These functions are useful if you make a mistake when entering data in a field.

KEY	FUNCTION
BACKSPACE	Delete the Previous Character
←	Move Cursor to Previous Character
→	Move Cursor to Next Character
F6 CLEAR FIELD	Clear the Field
INS	Go out/into Insert Mode
DEL	Delete the Current Character

SAVING THE RECORD

As you type information into the form, it appears on the screen, but it is not saved to the disk. If you want to erase the information, press the F5 FORM CLEAR or the F4 EXIT key. To save the record, press the F2 ENTER key. The record is now saved.

If you try to save a record that has missing required data, you will get the message

```
required field not entered
```

You must then fill in all required fields before you can save the record.

If you are trying to save a record with duplicate unique values, the computer will tell you that the record already exists. It will then ask if you wish to modify the record or not. Since DataEase does not save each record individually, it waits until about 10 records are in memory or until approximately 30 seconds have passed with no keyboard activity. If you leave the keyboard for at least 30 seconds without typing, the information that is then in memory will be saved to disk. **Do not remove your Data disk until you exit to the Records Menu or exit DataEase.** Otherwise, you might loose some data.

PRINTING THE RECORD

If you press the SHIFT F9 PRINT keys, the printer will print out the record that is on the screen. You may then continue entering records or performing any other record operations.

VIEWING RECORDS IN A FILE

VIEW	KEYS
First Record	F5 FORM CLEAR followed by F3 VIEW
Last Record	F5 FORM CLEAR followed by SHIFT F3 VIEW BACK
Next Record	F3 VIEW
Previous Record	SHIFT F3 VIEW BACK
By Record Number	CTRL F3 VIEW RECORD, type record number, followed by RETURN

After you view a record, you may modify, delete, or print the record.

MODIFYING A RECORD

Any record that is on the screen may be modified. To modify a record, make any necessary changes, then press the F8 MODIFY key. **Be very careful!** If you press the F2 ENTER key after you modify a record, you may have two records on the disk with the same information except for minor changes. This can happen quite frequently if you are changing records that you are viewing.

DELETING A RECORD

Any record on the screen may be deleted by pressing the F7 DELETE key. DataEase will always ask

```
Are you sure you want to delete the record?
```

If you answer

```
yes
```

the record is deleted, the message

```
Record deleted
```

appears, and the record data remains on the screen.

VIEWING SELECTED RECORDS

If you specify criteria in one or more fields, selected records can be found. First, clear the form by pressing the F5 FORM CLEAR key. Then type in the selection criteria. For example, if you wanted to find all the information in the **EMPLOYEES** file about a salesperson whose last name was Braun, you would type

```
Braun
```

in the **Last Name** field, as shown in Figure 3.19. After you type in the selection criteria, press the F3 VIEW key to see if any records match your criteria.

In you weren't sure of the spelling of the last name, you could have typed

```
Br??n
```

in the field. The **?** character is called a wildcard character, because it takes the place of any single character. Therefore, the computer would indicate records for Braun, Brown, Brain, etc.

```
Employees

   Employee #:                      Position:

   Last Name:  Braun                First Name:

   Address:                         City:

   State:                           Zip:

   Date of Birth:    / /            Date Hired:    / /

   Phone #:  (   )-   -             Social Security Number:     - -

   Salary:

   Marital Status:



F2ENTER F3VIEW F4EXIT F5FORM CLR F6FLD CLR F7DELETE F8MODIFY F9REPORT F10MULTI
```
FIGURE 3.19

Another wildcard character is the *. It is used to represent any number of characters, instead of a single character. For example, if you typed **Br*n**, the resulting search might bring up Braun, Bran, Branagan, Browen, etc. If you typed in **Br***, this would have the same effect as **Br*n**. Typing the letter **n** would be meaningless.

The wildcard searches are very useful if you are unsure of the spelling of a name, address, etc.

If you are typing selection criteria into a prevent data-entry field or want to suppress the automatic derivation of these data-entry fields, use the ALT F5 UNCHECKED keys to go into the Unchecked mode. Then type in the selection criteria and press the F3 VIEW key.

After the first record is found that satisfies that criteria, press the ALT-F3 CONTINUE keys to find the next record that satisfies that criteria. If a record is found, you may modify, delete, or print the record.

MULTI-VIEW

In your computer store simulation, the four files you are using are related to each other based on match fields. Remember the relationship forms! Multi-View allows you to view related records in multiple files. It also allows you to enter, modify, or delete records in multiple files.

In order to learn how to use Multi-View, you will now locate a customer's record, view their order, find out what products they purchased, and find out what salesperson waited on him/her. All of this information is located in related files. The only information you know is that the person's last name begins with "Vul."

From the Main Menu, type **2** for **Record Entry and Quick Reports.** Type **3** for the **CUSTOMER** file and press the RETURN key. On the screen you will see a blank customer form. Move the cursor to the field **Last Name**. As the cursor moves to this field, you will notice that the field **Cust ID** becomes C-0011. Ignore this now. You will get back to it in a minute.

While in the **Last Name** field, type

```
Vul*
```

```
Customer
No record on screen

Cust ID:

Last Name:  Vul*                   First Name:

Street:

City:                         State:        Zip:

Phone #:  (    )-    -











F2ENTER F3VIEW F4EXIT F5FORM CLR F6FLD CLR F7DELETE F8MODIFY F9REPORT F10MULTI
```

FIGURE 3.20

using the wildcard character to find any name that begins with "Vul." If you are typing selection criteria in a prevent data-entry field, press the ALT F5 UNCHECKED keys to go into the Unchecked mode. Then type in the selection criteria and press the F3 VIEW key. The result is shown in Figure 3.20.

To locate a record that matches this selection criteria, press the F3 VIEW key. Figure 3.21 should appear.

To access any related files, press the F10 MULTI-VIEW key. This will give you the screen shown in Figure 3.22. Notice that the two files **CUSTOMER** and **ORDERS** are related by having the same field—**Cust ID**. Notice that the **Cust ID** C-0011 appears in the two figures. Press the F4 key, and you will return to the **ORDERS** file, with Record 4 on screen, as shown in Figure 3.23.

```
Customer                                    Returned to Customer
Record 22 on screen

Cust ID:  C-ØØ11

Last Name:  Vultaggio              First Name:  Brema

Street:  33 Bay Drive

City:  Massapequa            State:  NY     Zip:  11758

Phone #:  (516)-795-7914








F2ENTER F3VIEW F4EXIT F5FORM CLR F6FLD CLR F7DELETE F8MODIFY F9REPORT F1ØMULTI
```

FIGURE 3.21

```
Orders
Record 4 on screen

Order #:  O-ØØ3                    Cust ID:  C-ØØ11

Stock #:  ØØØØØ2                   Quantity Ordered:      4

Total Order:       8,8ØØ.ØØ

Date:  Ø2/22/87                    Emp #:  Ø4545








F2ENTER F3VIEW F4EXIT F5FORM CLR F6FLD CLR F7DELETE F8MODIFY F9REPORT F1ØMULTI
```

FIGURE 3.22

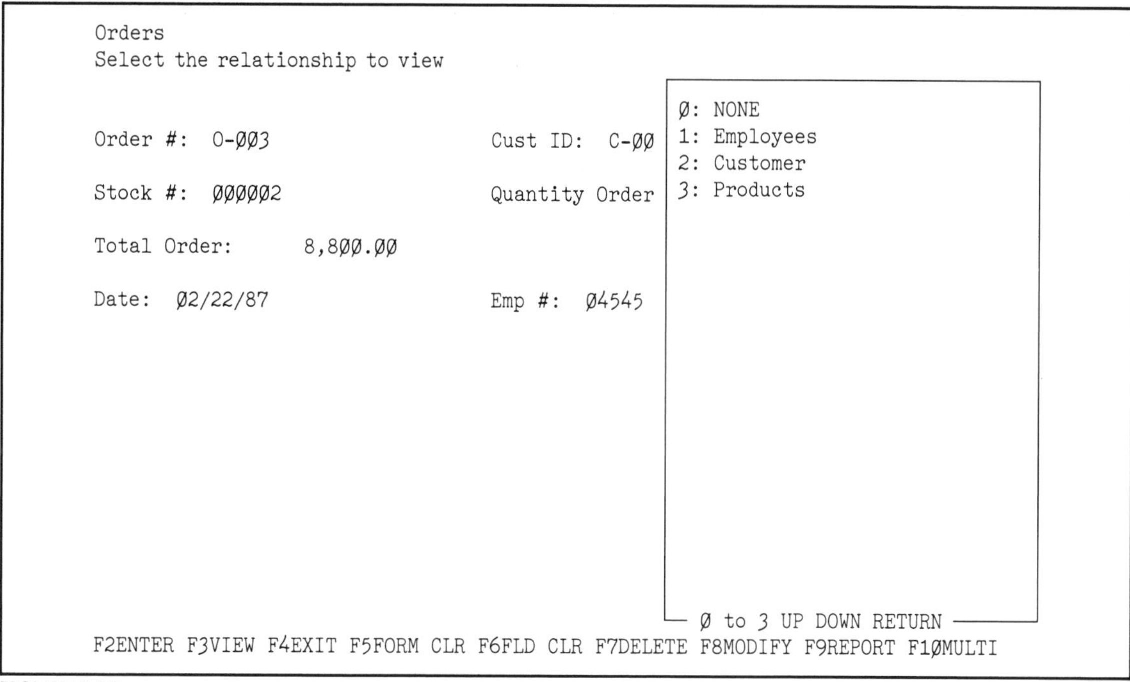

FIGURE 3.23

Press the F10 MULTI-VIEW key, and the Form or Relationships Menu will appear in the window, as shown in Figure 3.23.

Press **3** for the **PRODUCTS** file, then press the RETURN key. Figure 3.24 shows the screen that appears. It indicates the product that Brema Vultaggio ordered.

Press the F4 key, and you will return to the **ORDERS** file, with Record 4 on screen. Press the F10 MULTI-VIEW key, and the File Menu will appear in the window. Press **1** for the **EMPLOYEES** file, then press the RETURN key. The screen shown in Figure 3.25 appears. It indicates the salesperson who waited on Brema Vultaggio.

In this example, you had to keep returning to the **ORDERS** file to access the other files because three of its fields are linked to the other files, as shown below. Refer also to Figure 3.1.

```
Products
Record 2 on screen

Stock #:  ØØØØØ2

Description:  IBM Personal Computer System - Color

Quantity:   25

Price        2,2ØØØ.ØØ


F2ENTER F3VIEW F4EXIT F5FORM CLR F6FLD CLR F7DELETE F8MODIFY F9REPORT F1ØMULTI
```

FIGURE 3.24

```
Employees
Record 5 on screen

   Employee #:  Ø4545            Position:  Salesperson

   Last Name:   Krawiec          First Name:  Agnes

   Address:  288-11th Street     City:  Brooklyn

   State:  NY                    Zip:  11215

   Date of Birth:  Ø1/Ø2/44      Date Hired:  Ø2/13/75

   Phone #:  (212)-788-7114      Social Security Number:  112-54-2853

   Salary:         27,5ØØ.ØØ

   Marital Status:  Married


F2ENTER F3VIEW F4EXIT F5FORM CLR F6FLD CLR F7DELETE F8MODIFY F9REPORT F1ØMULTI
```

FIGURE 3.25

FILE 1	FIELD 1	FILE 2	FIELD 2
ORDERS	Cust ID	CUSTOMER	Cust ID
ORDERS	Stock #	PRODUCTS	Stock #
ORDERS	Emp #	EMPLOYEE	Employee #

By going through the **ORDERS** file, you can access information in any of the other three files. If you would like to go back to a particular menu, simply press the F4 EXIT key.

QUICK REPORTS—A SIMPLE REPORT

In this chapter you will learn the difference between quick and full reports. The use of record selection, field selection, and report formats to generate a simple quick report will be discussed. You will learn how to do statistics on a field and search for selected fields. You will also learn how to print a report definition and how to save and load a report.

DIFFERENCE BETWEEN QUICK AND FULL REPORTS

While in the Record Entry mode, you may access the Quick Reports Menu at any time by pressing the F9 REPORTS key. There are two types of reports: quick reports and full reports. Quick reports, which are discussed in this chapter, let you define reports with very little effort. Full reports let you use the DataEase query language to generate sophisticated reports. Quick reports use a query by example to let you specify your requirements. For example, you can find all the people who live in Massapequa and who make more than $35,000 a year.

You can enter the Reports Menu in two ways. From the Main Menu, you can select **3**, **Full Reports**, and press the F9 QUICK key to access the Quick Reports Menu. You can also press the F9 REPORTS key in the Record Entry mode. You can switch from quick reports to full reports by pressing the F9 REPORTS key. The menus for the two types of reports are very similar.

QUICK REPORTS MENU

You will now create a simple report to print out a list of all the employees in the computer company, including their **Employee #**, **Position**, **Last Name**, **First Name**, and **Salary**. The last names of the employees will be printed in alphabetical order. The first thing you must do is enter the **EMPLOYEES** file. To enter the Quick Reports Menu press the F9 REPORTS key. The Quick Reports Menu appears, as shown in Figure 4.1.

Since you are in the Record Entry mode, the quick report will be based on the record entry form. To define a quick report, you must first select the records that you wish to view or print. You can select certain information or all the information about a file of records. If you don't select any records, the system will default to all records.

SELECTING ALL RECORDS

From the Quick Reports Menu, select **2**, **Start New Report**. Next, select **3**, **Define Record Selection**. This function allows you to select certain records from the primary file, in this case, **EMPLOYEES**. (In a future

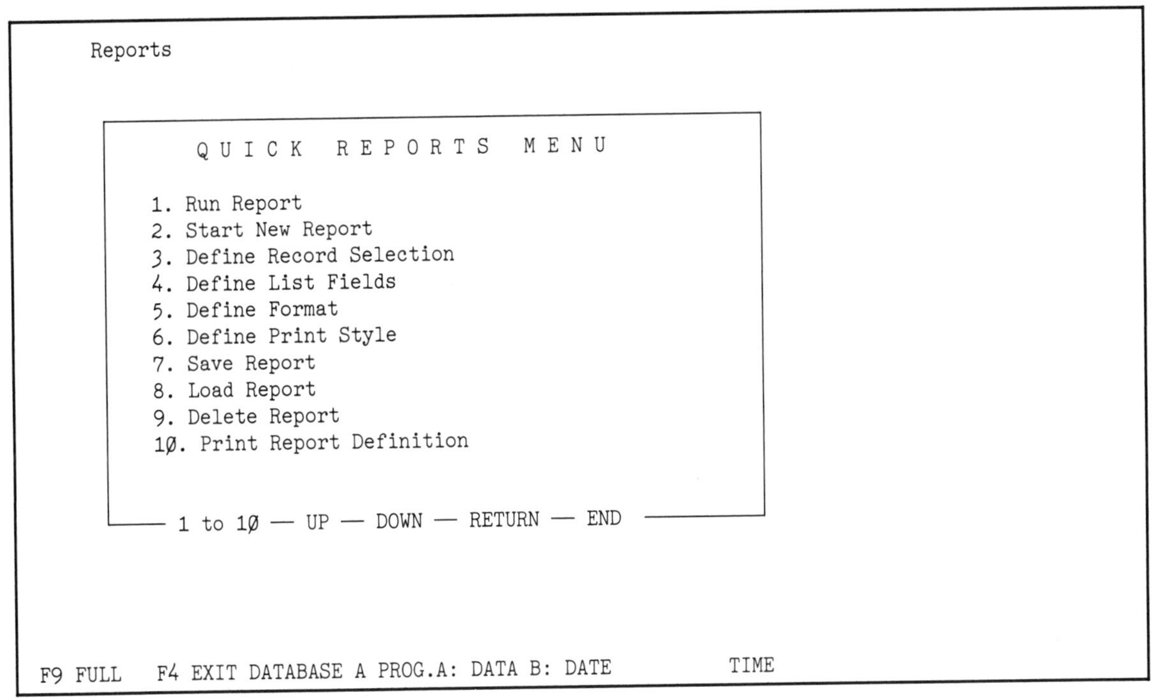

FIGURE 4.1

chapter you will learn how to generate a quick report that has information in several files.)

DataEase will show you a blank form. Since you want to generate a list of all the people in the **EMPLOYEES** file, you will enter any information into this form. Press the F2 ENTER key.

DEFINING WHICH FIELDS ARE TO BE LISTED

Pressing the F2 ENTER key will cause a blank record form to appear. The prompt line says:

```
    Press Space to mark field. Then specify Order Reverse
Group Sum Mean Max or Min
```

Move the cursor to the **Last Name** field and press the SPACEBAR. The number **1** appears in that field. This will be the first field that will be printed in the report. Since you want the report to be sorted by **Last**

Name in alphabetical order, you will type:

```
order
```

to the right of the number **1**, as shown in Figure 4.2.

In a similar manner, move the cursor to the **First Name** field and press the SPACEBAR. The number **2** appears in the field. This will be the second field that will be printed in the report. Move the cursor to the **Employee #** field and press the SPACEBAR. The number **3** appears in the field. This will be the third field printed. Move the cursor to the **Position** field and press the SPACEBAR. The number **4** appears in that field. This will be the fourth field that will be printed. Move the cursor to the **Salary** field and press the SPACEBAR. The number **5** appears in that field. This will be the fifth and last field that will be printed in this report.

When you typed the word **order** into the **Last Name** field, you instructed DataEase to sort that field into alphabetical order. If you

```
Select Fields
Press Space to mark field. Then specify Order Reverse Group Sum Mean Max or Min

   Employee #  3                   Position:  4

   Last Name:  1 order             First Name:  2

   Address:                        City:

   State:                          Zip:

   Date of Birth:                  Date Hired:

   Phone #:                        Social Security Number:

   Salary:  5

   Marital Status:



F2ENTER F4EXIT F5FORM CLR F6FLD CLR F10MULTI
```

FIGURE 4.2

wanted to have the field printed in reverse alphabetical order, you could have typed in the word **reverse**. If you typed in the word **group**, DataEase would sort the records and separate them into groups. In your example, **group** could have been typed in the **Position** field. DataEase would have sorted the field by manager, assistant manager, secretary, and salesperson. When you group a field, the field is listed only once. Statistics can be performed for each group. Each group can be formatted with its own headers and footers. (This will be discussed later.)

After you have selected the fields, as shown in Figure 4.2, press the F4 ENTER key to save the selection criteria.

DEFINING REPORT FORMAT

You can now define the format in which you want the data to be presented. The default format is columnar. You may select a system form or design your own. Press **5**, **Define Format**. DataEase defaults to a columnar format and displays the following message:

```
Minimum line length for a columnar report is 78
```

DataEase calculates this for you by adding the length of each of the five fields, allowing one space between each one of them. The format screen with the line length and format options is shown in Figure 4.3.

DataEase then responds with:

```
What type of report format do you want:
```

You will notice that at the top of Figure 4.3 the six report formats are shown. The default setting for any report is columnar. (Some of the other report formats will be discussed and illustrated in later chapters.) The columnar report has headings and one record per line. Choice **2**, **Field per Line**, places each field on a separate line. Figures 3.12, 3.14, 3.16, and 3.18 in the last chapter are examples that were printed using the field per line format. If you look at those figures, you will notice that the field titles occupy the left-hand column, while the right-hand column contains the field information. There is one blank line between each of the records.

Choice **3**, **Export format**, is used to export data to other programs—such as Lotus 1-2-3 and Multimate—and to a mainframe computer.

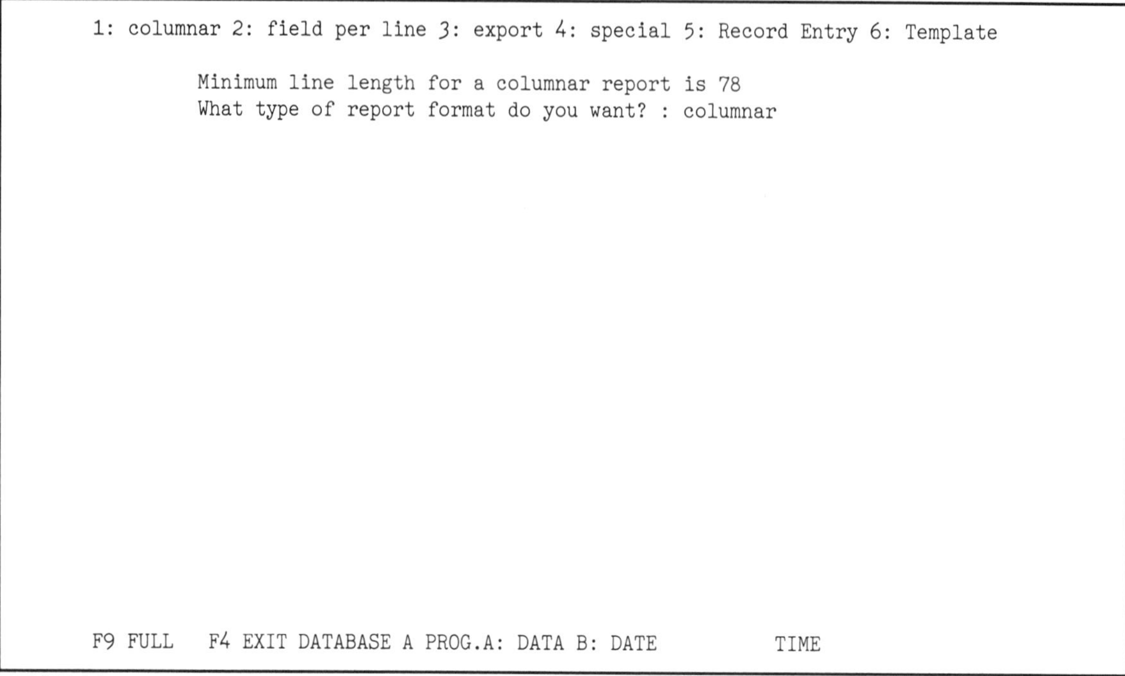

FIGURE 4.3

Choice 4, **Special format**, allows you to create your own format. Choice 5, **Record Entry format**, uses its own form for the report format. Choice 6, **Template format**, allows you to use a template or format that was created by you or another user. Since you want the report to be in columnar form, press the RETURN key to accept the format.

DataEase will show you an outline of the output format, as shown in Figure 4.4.

In the columnar report, DataEase provides all the headings. Some of these headings may be abbreviated or continued on the next line. In your example, the heading **Employee #** exceeds the length of the field and must be continued on the next line. (You will be shown how to correct this later.) You will notice that two words below the title headings begin with a period. A period signifies a Report Format command. The Report Format command **.items** shows where the individual record information will be printed. Each record will be printed on one

```
                              R  1 C   1

==============================================================================
      Last              First       Employe        Position             Salary
      Name              Name           e
                                       #
------------------------------------------------------------------------------
.items
  [          ]      [         ]    [   ]     [          ]         [           ]

.end
==============================================================================

F2ENTER F3CUT F4EXIT F5COPY F6PASTE F7DEL LINE F8INS LINE F9PRINT F10FIELD
```

FIGURE 4.4

blank line. There will be as many lines of data printed as there are records. The **.end** command signifies the end of the report. To save the Report format, press F2 ENTER.

DEFINING PRINT STYLE, RUNNING, AND SAVING REPORT

Press **6** to **Define Print Styles**. The Print Style specification now appears, as shown in Figure 4.5.

Notice in the top line of Figure 4.5 that you may have the report sent to the screen, printer, or disk. At the present time, have the report sent to the screen by pressing **1**. Notice the statement on the third line of the screen that says:

```
Allow Style modification at run-time
```

This statement allows you to change the menu when running the report. This would include redirecting the output of the report to the printer at a later time.

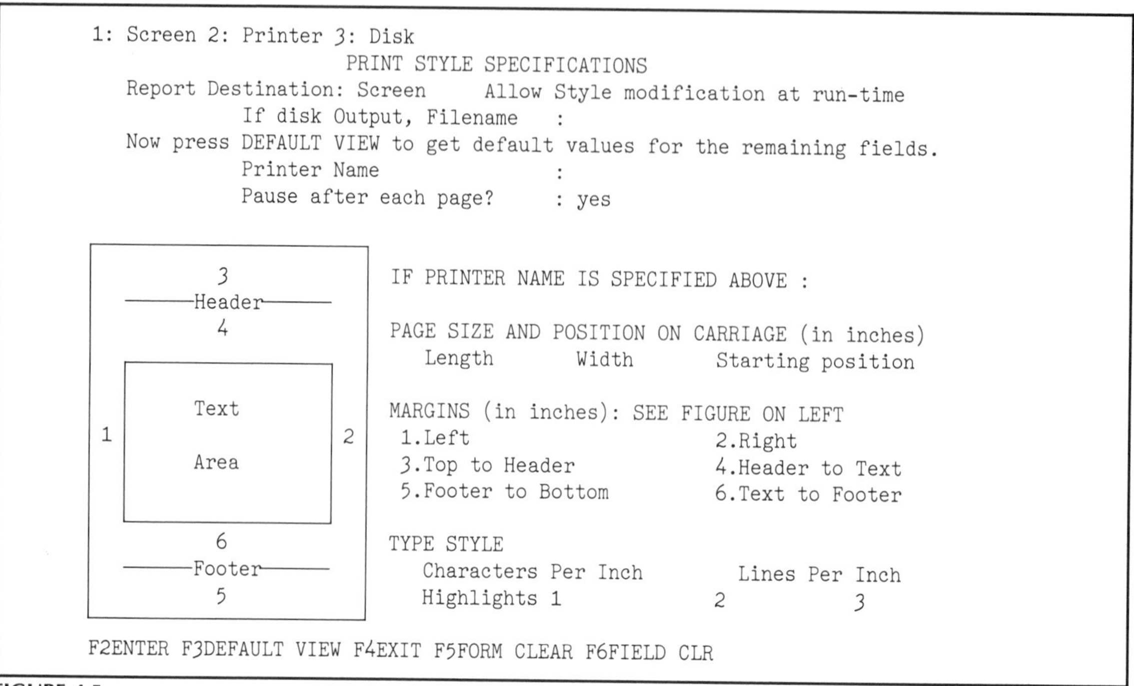

```
1: Screen 2: Printer 3: Disk
                 PRINT STYLE SPECIFICATIONS
  Report Destination: Screen     Allow Style modification at run-time
          If disk Output, Filename    :
  Now press DEFAULT VIEW to get default values for the remaining fields.
          Printer Name                :
          Pause after each page?      : yes

        3            IF PRINTER NAME IS SPECIFIED ABOVE :
  -----Header-----
        4            PAGE SIZE AND POSITION ON CARRIAGE (in inches)
                        Length       Width        Starting position

       Text          MARGINS (in inches): SEE FIGURE ON LEFT
  1                2  1.Left                        2.Right
       Area           3.Top to Header               4.Header to Text
                      5.Footer to Bottom            6.Text to Footer

        6            TYPE STYLE
  -----Footer-----      Characters Per Inch          Lines Per Inch
        5               Highlights 1               2           3

F2ENTER F3DEFAULT VIEW F4EXIT F5FORM CLEAR F6FIELD CLR
```

FIGURE 4.5

The rest of the Print Style specifications relate to the printer. They do not apply if you are sending your data to the screen, unless you are changing margins or page lengths. However, at a later point, you should experiment with Print Style specifications by changing some of the values and seeing how the output appears on the paper and screen. It is imperative that you have your printer manual nearby to use as a reference if you need help. Since you are finished with the Print Style specifications, press F2 ENTER to save this information. Press **7** to save and name the report or **1** to run the report. If you run the report, option **1**, the status, or top, line of the screen will now say:

```
Running report
```

When the computer has finished, the final report will be displayed on the screen, as shown in Figure 4.6.

```
                              Running report
END OF REPORT   SPACE: Return to Menu   LEFT and RIGHT Arrows: Scroll

================================================================================
      Last           First       Employe       Position             Salary
      Name           Name           e
                                    #
--------------------------------------------------------------------------------
 Braun           Sheila           98798  Salesperson              33,ØØØ.ØØ
 Caravan         Peggy            65456  Secretary                27,5ØØ.ØØ
 Comforto        Anthony          Ø3999  Salesperson              31,ØØØ.ØØ
 DeTrinis        Joan             21346  Ass't Manager            45,ØØØ.ØØ
 DeTrinis        Vincent          12121  Manager                  56,ØØØ.ØØ
 DiToro          Hank             29952  Salesperson              39,ØØØ.ØØ
 Duke            Joan             34343  Salesperson              28,ØØØ.ØØ
 Krawiec         Agnes            Ø4545  Salesperson              27,5ØØ.ØØ
 Talamo          Louis            87698  Salesperson              29,25Ø.ØØ
 Wasniewski      Joann            76723  Salesperson              31,5ØØ.ØØ
================================================================================


      F4 EXIT     DATABASE A PROG.A: DATA B: DATE          TIME
```

FIGURE 4.6

In your case, the report is pictured on one screen. If the report had been on several screens, the message **END OF REPORT**, shown on the prompt line, would have been displayed only on the last screen that contained data. Your report was only 78 characters long (see Figure 4.3). If it were longer, the entire report output could not be seen on the screen. In that situation, you could use the LEFT and RIGHT ARROW keys to scroll across the screen to view the data and the message on the prompt line. Press the SPACEBAR either to exit this screen and return to the Quick Reports Menu or to continue viewing the report.

You can now save this report by pressing **7**, **Save Report**. If you ran the report without saving it, DataEase will comment:

```
Hit F2 to Save Report
```

After you press F2, DataEase will ask:

```
Please enter the report name:
```

```
Reports
Current Report :

        Q U I C K   R E P O R T S   M E N U

    1. Run Report
    2. Start New Report
    3. Modify Record Selection
    4. Modify List Fields
    5. Modify Format
    6. Modify Print Style
    7. Save Report
    8. Load Report
    9. Delete Report
    1Ø. Print Report Definition

    1 to 1Ø — UP — DOWN — RETURN — END

 Please enter the report name: Emp1

F9 FULL   F4 EXIT DATABASE A PROG.A: DATA B: DATE          TIME
```

FIGURE 4.7

Enter the report name as

```
Emp1
```

and press the RETURN key, as shown in Figure 4.7. This report will now be saved to the Data disk and can be used anytime in the future.

If you would like to print the report definition, return to the output format, as shown in Figure 4.4, and press F9 PRINT or press **10**, **Print Report Definition**, in the Quick Reports Menu. The report definition of **Emp1** will now be printed, as shown in Figure 4.8. It is a good idea to print and file for future use all report definitions that you save. The report definition shows the record selections (none in this case), the field selections, report format, and field descriptions.

```
REPORT Emp1
------------------------------

RECORD SELECTION
----------------

  File Employees
  ----------------------------

FIELD SELECTION
---------------
Last Name              : 1 order
First Name             : 2
Employee #             : 3
Position               : 4
Salary                 : 5
       REPORT FORMAT
       -------------

1       1Ø        2Ø        3Ø        4Ø        5Ø        6Ø        7Ø        8Ø
----+----+----+----+----+----+----+----+----+----+----+----+----+----+----+----+

================================================================================
      Last            First       Employe       Position          Salary
      Name            Name           e
                                     #
--------------------------------------------------------------------------------
.items
  ______________  _______________  _____  ____________________  _______________
.end
================================================================================
----+----+----+----+----+----+----+----+----+----+----+----+----+----+----+----+
1       1Ø        2Ø        3Ø        4Ø        5Ø        6Ø        7Ø        8Ø
        FIELD DESCRIPTIONS
        ------------------

No.  Name                    Type              Length  Remove
                                                       Spaces?

---  ----------------------- ----------------  ------  -------
  1  Last Name               Text                15      No
  2  First Name              Text                15      No
  3  Employee #              Numeric String       5      No
  4  Position                Text                20      No
  5  Salary                  Number              16      No
       Number Type : Fixed point
       Digits to left of decimal  =  13

Memory required:
  Report Definition:         962
```

FIGURE 4.8

STATISTICS ON A FIELD

You can perform statistics on one or more fields by entering any of the words from the prompt line: **Sum**, **Mean**, **Min**, **Max**, **Variance**, **Std.Dev.**, or **Std.Err**.

OPERATION	MEANING
Sum	Total
Mean	Average
Min	Minimum
Max	Maximum
Variance	Variance
Std.Dev.	Standard Deviation
Std.Err.	Standard Error

To perform statistics on the field **Salary**, as shown in Figure 4.8, start a new report by pressing **2**, **Start New Report**, in the Quick Reports Menu. Ignore record selection and press **4**, **Define Line Fields**. Type in the fields with the codes, as shown in Figure 4.9.

Notice that the **Position** field is the first field that will be printed, but it will be printed in groups. In other words, all the salespersons will be in one group, secretaries in another, etc. The sum of the salaries, the mean salary, and the maximum salary will be printed for each group.

Press F2 ENTER to save this report and enter the select fields screen, as shown in Figure 4.9. Figure 4.10 shows how the report will be printed.

The fields are listed at the top of the screen. After the Report command **.end**, the words **sum**, **max**, and **mean** are printed out, to indicate that they will be printed in the final report. Compare Figure 4.10 to Figure 4.4. Notice that in this example the statistics will be printed at the end of the report.

Press F2 ENTER to save this information and exit to the Quick Reports Menu. Press **1**, **Run Report**, and have the report directed to the screen by pressing **1** again. The report is now shown in Figure 4.11. Notice that the sum, maximum, and mean of each salary is printed out by group. The bottom of the page contains the total sum of all salaries, the largest of all the salaries, and the mean of all the salaries.

```
Select Fields
Press Space to mark field. Then specify Order Reverse Group Sum Mean Max or Min

   Employee #:                     Position:  1  group

   Last Name:   2 order            First Name:  3

   Address:                        City:

   State:                          Zip:

   Date of Birth:                  Date Hired:

   Phone #:                        Social Security Number:

   Salary:  4 sum mean max

   Marital Status:



F2ENTER F4EXIT F5FORM CLR F6FLD CLR F1ØMULTI
```

FIGURE 4.9

```
                                   R  1 C   1

================================================================================
       Position                 Last           First              Salary
                                                Name
--------------------------------------------------------------------------------
.items

.end
--------------------------------------------------------------------------------
sum
max
mean
================================================================================




F2ENTER F3CUT F4EXIT F5COPY F6PASTE F7DEL LINE F8INS LINE F9PRINT F1ØFIELD
```

FIGURE 4.10

Position	Last Name	First Name	Salary
Ass't Manager	DeTrinis	Joan	45,000.00
sum			45,000.00
max			45,000.00
mean			45,000.00
Manager	DeTrinis	Vincent	56,000.00
sum			56,000.00
max			56,000.00
mean			56,000.00
Salesperson	Braun	Sheila	33,000.00
	Comforto	Anthony	31,000.00
	DiToro	Hank	39,000.00
	Duke	Joan	28,000.00
	Krawiec	Agnes	27,500.00
	Talamo	Louis	29,250.00
	Wasniewski	Joann	31,500.00
sum			219,250.00
max			39,000.00
mean			31,321.43
Secretary	Caravan	Peggy	27,500.00
sum			27,500.00
max			27,500.00
mean			27,500.00
sum			347,750.00
max			56,000.00
mean			34,775.00

FIGURE 4.11

Save this report by pressing **7, Save Report**, in the Quick Reports Menu. Type:

```
Emp2
```

and press the RETURN key to name this report. The report definition of **Emp2** is shown in Figure 4.12.

Figure 4.11 shows the grand totals at the bottom of the page, but it is confusing because the totals are not labelled. If you wanted to label the totals at the end of the report, press **5**, **Modify Format**. Then say

```
no
```

to keep the existing format. DataEase asks if you would like group headers and group trailers. Respond by typing

```
yes
```

The format that is produced looks like Figure 4.13.

For each group, the system produces a group header and group trailer. **Position** (the group level) is the group header. The group trailer produces the statistics for each group. At the end of the report, the group statistics will be labelled. To label the statistics, position the CURSOR key where you want the label and type the label in. You can customize group headers and group labels so the output is as clear and readable as you would like it to be. When the report is run, it will look like Figure 4.14. Notice that the summary data is clearly labelled.

PRINTING SELECTED RECORDS

In the above two examples, you did not specify any selective criteria in choosing fields. To specify criteria (such as any employee who earns over $35,000), move the cursor over to that field and enter the criteria in the space following that field. You may type criteria in more than one field (such as any salesperson who lives in Massapequa and makes more than $35,000). Only those records that satisfy all the criteria in all fields will be displayed.

If you make any errors typing in criteria, you can use the BACKSPACE, LEFT ARROW, RIGHT ARROW, INS, and DEL keys to make corrections.

```
REPORT Emp1
------------------------------

RECORD SELECTION
----------------

  File Employees
  ----------------------------

FIELD SELECTION
---------------
Position                      : 1  group
Last Name                     : 2  order
First Name                    : 3
Salary                        : 4 sum mean max
       REPORT FORMAT
       -------------

1       1Ø        2Ø        3Ø        4Ø        5Ø        6Ø        7Ø        8Ø
----+----+----+----+----+----+----+----+----+----+----+----+----+----+----+----+

================================================================================
       Position              Last          First               Salary
                             Name           Name
--------------------------------------------------------------------------------
.items
 ____________________  _______________  _______________     ________________
.end
--------------------------------------------------------------------------------
sum                                                    _____________________
max                                                         ________________
mean                                                        ________________
================================================================================
----+----+----+----+----+----+----+----+----+----+----+----+----+----+----+----+
1       1Ø        2Ø        3Ø        4Ø        5Ø        6Ø        7Ø        8Ø
        FIELD DESCRIPTIONS
        ------------------

No.  Name                    Type             Length  Remove
                                                      Spaces?
---  ----------------------  ---------------- ------  -------
  1  Position                Text              2Ø      No
  2  Last Name               Text              15      No
  3  First Name              Text              15      No
  4  Salary                  Number            16      No
      Number Type : Fixed point
      Digits to left of decimal  =  13
  5  Salary                  Number            2Ø      No
       Number Type : Fixed point
      Digits to left of decimal  =  17
  6  Salary                  Number            16      No
      Number Type : Fixed point
      Digits to left of decimal  =  13
  7  Salary                  Number            16      No
      Number Type : Fixed point
      Digits to left of decimal  =  13
Memory required:
  Report Definition:         1183
```

FIGURE 4.12

```
Emp1                      R  1 C   1

================================================================================
                Last              First                 Salary
                Name               Name
--------------------------------------------------------------------------------
.Group Header
Position
.items

.Group Trailer
sum
max
mean
.end
--------------------------------------------------------------------------------
sum                 The grand total is:
max             The greatest salary is:
mean             The average salary is:
================================================================================


F2ENTER F3CUT F4EXIT F5COPY F6PASTE F7DEL LINE F8INS LINE F9PRINT F1ØFIELD
```

FIGURE 4.13

In some cases the criteria will be more than the length of a field. DataEase allows you to type up to 500 characters in each field. As soon as you leave the field, the computer will reduce the field size to its original length and display only that criteria that fits in its space.

You can search for any constants, as shown below.

FIELD TYPE	EXAMPLE	REMARKS
Text	"Salesperson"	Must be enclosed in quotes
Number, Dollar	2345.67	Do not type any commas
Numeric String	Ø5Ø366989	Do not type formatting characters, such as the "/"
Date	1Ø/17/87	Type slashes
Time	11:ØØ:ØØ	Type colons
Choice	Married	Type in choice rather than number of choice

```
================================================================================
                Last              First                  Salary
                Name               Name
--------------------------------------------------------------------------------
Position Ass't Manager
          DeTrinis           Joan                          45,000.00
sum                                                       45,000.00
max                                                   45,000.00
mean                                                  45,000.00
Position Manager
          DeTrinis           Vincent                       56,000.00
sum                                                       56,000.00
max                                                   56,000.00
mean                                                  56,000.00
Position Salesperson
          Braun              Sheila                        33,000.00
          Comforto           Anthony                       31,000.00
          DiToro             Hank                          39,000.00
          Duke               Joan                          28,000.00
          Krawiec            Agnes                         27,500.00
          Talamo             Louis                         29,250.00
          Wasniewski         Joann                         31,500.00
sum                                                      219,250.00
max                                                   39,000.00
mean                                                  31,321.43
Position Secretary
          Caravan            Peggy                         27,500.00
sum                                                       27,500.00
max                                                   27,500.00
mean                                                  27,500.00
--------------------------------------------------------------------------------
sum                    The grand total is:                347,750.00
max                The greatest salary is:                 56,000.00
mean                The average salary is:                 34,775.00
================================================================================
```

FIGURE 4.14

You can also search for ranges, as shown below.

OPERATOR	EXAMPLE	REMARKS
=	=10	equal to 10
>	>50	greater than 50
<	<"Bob"	less than Bob (must be in quotes)
>=	>=100	greater than or equal to 100
<=	<=100	less than or equal to 100
between...to...	between 50 to 100	between 50 and 100, inclusive
not	not=100	not equal to 100

When selecting criteria, you may use the wildcard characters **?** and * except when you select dates that must use the ??/??/?? format. You may use the word **or** if a field can have more than one value. For example:

```
"Rita" or "Debra"

Married or Single
```

You may also use the word **and** if you need to use both operators in the same criteria. You may use parentheses to indicate the order of operation. For example:

```
>50 and <100

(>50 and <100) or (>150 and <200)
```

Start a new report by pressing **2**, **Start New Report**, in the Quick Reports Menu. After you press **3**, **Define Record Selection**, type:

```
= "Salesperson"
```

in the **Position** field, as shown in Figure 4.15. The previous two examples dealt with all records. In this example you will be using records that pertain to people who hold the position of salesperson. Press F2 ENTER to save the field selection criteria.

```
Select Records
Specify the Field Selection Criteria

   Employee #:                       Position:   = "Salesperson"

   Last Name:                        First Name:

   Address:                          City:

   State:                            Zip:

   Date of Birth:                    Date Hired:

   Phone #:                          Social Security Number:

   Salary:

   Marital Status:



F2ENTER F4EXIT F5FORM CLR F6FLD CLR F1ØMULTI
```

FIGURE 4.15

Select the fields, as shown in Figure 4.16. In the **Salary** field, type:

```
min
```

for minimum. Press F2 ENTER to save and exit the selected fields.

When you run the report by pressing **1**, **Run Report**, the screen should look like Figure 4.17. Notice that the statistics for the **Salary** field are shown at the bottom of the report, after the **.end** command. These statistics apply only to those people who hold the position of salesperson.

If you press **10**, **Print Report Definition**, the report definition will be printed, as shown in Figure 4.18.

If at any time in the future you wish to load a certain report, press **8**, **Load Report**, in the Quick Reports Menu. A list of the names of the reports will appear in the window at the right. You select the report that you wish to execute by pressing the number next to the report name.

```
Select Fields
Press Space to mark field. Then specify Order Reverse Group Sum Mean Max or Min

   Employee #:                       Position:

   Last Name:   1  order             First Name:  2

   Address:                          City:

   State:                            Zip:

   Date of Birth:                    Date Hired:  3

   Phone #:                          Social Security Number:

   Salary:  4 sum mean max min

   Marital Status:



F2ENTER F4EXIT F5FORM CLR F6FLD CLR F10MULTI
```

FIGURE 4.16

```
================================================================================
       Position              Last            First              Salary
                             Name             Name
--------------------------------------------------------------------------------
                        Braun           Sheila                   33,000.00
                        Comforto        Anthony                  31,000.00
                        DiToro          Hank                     39,000.00
                        Duke            Joan                     28,000.00
                        Krawiec         Agnes                    27,500.00
                        Talamo          Louis                    29,250.00
                        Wasniewski      Joann                    31,500.00
--------------------------------------------------------------------------------
sum                                                             219,250.00
max                                                              39,000.00
mean                                                             31,321.43
================================================================================
```

FIGURE 4.17

```
REPORT
------------------------------
RECORD SELECTION
----------------
  File Employees
  ----------------------------
Position               : = "Salesperson"
FIELD SELECTION
---------------
Last Name              : 1  order
First Name             : 2
Date Hired             : 3
Salary                 : 4  sum mean max
       REPORT FORMAT
       -------------
1       10        20        30        40        50        60        70        80
----+----+----+----+----+----+----+----+----+----+----+----+----+----+----+----+

================================================================================
       Position              Last              First             Salary
                             Name               Name
--------------------------------------------------------------------------------
.items
                       _______________  _______________     ________________
.end
--------------------------------------------------------------------------------
sum                                                     ____________________
max                                                         ________________
mean                                                        ________________
================================================================================
----+----+----+----+----+----+----+----+----+----+----+----+----+----+----+----+
1       10        20        30        40        50        60        70        80
        FIELD DESCRIPTIONS
        ------------------

No.  Name                     Type              Length  Remove
                                                        Spaces?
---  ----------------------- ---------------- ------  -------
  1  Last Name                Text               15     No
  2  First Name               Text               15     No
  3  Salary                   Number             16     No
      Number Type : Fixed point
      Digits to left of decimal  =  13
  4  Salary                   Number             20     No
       Number Type : Fixed point
      Digits to left of decimal  =  17
  5  Salary                   Number             16     No
      Number Type : Fixed point
      Digits to left of decimal  =  13
  6  Salary                   Number             16     No
      Number Type : Fixed point
      Digits to left of decimal  =  13
Memory required:
  Report Definition:         1249
```

FIGURE 4.18

Quick reports use the query-by-example approach, which lets you specify the conditions you wish to see. Full reports use a procedural query language that allows you to write procedures to generate reports and manipulate data. Quick reports let you generate routine reports, while full reports solve more comprehensive business problems. Quick reports can be converted to full reports to utilize the power of the procedural language.

SPECIAL FORMATS—MAILING LABELS—MAILMERGE

As part of your simulated computer store advertising, you will send a special mailing to all of your customers. This involves creating reports. The first report will be a mailing list of all customers in your database. The names and addresses of these customers will be printed on mailing labels that are two across. The second operation involves the creation of a form letter that will pull the names and addresses from the database.

CREATING MAILING LABELS

To create mailing labels, you can first create the report format that will generate these labels. A report format consists of text that remains fixed on a form, data and output fields where information will be filled in later, and command lines that control the format. You enter the text and command lines by moving the cursor anywhere on the form and typing. You define fields by placing the cursor at the starting position of the field, then pressing the F10 FIELD key.

The process for typing and correcting text is identical to the one used for designing record entry forms. Command lines are used to divide a report into report format areas. They can also be used to indicate page breaks. Each command line starts with a period in the first column, followed by the command name.

Since you want to create a mailing list from the **CUSTOMER** file, access the Quick Reports Menu by selecting the **CUSTOMER** file, pressing **4**, and pressing the RETURN key. You can produce a quick report by selecting any one of the four options in the Quick Reports Menu: **Define Record Selection**, **Select List Fields**, **Modify Format**, or **Print Style Specs**. When you select any one of those options, the system will be able to generate a quick report. The other three options will default. No record selection means all records; no selection of list fields will give you all fields in the form; no format will default to the columnar format; and no specification on report output will default to the screen.

Press the F9 REPORTS key to enter the Quick Reports Menu. Press **2**, **Start New Report**, to start the report for printing mailing labels. Press **4**, **Define List Fields**, to select the fields you want printed on the mailing labels. The order of the selected fields is shown in Figure 5.1. If you accidentally select the wrong fields, you should retype the correct number in the field you want.

```
Select Fields
Press Space to mark field. Then specify Order Reverse Group Sum Mean Max or Min

Cust ID:

Last Name:  2                    First Name:  1

Street:  3

City:  4                  State:  5     Zip:  6 order

Phone #:









F2ENTER F4EXIT F5FORM CLR F6FLD CLR F1ØMULTI
```

FIGURE 5.1

After you have finished selecting the fields, press F2 ENTER. Next, define the format. This falls under the category of **4**, **Special**. You will use the special format to design mailing labels and form letters. It may also be used to create custom columnar reports and reports that will be run on preprinted business forms. As shown in the Figure 5.2 prompt, type:

DataEase then displays the window shown on the right side of Figure 5.2.

If you press **1** then the RETURN key, the word **items** will appear. Continue by typing:

```
across 2 wide 38
```

as shown in the top line of Figure 5.3.

```
                               R  1 C   1
Select a Command.

                                                       ┌──────────────────────┐
                                                       │ Ø: NONE              │
                                                       │ 1: items             │
                                                       │ 2: end               │
                                                       │ 3: page              │
                                                       │ 4: header            │
                                                       │ 5: footer            │
                                                       │ 6: group header      │
                                                       │ 7: group trailer     │
                                                       │                      │
                                                       └─ Ø to 7 UP DOWN RETURN ─┘
F2ENTER F3CUT F4EXIT F5COPY F6PASTE F7DEL LINE F8INS LINE F9PRINT F1ØFIELD
```

FIGURE 5.2

```
mail                           R  3 C   1

.items across 2 wide 38




.end




F2ENTER F3CUT F4EXIT F5COPY F6PASTE F7DEL LINE F8INS LINE F9PRINT F1ØFIELD
```

FIGURE 5.3

The basic command lines are **.items** and **.end**. They **must** be present in every report format. The word **.items** signifies the information printed for each record. The area following **.items** will be repeated for each record, which is to print two records across and 38 columns wide. The command **.end** signifies the end of the basic report. It also signals the beginning of the report area in which summary data may be placed.

You have told DataEase to print two records across, each 38 columns wide. If you use three across, make sure that your mailing labels are three or more across. Also be sure that your printer has a wide carriage, so that it can print 114 columns across (3 times 38 columns equals 114 columns). A report format may be up to 4000 columns wide. On the computer screen, 80 columns are visible at one time. If you wish to see the rest of the columns, you may scroll by using the LEFT ARROW and RIGHT ARROW keys.

You will now specify the fields that are to be printed. Move the cursor to R 3 C 1. Press the F10 FIELD key. As shown in Figure 5.4, you would like the field **First Name** to be printed here. Finish completing Figure 5.4. Answer **yes** to the last question, which asks if you would like to remove leading and trailing spaces. This will cause DataEase to properly space between names, some of which are short and some of which are long. When you are finished, press F2 ENTER to save the field.

In a similar manner, move the cursor to R 3 C 17, press the F10 FIELD key, and enter the specifications for the **Last Name** field. Move the cursor to R 4 C 1, press F10 FIELD, and enter the specification for the **Street** field. Move the cursor to R 5 C 1, press F10 FIELD, and type in the specifications for the **City** field. Move the cursor to R 5 C 22, press F10 FIELD, and type in the specification for the **State** field. Move the cursor to R 5 C 25, press the F10 FIELD key, and type in the specification for the **Zip** field. You will notice that Figure 5.3 does not show the fields. They are shown on the screen as an underline (on a monochrome screen) or a blue highlight (on a color monitor). They are not printed out in screen dumps. You can press the **F2** key to save this format.

The complete report definition is shown in Figure 5.5. Remember that you can obtain this information by pressing the F9 PRINT key in the **Define Format** option of the menu. In Figure 5.5 you see the field names, their order or selection, the report format, the length of each field (try placing one of your mailing labels over it to see if it is the

```
mail
Please hit Enter, Delete or Modify key
     Field name :                             First Name
     Field type :                             Text
     Maximum length of the field :             15
     Remove Leading and Trailing spaces? :    yes

F2ENTER F7 DELETE F8 MODIFY
```

FIGURE 5.4

right size), and the field descriptions. In Figure 5.5 the length of the field is shown with an underline.

To run the report, press **1**, **Run Report** from the Quick Reports Menu. The output—the mailing labels—will now be printed, as shown in Figure 5.6. If the labels are too small or too large, you can go back and adjust the width in the Report Format, as discussed above. To save this report, press the F2 SAVE key.

MAILMERGE LETTER

You will now take the name and address of each customer that is shown in Figure 5.6 and merge the information with a form letter that announces an upcoming sale. You must first create a form letter. In the Quick Reports Menu, while still using the **CUSTOMER** file, press **2**, **Start New Report**. Press **4**, **Define List Fields**, to list the information that will be included in the letter. The six fields and their order are shown in Figure 5.7.

```
REPORT mail
------------------------------

RECORD SELECTION
----------------

  File Customer
  ----------------------------

FIELD SELECTION
---------------
First Name              : 1
Last Name               : 2
Street                  : 3
City                    : 4
State                   : 5
Zip                     : 6 order
       REPORT FORMAT
       -------------

1       10        20        30        40        50        60        70        80
----+----+----+----+----+----+----+----+----+----+----+----+----+----+----+----+

--------------------------------------------------------------------------------
.items across 2 wide 38

_______________ _________________
____________________
____________________ __ _________

.end
----+----+----+----+----+----+----+----+----+----+----+----+----+----+----+----+
1       10        20        30        40        50        60        70        80
        FIELD DESCRIPTIONS
        ------------------

No.  Name                   Type              Length  Remove
                                                      Spaces?
---  ---------------------- ----------------  ------  -------
  1  First Name             Text                15     Yes
  2  Last Name              Text                15     Yes
  3  Street                 Text                20     Yes
  4  City                   Text                20     Yes
  5  State                  Text                 2     Yes
  6  Zip                    Numeric String       5     Yes

Memory required:
 Report Definition:        612
```

FIGURE 5.5

```
Marge Swietnicki
29Ø 11th Street
Brooklyn NY 11215

Lisa Fitzgerald
9292 Shore Road
Brooklyn NY 11215

Malcolm Willoughby
9876 Molloy Way
Rockville Center NY 11355

Vincent Strongly
214-1Ø 24th Avenue
Bayside NY 1136Ø

Mary Ellen Herbold
793 Long Island Ave
Deer Park NY 11729

Timothy Swartarm
541 Shoreham Road
Massapequa NY 11758

Brema Vultaggio
33 Bay Drive
Massapequa NY 11758

Carol Bergen
37 Wilson Street
Massapequa Park NY 11762

Toni Tabone
Rd. 3, Box 124C
New Berlin NY 13411

Jeff Glass
1754 Apple Hollow Rd
Hamlin NY 14464

Paul Mena
7 Inverary Court
Charleston NC 294Ø7
```

FIGURE 5.6

```
Select Fields
Press Space to mark field. Then specify Order Reverse Group Sum Mean Max or Min

Cust ID:

Last Name:  1                  First Name:  2

Street:  3

City:  4                    State:  5      Zip:  6

Phone #




F2ENTER F4EXIT F5FORM CLR F6FLD CLR F1ØMULTI
```

FIGURE 5.7

You would like the name and address of each person to be printed in the letter. When you are finished marking the six fields, press F2 ENTER.

The letter that you wish to merge with the names and addresses will now be created. Select **5**, **Define Format** from the Quick Reports Menu. Figure 5.8 shows the letter that will be merged with the data from the **CUSTOMER** file. Notice again that DataEase will prompt you by displaying possible commands in the window at the right.

You will notice that a new word **page** appears at the beginning and end of the letter. This causes the printer to advance to a new page every time a new letter is printed. Therefore, a single letter will be printed on each page. You notice that **page** is one of the command words, as shown in the right-hand window of Figure 5.8. To select that **page** command, press **3**.

Looking at Figure 5.8, notice that the fields to be merged are not shown in the letter to be merged. How does DataEase know which fields are to be integrated, or merged, with the letter? If you look at the bottom

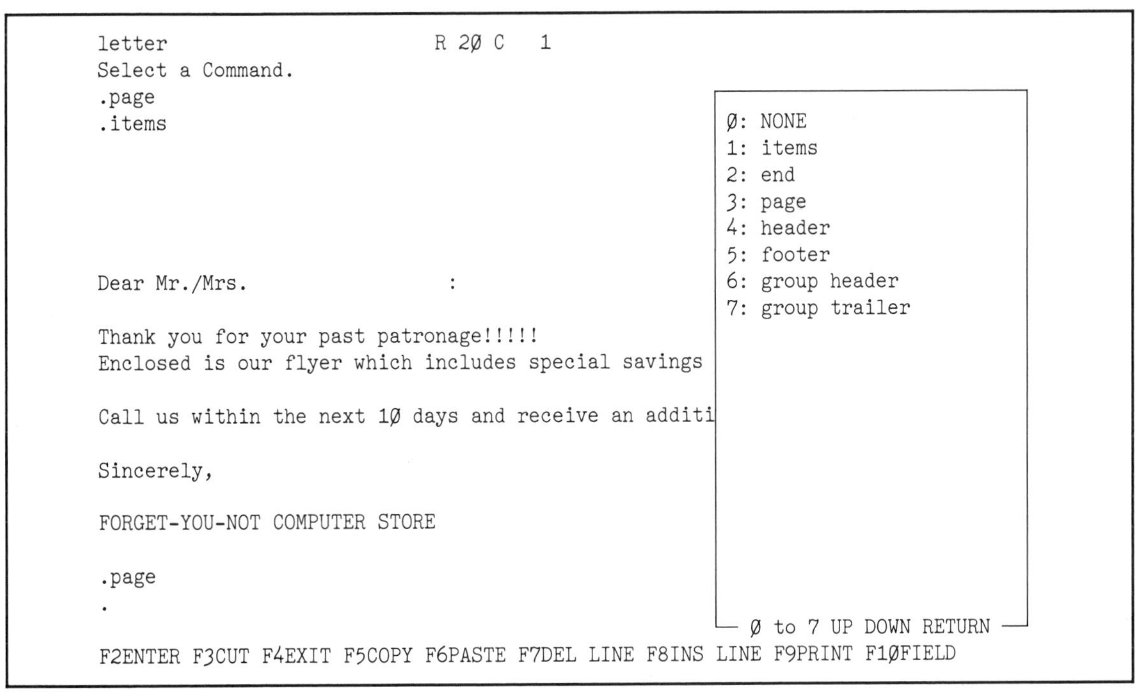

FIGURE 5.8

line of Figure 5.8, which shows the Command Menu, you see the F10 FIELD key is used to designate the fields you want merged. To designate a field that you want merged, place the cursor in the row and column of the letter where you want a field to appear and press F10 FIELD. From the menu that is given at the top of the screen type in the number of the field that you want merged. Place the cursor at R 4 C 1, press the F10 FIELD key, and type in the field specifications for the **First Name** field. This is shown in Figure 5.9. The abbreviated field specification is shown at the top of the figure. To obtain it, press the SPACE-BAR anywhere on the underline for that particular field. Figure 5.9 shows the cursor position with an abbreviated field specification.

In a similar manner, place the cursor at R 4 C 17, press the F10 FIELD key, and type in the field specifications for the **Last Name** field. Place the cursor at R 5 C 1, press the F10 FIELD key, and type in the field specifications for the **Street** field. Place the cursor at R 6 C 1, press the F10 FIELD key, and type in the field specifications for the **City** field. Place the cursor at R 6 C 22, press the F10 FIELD key, and type in the field specifications for the **State** field. Place the cursor at R 6 C 25,

```
letter                      R  4 C   1
FIELD First Name, TYPE Text
.page
.items






Dear Mr./Mrs.                :

Thank you for your past patronage!!!!!
Enclosed is our flyer which includes special savings for our past customers.

Call us within the next 10 days and receive an additional 5% discount.

Sincerely,

FORGET-YOU-NOT COMPUTER STORE

.page
.end

F2ENTER F3CUT F4EXIT F5COPY F6PASTE F7DEL LINE F8INS LINE F9PRINT F10FIELD
```

FIGURE 5.9

press the F10 FIELD key, and type in the field specifications for the **Zip** field. Place the cursor at R 8 C 15, press the F10 FIELD key, and type in the specification for the **Last Name** field. If you get lost, you can print out the report definition, which is shown in Figure 5.10.

The actual placement of the fields is indicated by an underline on a monochrome monitor or a blue highlight on a color monitor. At the botttom of Figure 5.10, you will notice that in the field descriptions the **Last Name** field appears twice. This indicates that the field will appear twice in the letter. The final form letter is shown in Figure 5.11. When you have finished entering it, press F2 ENTER to save it in the computer's memory. It is a good idea to save it onto disk, so it can be used at a later date. To save it, press **7**, **Save Report**, and give it a name. In this case, call it **letter**.

Figure 5.12 shows the merged letter after you have run this report.

Notice that the last name of this person, in this case Bergen, is repeated in the letter. You may repeat the name of any field as often as you wish to make your letter more personal. DataEase will adjust the spacing of the fields so that there aren't any large gaps or openings in the letter. In other words, DataEase will insert spaces around names, whether they are long or short, and adjust the surrounding text. Again, the field names may be repeated as many times as needed by pressing the F10 FIELD key in the **5**, **Define Format** mode and selecting the number of the field that will be inserted into the letter.

The mailmerge function is a very powerful feature of DataEase. In essence, DataEase has a mini word processor that can be used to write any report or letter. You can select data from any file and merge it with this letter.

```
REPORT letter
------------------------------

RECORD SELECTION
----------------

  File Customer
  ----------------------------

FIELD SELECTION
---------------
First Name          : 1
Last Name           : 2
Street              : 3
City                : 4
State               : 5
Zip                 : 6
       REPORT FORMAT
       -------------

1        10        20        30        40        50        60        70        80
----+----+----+----+----+----+----+----+----+----+----+----+----+----+----+----+

.page
.items

_______________ _______________
____________________
____________________ __ _____

Dear Mr./Mrs._______________:

Thank you for your past patronage!!!!!
Enclosed is our flyer which includes special savings for our past customers.

Call us within the next 10 days and receive an additional 5% discount.

Sincerely,

FORGET-YOU-NOT COMPUTER STORE

.page
.end
----+----+----+----+----+----+----+----+----+----+----+----+----+----+----+----+
1        10        20        30        40        50        60        70        80
        FIELD DESCRIPTIONS
        ------------------

No.  Name                    Type             Length  Remove
                                                      Spaces?
---  ----------------------  ---------------  ------  -------
  1  First Name              Text               15     Yes
  2  Last Name               Text               15     Yes
  3  Street                  Text               20     Yes
  4  City                    Text               20     Yes
  5  State                   Text                2     Yes
  6  Zip                     Numeric String      5     Yes
  7  Last Name               Text               15     Yes

Memory required:
 Report Definition:         863
```

FIGURE 5.10

```
letter                      R  1 C   1

.page
.items





Dear Mr./Mrs.                :

Thank you for your past patronage!!!!!
Enclosed is our flyer which includes special savings for our past customers.

Call us within the next 1Ø days and receive an additional 5% discount.

Sincerely,

FORGET-YOU-NOT COMPUTER STORE

.page
.end

F2ENTER F3CUT F4EXIT F5COPY F6PASTE F7DEL LINE F8INS LINE F9PRINT F1ØFIELD
```

FIGURE 5.11

```
Carol Bergen
37 Wilson Street
Massapequa Park NY 11762

Dear Mr./Mrs. Bergen:

Thank you for your past patronage!!!!!
Enclosed is our flyer which includes special savings for our past customers.

Call us within the next 1Ø days and receive an additional 5% discount.

Sincerely,

FORGET-YOU-NOT COMPUTER STORE
```

FIGURE 5.12

QUICK REPORTS FROM SEVERAL FILES

One very powerful feature of relational databases such as DataEase is their ability to integrate information from several files to produce reports. In this chapter you will produce a report that contains information found in several files.

PRINTING QUICK REPORTS FROM ONE FILE

In this section, you will review the procedures for printing out simple reports, then extend the concept to print out reports that contain information from several files. To review creating a simple quick report, you will create a report from the **CUSTOMER** file that prints out the names and identification numbers of the customers. The last names will be printed in ascending alphabetical order.

After you have accessed the **CUSTOMER** file, enter the Quick Reports Menu by pressing F9 QUICK REPORTS. Start a new report by pressing **2**, **Start New Report**. Since you want all records, press **4**, **List Fields** to view the fields of the **CUSTOMER** file. You will notice that the first field to be printed is **Last Name**. It will be printed in alphabetical order (notice the word **order**, as shown in Figure 6.1).

```
Select Fields
Press Space to mark field. Then specify Order Reverse Group Sum Mean Max or Min

Cust ID:  3

Last Name:  1 order              First Name:  2

Street:

City:                       State:        Zip:  6 order

Phone #:



F2ENTER F4EXIT F5FORM CLR F6FLD CLR F1ØMULTI
```

FIGURE 6.1

```
Cust1                                        Running report Cust1
END OF REPORT.  SPACE: Return to Menu

==================================================
        Last                 First          Cust
        Name                  Name           ID
--------------------------------------------------
  Bergen              Carol                C-ØØØ1
  Fitzgerald          Lisa                 C-ØØØ6
  Glass               Jeff                 C-ØØØ7
  Herbold             Mary Ellen           C-ØØØ8
  Mena                Paul                 C-ØØØ9
  Strongly            Vincent              C-ØØØ2
  Swartarm            Timothy              C-ØØ1Ø
  Swietnicki          Marge                C-ØØØ4
  Tabone              Toni                 C-ØØØ5
  Vultaggio           Brema                C-ØØ11
  Willoughby          Malcolm              C-ØØØ3
==================================================


      F4 EXIT     DATABASE A PROG.A: DATA B: DATE          TIME
```

FIGURE 6.2

When the report is run, it appears as shown in Figure 6.2.

If you order the fields, as shown in Figure 6.3, the printout will place the **Cust ID** field as the first field in numeric order. In this report, the **Phone #** field was added as the fourth field.

When you run the report format, it appears as shown in Figure 6.4.

PRINTING QUICK REPORTS FROM SEVERAL FILES

In your computer store, you would like to print a report that shows which customers were waited on by a salesperson named Braun and what was the total value of their order. This information is contained in three files: **EMPLOYEES, ORDERS,** and **CUSTOMER**. To accomplish this task, you can start by typing in the field selection criteria of the **EMPLOYEES** file. Go to the DataEase Records Menu by pressing the F4 EXIT key until you reach it. Press **3** to access the **EMPLOYEES** file. Press F9 QUICK REPORTS to access the Quick Reports Menu. Press **2**, **Start New Report** to start a new report. Press **3**, **Define Record**

```
Select Fields
Press Space to mark field. Then specify Order Reverse Group Sum Mean Max or Min

Cust ID:  1  order

Last Name:  2                    First Name:  3

Street:

City:                       State:        Zip:

Phone #:  4





F2ENTER F4EXIT F5FORM CLR F6FLD CLR F1ØMULTI
```

FIGURE 6.3

```
Cust2                                       Running report Cust2
END OF REPORT.  SPACE: Return to Menu

=========================================================
  Cust       Last           First          Phone
   ID        Name            Name            #
---------------------------------------------------------
 C-ØØØ1 Bergen          Carol          (516)-798-8632
 C-ØØØ2 Strongly        Vincent        (718)-224-5443
 C-ØØØ3 Willoughby      Malcolm        (516)-678-23Ø6
 C-ØØØ4 Swienicki       Marge          (718)-213-4299
 C-ØØØ5 Tabone          Toni           (6Ø7)-847-4289
 C-ØØØ6 Fitzgerald      Lisa           (718)-68Ø-1Ø26
 C-ØØØ7 Glass           Jeff           (716)-964-7322
 C-ØØØ8 Herbold         Mary Ellen     (515)-243-23Ø
 C-ØØØ9 Mena            Paul           (8Ø3)-556-1336
 C-ØØ1Ø Swartarm        Timothy        (516)-798-87Ø7
 C-ØØ11 Vultaggio       Brema          (516)-795-7914
=========================================================


     F4 EXIT     DATABASE A PROG.A: DATA B: DATE          TIME
```

FIGURE 6.4

Selection to select the name of the salesperson. For the **Last Name** field, type:

```
= "Braun"
```

to specify that you would like information only on the salesperson whose name is Braun, as shown in Figure 6.5. You must include the quotes in the command, because you are searching a text field, which can contain not only alphabetic data but numeric or alphanumeric data as well. To exit the record selection, press F2 ENTER.

You will now list the fields you wish to print in the report by pressing F4 DEFINE LIST FIELDS. Move the cursor to the **Last Name** field by pressing the TAB or RETURN key. After you arrive at the **Last Name** field, either press the SPACEBAR or press **1** to tell DataEase that **Last Name** is the first field to be listed, as shown in Figure 6.6.

If you make an error, just type in the correct number. At the bottom of the screen, you will notice that if you press the F10 MULTI key, you

```
Select Records
Specify the Field Selection Criteria

   Employee #:                    Position:

   Last Name:    = "Braun"        First Name:

   Address:                       City:

   State:                         Zip:

   Date of Birth:                 Date Hired:

   Phone #:                       Social Security Number:

   Salary:

   Marital Status:



F2ENTER F4EXIT F5FORM CLR F6FLD CLR F1ØMULTI
```

FIGURE 6.5

```
Select Fields
Press Space to mark field. Then specify Order Reverse Group Sum Mean Max or Min

   Employee #:                      Position:

   Last Name:    1                  First Name:

   Address:                         City:

   State:                           Zip:

   Date of Birth:                   Date Hired:

   Phone #:                         Social Security Number:

   Salary:

   Marital Status:




F2ENTER F4EXIT F5FORM CLR F6FLD CLR F1ØMULTI
```

FIGURE 6.6

will get a multiview of other files that are related to the **EMPLOYEES** file. Press the F10 MULTI key. The window at the right tells you the names of the files that are linked, or related to, the **EMPLOYEES** file, as shown in Figure 6.7.

In this case, it tells you that if you press **1**, you can access the **ORDERS** file. Press **1**, then press the RETURN key to access the **ORDERS** file. The screen will look like Figure 6.8. Remember that the **Employee #** field of the **EMPLOYEES** file is related to the **Emp #** field of the **ORDERS** file.

Move the cursor to the **Total Order** field and press the SPACEBAR. The number **2** will appear, as shown in Figure 6.8.

If you press the F10 MULTI key again, you will obtain a list of all the files related to the **ORDERS** file, as shown in the window at the right-hand side of Figure 6.8. You would now like to access the **CUSTOMER** file to obtain the last names, first names, and phone numbers of customers who were served by and bought merchandise from the salesperson

```
Select Fields
Select the relationship

  Employee #:                 Position:      Ø: NONE
                                             1: Orders
  Last Name:  1               First Name:

  Address:                    City:

  State:                      Zip:

  Date of Birth:              Date Hired:

  Phone #:                    Social Secur

  Salary:

  Marital Status:

                                             Ø to 1 UP DOWN RETURN
F2ENTER F4EXIT F5FORM CLR F6FLD CLR F1ØMULTI
```

FIGURE 6.7

```
Select Fields
Select the relationship

                                             Ø: NONE
Order  #:                    Cust ID:        1: Employees
                                             2: Customer
Stock #:                     Quantity Order  3: Products

Total Order:  2

Date:                        Emp #:

                                             Ø to 3 UP DOWN RETURN
F2ENTER F4EXIT F5FORM CLR F6FLD CLR F1ØMULTI
```

FIGURE 6.8

Braun. Press **2** to access the **CUSTOMER** file. The field that links these two files is the **Cust ID** field.

Press the SPACEBAR to mark the three fields, as shown in Figure 6.9.

The **Last Name** field is the third field to be listed, the **First Name** field is the fourth field to be listed, and the **Phone #** field is the fifth and final field to be listed. When you are finished press F2 ENTER to get to the Quick Report Menu.

When you run the report by pressing **1**, **Run Report**, the results appear as shown in Figure 6.10.

This report shows how simple it is to obtain information from three separate files by using DataEase. The first field, **Last Name**, is the name of the salesperson in the **EMPLOYEES** file. The last three fields—**Last Name**, **First Name**, and **Phone #**—are fields about the customer in the **CUSTOMER** file. Even though two files have the same field name, **Last Name**, DataEase can distinguish between them by the way they

```
Select Fields
Press Space to mark field. Then specify Order Reverse Group Sum Mean Max or Min

Cust ID:

Last Name:  3                    First Name:  4

Street:

City:                         State:        Zip:

Phone #:  5




F2ENTER F4EXIT F5FORM CLR F6FLD CLR F1ØMUTLI
```

FIGURE 6.9

```
qr1                                        Running report qr1
END OF REPORT.  SPACE: Return to Menu

================================================================================
      Last           Total          Last             First           Phone
      Name           Order          Name             Name              #
--------------------------------------------------------------------------------
 Braun                  1,4ØØ.ØØ Willoughby       Malcolm         (516)-678-23Ø6
 Braun                    45Ø.ØØ Vultaggio        Brema           (516)-795-7914
================================================================================

      F4 EXIT     DATABASE A PROG.A: DATA B: DATE          TIME
```

FIGURE 6.10

are selected. The second field, **Total Order**, is a field in the **ORDERS** file. It is the "bridge" or relation between the other two files. If you press the F10 MULTI key in the selection of any fields of a file, DataEase will give you a list of all the related fields in the window on the right of the screen. If no window appears, no relation exists between that file and any other file.

Figure 6.11 shows the report definition for this file, which was saved under the name **qr1**. You can print out the report definition by pressing **10**, **Print Report Definition** in the Quick Reports Menu. As shown at the top of Figure 6.11, the report definition gives the report selection. Below that, it indicates all the files related to **EMPLOYEES**. It then gives the five fields that were selected from the various files.

This example shows the power of DataEase in extracting information from several files. Through the information in the on-screen windows, DataEase will always prompt you with the names of the files and fields that are related. Thus, an inexperienced user or a user who has been

```
REPORT qr1
------------------------------

RECORD SELECTION
----------------

  File Employees
  ----------------------------

Last Name              : = "Braun"
  Relationship Orders
  ----------------------------
  Relationship Customer
  ----------------------------
  Relationship Products
  ----------------------------

FIELD SELECTION
---------------
Last Name              : 1
Total Order            : 2
Last Name              : 3
First Name             : 4
Phone #                : 5
       REPORT FORMAT
       -------------

1        1Ø        2Ø        3Ø        4Ø        5Ø        6Ø        7Ø        8Ø
----+----+----+----+----+----+----+----+----+----+----+----+----+----+----+----+

================================================================================
      Last          Total          Last            First          Phone
      Name          Order          Name             Name          #
--------------------------------------------------------------------------------
.items
 _______________ ____________ _______________ _______________ ______________

.end
================================================================================
----+----+----+----+----+----+----+----+----+----+----+----+----+----+----+----+
1        1Ø        2Ø        3Ø        4Ø        5Ø        6Ø        7Ø        8Ø
        FIELD DESCRIPTIONS
        ------------------

No.  Name                    Type              Length  Remove
                                                       Spaces?
---  ----------------------- ----------------- ------  -------
  1  Last Name               Text               15      No
  2  Total Order             Number             12      No
      Number Type : Fixed point
      Digits to left of decimal = 9
  3  Last Name               Text               15      No
  4  First Name              Text               15      No
  5  Phone #                 Numeric String     14      No

Memory required:
 Report Definition:          133Ø
```

FIGURE 6.11

away from the system for a long time can always receive help. As mentioned several times before, it is always a good idea to print out and file the report definitions. These summaries are extremely useful when you need to refresh your memory about what is being printed out.

Introduction to Full Reports

In this chapter you will learn what a full report is and how it differs from a quick report. You will learn how to create and print out two simple full reports that perform statistics on certain fields. You will be introduced to the DataEase query language (DQL), which enables you to ask questions of the database to obtain information or generate reports. The DQL can be menu driven. In the beginning, it will help you write queries to generate reports. As you become more proficient in DataEase, you may turn off the menu and write your reports with little or no help from DataEase.

BACKGROUND

The full report is very similar to the quick report, except that it has more features and possesses a procedural language. It can be used in transaction processing and batch updates. These are powerful features that are available only in a major programming language, such as COBOL. DataEase allows you to perform these complex functions using only a minimum of computer background and skill.

ACCESSING THE FULL REPORTS MENU

The Main Menu of DataEase shows how to access the Full Reports Menu by pressing **3**, as shown in Figure 7.1.

You can also access the Full Reports Menu from the Quick Reports Menu, by pressing the F9 FULL key. The Full Reports Menu and the Quick Reports Menu are very similar. Figure 7.2 shows the Full Reports Menu and Figure 7.3 shows the Quick Reports Menu.

If you look at Figures 7.2 and 7.3, you will notice that they differ in only two of the menu selections. These are choices **3** and **4**. All of the other choices are identical. Choice **3** of the Full Reports Menu is **Define Data-entry Form**. This allows you to enter information before you run the report. The information that you type in can be used in selecting records or used as information in printing reports. (You will learn how to use this in a later chapter.)

Choice **4**, **Define Query** of the Full Reports Menu enables you to ask questions of the database to obtain information.

```
DATAEASE

        D A T A E A S E - M A I N   M E N U

        1. Form Definition and Changes

        2. Record Entry and Quick Reports

        3. Full Reports

        4. Data Base Maintenance

        5. Data Base Utilities

        6. Menus and Relationships

        7. System Administration

    ——— 1 to 7 — UP — DOWN — RETURN — END ———

    F4EXIT    DATABASE A PROG.A: DATA B: DATE        TIME
```

FIGURE 7.1

```
Reports

        F U L L   R E P O R T S   M E N U

    1. Run Report
    2. Start New Report
    3. Define Data-entry Form
    4. Define Query
    5. Define Format
    6. Define Print Style
    7. Save Report
    8. Load Report
    9. Delete Report
    1Ø. Print Report Definition

  ——— 1 to 1Ø — UP — DOWN — RETURN — END ———

F9 QUICK  F4 EXIT DATABASE A PROG.A: DATA B: DATE        TIME
```

FIGURE 7.2

```
Reports

    Q U I C K   R E P O R T S   M E N U

  1. Run Report
  2. Start New Report
  3. Define Record Selection
  4. Define List Fields
  5. Define Format
  6. Define Print Style
  7. Save Report
  8. Load Report
  9. Delete Report
  1Ø. Print Report Definition

 ── 1 to 1Ø — UP — DOWN — RETURN — END ──

F9 FULL   F4 EXIT DATABASE A PROG.A: DATA B: DATE        TIME
```

FIGURE 7.3

CREATING A SIMPLE QUERY

One of the best ways to learn the DataEase query language is by doing a simple exercise and observing what happens. You will access the **CUSTOMER** file and print out the last names of the customers in alphabetical order, along with their first names, ID numbers, and phone numbers.

Access the Full Reports Menu by pressing **3** from the DataEase Main Menu or by pressing the F9 FULL key from the Quick Reports Menu. When you are in the Full Reports Menu, press **2**, **Start New Report**. You can also use **2**, **Start New Report** if you are finished with a report and want to start another one. This enables you to delete the previous report (from memory and not from disk) and start another one. Next, press **4** to **Define Query**. (As mentioned previously, you will look at choice **3**, **Define Data-entry Form** in a later chapter.)

When you press **4**, **Define Query**, the screen should look like Figure 7.4.

```
                         R  1 C   5

Select form name

1: System 2: Employee 3: Employees 4: Customer 5: Products 6: Orders
for











F1 MORE F4EXIT F9LEVEL QUERY LEVEL Low    MODE Interactive
```

FIGURE 7.4

At the top of the screen, DataEase prompts you to select a form and lists all the files that are in your database. At the bottom of the screen it lists more options in a menu. If you have more files, press the F1 MORE key. The names will appear in a window at the right of the screen. If you want to exit this screen, press the F4 EXIT key to remove the window menu. Pressing the F9 QUERY LEVEL key enables you to change the query level from low to high, which makes available all query features, including enter, modify, and delete records, perform statistics, etc. This feature is useful if you are changing or updating records. At the bottom right of the screen DataEase tells you that the mode is interactive, which means that DataEase will help you compose the query. As you become more proficient, you can turn this mode off. One advantage of using the interactive mode is that DataEase will prompt you for each command and check to make sure that each command is acceptable as you compose your query.

You will notice that the word **for** is below the list of files in the database. It allows you to select a file and choose selected records from that file. The **for** statement is almost always the first word in the query. Be sure to notice all the prompts that DataEase gives you and notice how the prompts change after you select one.

Since you want to work with the **CUSTOMER** file, press **4** for **CUSTOMER**. DataEase immediately prints it to the right of the **for** statement, as shown in Figure 7.5.

At the top of the screen, DataEase asks you:

```
Any record selection criteria?
```

Another menu item also appears:

```
Ø: NONE 1: with
```

DataEase is asking you if you would like only selected customer records or all customer records. As you can see, the procedure for selecting reports in the Full Reports mode is similar to that for quick reports,

```
                    R  2 C   1

Any record selection criteria?


Ø: NONE 1: with
for Customer








F1 MORE F4EXIT F9LEVEL QUERY LEVEL Low    MODE Interactive
```

FIGURE 7.5

```
                    R  4 C   3

Specify the items to be listed.
Select field name

Ø: NONE 1: Cust ID 2: Last Name 3: First Name 4: Street 5: City 6: State F1 MORE
for Customer
;
list records









F1 MORE F4EXIT F9LEVEL QUERY LEVEL Low    MODE Interactive
```

FIGURE 7.6

as explained in the last chapter. Since you would like a list of all the customers, press **0**. The screen now appears as in Figure 7.6. Notice that DataEase inserts a **;** in a query and types out **list records**.

When you are in the low query level, DataEase assumes that you automatically wish to list the records. Other options are enter records, modify records, and delete records. You must switch to high query level to access these functions.

At the top of Figure 7.6, notice that DataEase asks what fields are to be listed or printed in the output report. It also lists all the fields in the **CUSTOMER** file across the top of the screen. If you press the F1 MORE key, it shows a complete list of all the fields in the window at the right-hand side of the screen, as shown in Figure 7.7. Press **2** and the RETURN key to insert the **Last Name** field as one of the fields to be listed.

Figure 7.8 shows what the query looks like so far.

```
                              R  4 C   3

     Select field name                              ┌──────────────────┐
                                                    │ Ø: NONE          │
     Ø: NONE 1: Cust ID 2: Last Name 3: First Name 4: Stre│ 1: Cust ID │
     for Customer                                   │ 2: Last Name     │
     ;                                              │ 3: First Name    │
     list records                                   │ 4: Street        │
                                                    │ 5: City          │
                                                    │ 6: State         │
                                                    │ 7: Zip           │
                                                    │ 8: Phone #       │
                                                    │                  │
                                                    └ Ø to 8 UP DOWN RETURN ┘
     F1 MORE F4EXIT F9LEVEL QUERY LEVEL Low    MODE Interactive
```

FIGURE 7.7

```
                              R  4 C  13

     Select any ordering, grouping, or group-totals for this item?

     Ø: NONE 1: in order 2: in reverse 3: in groups 4: in groups with group-totals
     for Customer
     ;
     list records
       Last Name

     F1 MORE F4EXIT F9LEVEL QUERY LEVEL Low    MODE Interactive
```

FIGURE 7.8

At the top of the screen, DataEase prompts:

```
 Select any ordering, grouping, or group-totals for this
item?
```

Since you want the last names to be printed in alphabetical order, press **1**, **In Order**. The screen will now appear as in Figure 7.9.

If you wanted the names printed in reverse alphabetical order, you would have typed **2**, **In Reverse**. If you had a field that you wanted grouped, such as **State**, you would press **3**, **In Groups**. DataEase would list all the customers by state. Finally, if you wanted to list total sales for each state, you would press **4**, **In Groups with Group-Totals**. This would produce statistics, such as sum, mean, etc., every time a different state name appears, for all numeric fields in the query.

To continue adding fields, you must enter

;

If you want to end the query, you type in

.

Press **1** to tell DataEase that you wish to add more items. Continue adding the fields by pressing **3** for **First Name**, the RETURN key, **0** for **None**, **1** for the **;**. A short cut is to type **;** to avoid the **0** and **1**. Press **1** for the **Cust ID**, **0** for **None**, and **1** for the **;**. Press **8** for the **Phone #,** **0** for **None**, and **0** for the **.**. The final query should look like Figure 7.10.

As soon as you enter the period, DataEase exits back to the Full Reports Menu, highlighting **5**, **Define Format** as the next probable choice. The query now is in the computer's memory but is **not** saved on disk. Press the RETURN key to enter the **Define Format** selection. You will choose the columnar format, as shown in Figure 7.11. Press the F2 ENTER key to save the format.

The output format is now shown in Figure 7.12.

```
                                R  4 C  22

Any more items to be listed?

Ø: NONE 1: ;
for Customer
;
list records
  Last Name in order






F1 MORE F4EXIT F9LEVEL QUERY LEVEL Low    MODE Interactive
```

FIGURE 7.9

```
                                R  1 C   1

for Customer
;
list records
  Last Name in order ;
  First Name ;
  Cust ID ;
  Phone # .






F1INTERACTIVE F2ENTER F3CUT F4EXIT F5COPY F6PASTE F7DEL LINE F8INS LINE F9LEVEL
```

FIGURE 7.10

```
1: columnar 2: field per line 3: export 4: special 5: Record Entry 6: Template

        Minimum line length for a columnar report is 56
        What type of report format do you want? : columnar






F9 QUICK  F4 EXIT DATABASE A PROG.A: DATA B: DATE          TIME
```

FIGURE 7.11

```
                              R  1 C   1

================================================================================
        Last              First          Cust          Phone
        Name              Name           ID            #
--------------------------------------------------------------------------------
.items
  [              ]   [                ]  [     ]    [            ]
.end
================================================================================




F2ENTER F3CUT F4EXIT F5COPY F6PASTE F7DEL LINE F8INS LINE F9PRINT F1ØFIELD
```

FIGURE 7.12

You would now like to save the report on the disk; press **7**, **Save Report** on the Full Reports Menu. As shown in Figure 7.13, DataEase asks for the name of the report. You type

```
FR1
```

for Full Report #1, or whatever name you would like to call it. **Begin all report names with a letter.** DataEase attempts to match report lists by item number first, then by item name. Names beginning with a number produce unexpected results. After you've named the report, press the ENTER or the RETURN key.

At a later time you can retrieve the report format by pressing **8**, **Load Report** and typing in either the name of the report or the report's item number, which appears in the Window Menu. To retrieve the report itself, you can either type in the first few letters of the report name and press the ENTER or the RETURN key, or you can type in the record number, highlight the report, and press the ENTER or the RETURN key. Any report can be deleted by pressing **9**, **Delete Report**, then typing

```
Reports
Current Report :

        F U L L   R E P O R T S   M E N U

    1. Run Report
    2. Start New Report
    3. Define Data-entry Form
    4. Modify Query
    5. Modify Format
    6. Define Print Style
    7. Save Report
    8. Load Report
    9. Delete Report
    1Ø. Print Report Definition

     1 to 1Ø — UP — DOWN — RETURN — END

 Please enter the report name: FR1

F9 QUICK  F4 EXIT DATABASE A PROG.A: DATA B: DATE          TIME
```

FIGURE 7.13

```
FR1                                          Running report FR1
END OF REPORT.  SPACE: Return to Menu

==========================================================================================
         Last              First               Cust           Phone
         Name               Name                ID              #
------------------------------------------------------------------------------------------
   Bergen              Carol               C-0001     (516)-798-8632
   Fitzgerald          Lisa                C-0006     (718)-680-1026
   Glass               Jeff                C-0007     (716)-964-7322
   Herbold             Mary Ellen          C-0008     (515)-243-2308
   Mena                Paul                C-0009     (803)-556-1336
   Strongly            Vincent             C-0002     (718)-224-5443
   Swartarm            Timothy             C-0010     (516)-798-8707
   Swietnicki          Marge               C-0004     (718)-213-4299
   Tabone              Toni                C-0005     (607)-847-4289
   Vultaggio           Brema               C-0011     (516)-795-7914
   Willoughby          Malcolm             C-0003     (516)-678-2306
==========================================================================================



      F4 EXIT    DATABASE A PROG.A: DATA B: DATE          TIME
```

FIGURE 7.14

in either the name of the report or the report's item number. To run the report, press **1**, **Run Report**. The final report should look like Figure 7.14.

If you press **10**, **Print Report Definition**, the complete query with report definition will be printed out as shown in Figure 7.15.

CORRECTING ERRORS—EXITING THE PROMPT MODE

As you create your query, you may press the wrong key to get the wrong field or symbol. DataEase keeps beeping and will not let you out of the menu. Don't panic! Simply press the UP ARROW key or the LEFT ARROW key to go backwards. When you do this, notice that the Top Menu disappears and the Bottom Menu says that you are no longer in the interactive mode. You can now correct any errors. When you want to get back into the interactive mode, position the cursor where you want to resume input and press the F1 key. DataEase will check what you have done, then prompt you to the next command.

If you want to type in your query without using the prompt mode, simply press the LEFT ARROW key until you exit the interactive mode.

```
REPORT FR1
------------------------------

      REPORT QUERY
      ------------

for Customer
;
list records
  Last Name in order ;
  First Name ;
  Cust ID ;
  Phone # .

        REPORT FORMAT
        -------------

1       1Ø        2Ø        3Ø        4Ø        5Ø        6Ø        7Ø        8Ø
----+----+----+----+----+----+----+----+----+----+----+----+----+----+----+----+

--------------------------------------------------------------------------------
==------------------------------------------------------------------------------
        Last              First          Cust            Phone
        Name               Name           ID               #
--------------------------------------------------------------------------------
.items
  _______________    _______________    ______    ________________

.end
================================================================================
----+----+----+----+----+----+----+----+----+----+----+----+----+----+----+----+
1       1Ø        2Ø        3Ø        4Ø        5Ø        6Ø        7Ø        8Ø

        FIELD DESCRIPTIONS
        ------------------

No. Name                     Type              Length  Remove
                                                       Spaces?
--- ------------------------ ---------------- ------  -------
  1 Last Name                Text               15      No
  2 First Name               Text               15      No
  3 Cust ID                  Text                6      No
  4 Phone #                  Numeric String     14      No

Memory required:
  Report Definition:        942
```

FIGURE 7.15

Type in your complete query. When you are finished, press F2 ENTER. DataEase will now check your query for any syntax errors. If there are any errors, it will highlight them, beginning with the first error, one at a time. If there are no errors, it will exit to the Full Reports Menu, if you are in a low level query.

ANOTHER EXAMPLE

You would now like to create another simple full report that breaks the data into groups and does group statistics. In this example, you will use the **EMPLOYEES** file to group by position, list the last name in alphabetical order, list the first name, and list the salary. On the **Salary** field, you will compute all the statistics that are available in DataEase.

In the Full Reports Menu, press **2**, **Start New Report**. Then press **4**, **Define Query** to create a new query. You will again be using the interactive mode, so DataEase will help you in writing the query. Press **3** for the **EMPLOYEES** file, press **0** for **None** (no other files need to be accessed), and press the RETURN key. Press **2** for **Position**, **3** for **In Groups**, and **1** for the **;**. Figure 7.16 shows a portion of the initial query that you should have so far. Notice that the window at the right contains

```
                          R  5 C   3

Select field name
                                                  Ø: NONE
Ø: NONE 1: Employee # 2: Position 3: Last Name 4: Fir 1: Employees #
for Employees                                     2: Position
;                                                 3: Last Name
list records                                      4: First Name
  Position in groups ;                            5: Address
                                                  6: City
                                                  7: State
                                                  8: Zip
                                                  9: Date of Birth
                                                  10: Date Hired
                                                  11: Phone #
                                                  12: Social Security Numb
                                                  13: Salary
                                                  14: Marital Status

                                                  Ø to 14 UP DOWN RETURN
F1 MORE F4EXIT F9LEVEL QUERY LEVEL Low    MODE Interactive
```

FIGURE 7.16

the list of all field names, which you can obtain by pressing the F1 MORE key.

Continue structuring the query until it matches Figure 7.17. Press **3**, **Last Name**, the RETURN key, **1** for **In Order**, and **1** for the **;**. Press **4**, **First Name**, **0** for **None**, and **1** for the **;**. Press **13**, **Salary**, then type:

:

The **:** signifies that you will perform some statistics on that field. The **Position** field will be printed within groups. The **Last Name** field will be printed in alphabetical order. The **First Name** and **Salary** fields will be printed along with certain statistics for the **Salary** field. The window on the right of Figure 7.17 shows all the statistics that may be performed on a number field only. Press **1** for **item**, **2** for **sum**, **3** for **mean** or average, **4** for **max**, **5** for **min**, **6** for **variance**, **7** for **standard deviation**, and **8** for **standard error**. You can select as many statistics on a field as you want. In this example, you will perform all statistics on the **Salary** field, so you can observe all the choices. The word **item** means that each individual salary will be printed out for each person. The word **sum** will give the total of all salaries for each group. The word **mean** will give the average of all salaries per group. **Max** will give you the highest salary in the group. **Min** will give you the lowest salary in the group. **Variance** will give you the variance among the salary values in the group. **Std.dev.** will give you the standard deviation of the group, and **Std.err.** will give you the standard error.

Finish typing the query by typing a period (**.**). The finished query should look like Figure 7.18. Save the query by pressing the F2 ENTER key.

The output format of the report appears as in Figure 7.19. Notice the basic formatting commands **.items** and **.end**. The statistics for the report are automatically inserted after the **.end** command, which means the summary statistics or data will be placed at the end or bottom of the report. No group headers or group trailers are to appear in this report. They are not required, but you may insert them if you wish. (The procedure will be discussed in a later chapter.)

Save the report by pressing **7**, **Save Report** and calling it **FR2**, for Full Report #2, or any other name you choose. Run the program in columnar format by pressing **1**, **Run Report**. The output should look like Figure 7.20.

```
                              R  7 C  28

Select the next statistical function.                 ┌──────────────────────┐
                                                      │ Ø: NONE              │
Ø: NONE 1: item 2: sum 3: mean 4: max 5: min 6: varia │ 1: item              │
for Employees                                         │ 2: sum               │
;                                                     │ 3: mean              │
list records                                          │ 4: max               │
  Position in groups ;                                │ 5: min               │
  Last Name in order ;                                │ 6: variance          │
  First Name ;                                        │ 7: std.dev.          │
  Salary : item sum mean                              │ 8: std.err.          │
                                                      │                      │
                                                      └─ Ø to 8 UP DOWN RETURN ─┘
F1 MORE F4EXIT F9LEVEL QUERY LEVEL Low    MODE Interactive
```

FIGURE 7.17

```
                              R  1 C   1

for Employees
;
list records
  Position in groups ;
  Last Name in order ;
  First Name ;
  Salary :  item sum mean  max min variance std.dev. std.err. .

F1INTERACTIVE F2ENTER F3CUT F4EXIT F5COPY F6PASTE F7DEL LINE F8INS F9LEVEL
```

FIGURE 7.18

```
                          R  1 C   1

=============================================================================
      Position              Last            First              Salary
                            Name             Name
-----------------------------------------------------------------------------
.items

.end
-----------------------------------------------------------------------------
sum
min
max
mean
variance
std.dev.
std.err.
=============================================================================



F2ENTER F3CUT F4EXIT F5COPY F6PASTE F7DEL LINE F8INS LINE F9PRINT F10FIELD
```

FIGURE 7.19

```
=============================================================================
      Position              Last            First              Salary
                            Name             Name
-----------------------------------------------------------------------------
 Ass't Manager         DeTrinis         Joan                       45,000.00
 Manager               DeTrinis         Vincent                    56,000.00
 Salesperson           Braun            Sheila                     33,000.00
                       Comforto         Anthony                    31,000.00
                       DiToro           Hank                       39,000.00
                       Duke             Joan                       28,000.00
                       Krawiec          Agnes                      27,500.00
                       Talamo           Louis                      29,250.00
                       Wasniewski       Joann                      31,500.00
 Secretary             Caravan          Peggy                      27,500.00
-----------------------------------------------------------------------------
sum                                                               347,750.00
min                                                                27,500.00
max                                                                56,000.00
mean                                                               34,775.00
variance                                                      87034027.77778
std.dev.                                                            9,329.20
std.err.                                                            2,950.15
=============================================================================
```

FIGURE 7.20

Notice that the last names are in alphabetical order and grouped by position. The group statistics are printed in the summary. Print the report definition by pressing **10**, **Print Report Definition**, as shown in Figure 7.21.

You will now delete the **item** from the query and run it to see the differences in the output. If you left the word **item** out of the statistics, each individual salary would not be printed. Only the statistics for the group would be printed. Go to **4**, **Modify Query**. DataEase has automatically placed you in the edit mode. You can now edit the query. Notice the report name in the top left-hand side of the screen. Move the cursor to the word **item** and delete it by pressing the DEL key four times. The final query should appear as in Figure 7.22.

Be sure to press **5**, **Modify Format** and **6**, **Modify Print Style** before you run the report. NOTE: If you run the report and there is no output on the screen or printer, you did not enter **5**, **Modify Format** and **6**, **Modify Print Style** before you ran the report.

When you select **6**, **Modify Print Style**, the print style form will appear, as shown in Figure 7.23.

In the print style form, you define where you would like the report to be sent. It can be sent to the screen, printer, or disk. It also shows the name of the destination printer or file, the pape size and position, page margins, and the global type style for the report. You can define the print style either when you define the report or when you modify it.

Fill in the report destination by specifying **1** for **Screen**, **2** for **Printer**, or **3** for **Disk**. Press the F3 DEFAULT VIEW key to obtain default values for the rest of the fields. You can accept these values or change them as you see fit.

You can allow the style modification at run time. This means that you can test the report to see if it runs properly on the screen, then direct the output to the printer after all corrections or changes have been made.

You can specify the printer name by typing in either the name of the printer or an *. The system will then use the default printer specified in the configuration form.

```
REPORT FR2
------------------------------

       REPORT QUERY
       ------------

for Employees
;
list records
  Position in groups ;
  Last Name in order ;
  First Name ;
  Salary :  item sum mean  max min variance std.dev. std.err. .

       REPORT FORMAT
       -------------

1       1Ø        2Ø        3Ø        4Ø        5Ø        6Ø        7Ø        8Ø
----+----+----+----+----+----+----+----+----+----+----+----+----+----+----+----+

================================================================================
       Position              Last             First              Salary
                             Name              Name
--------------------------------------------------------------------------------
.items
 ____________________  _______________  _______________       ________________
.end
--------------------------------------------------------------------------------
sum                                                       ____________________
min                                                           ________________
max                                                           ________________
mean                                                          ________________
variance                                                        ______________
std.dev.                                                      ________________
std.err.                                                      ________________
================================================================================
----+----+----+----+----+----+----+----+----+----+----+----+----+----+----+----+
1       1Ø        2Ø        3Ø        4Ø        5Ø        6Ø        7Ø        8Ø

        FIELD DESCRIPTIONS
        ------------------

No.  Name                     Type             Length  Remove
                                                       Spaces?
---  -----------------------  ---------------- ------  -------
  1  Position                 Text               20     No
  2  Last Name                Text               15     No
  3  First Name               Text               15     No
  4  Salary                   Number             16     No
      Number Type : Fixed point
      Digits to left of decimal  =  13
```

FIGURE 7.21

```
No.  Name                     Type             Length  Remove
                                                       Spaces?
---  -----------------------  ---------------- ------  -------
  5  Salary                   Number            2Ø      No
      Number Type : Fixed point
      Digits to left of decimal  =  17
  6  Salary                   Number            16      No
      Number Type : Fixed point
      Digits to left of decimal  =  13
  7  Salary                   Number            16      No
      Number Type : Fixed point
      Digits to left of decimal  =  13
  8  Salary                   Number            16      No
      Number Type : Fixed point
      Digits to left of decimal  =  13
  9  Salary                   Number            14      No
      Number Type : Floating point
 1Ø  Salary                   Number            16      No
      Number Type : Fixed point
      Digits to left of decimal  =  13
 11  Salary                   Number            16      No
      Number Type : Fixed point
      Digits to left of decimal  =  13

Memory required:
  Report Definition:         1646
```

FIGURE 7.21 (continued)

```
FR2                         (INSERT)

for Employees
;
list records
  Postion in groups ;
  Last Name in order ;
  First Name ;
  Salary :  sum mean  max min variance std.dev. std.err. .




F1INTERACTIVE F2ENTER F3CUT F4EXIT F5COPY F6PASTE F7DEL LINE F8INS LINE F9LEVEL
```

FIGURE 7.22

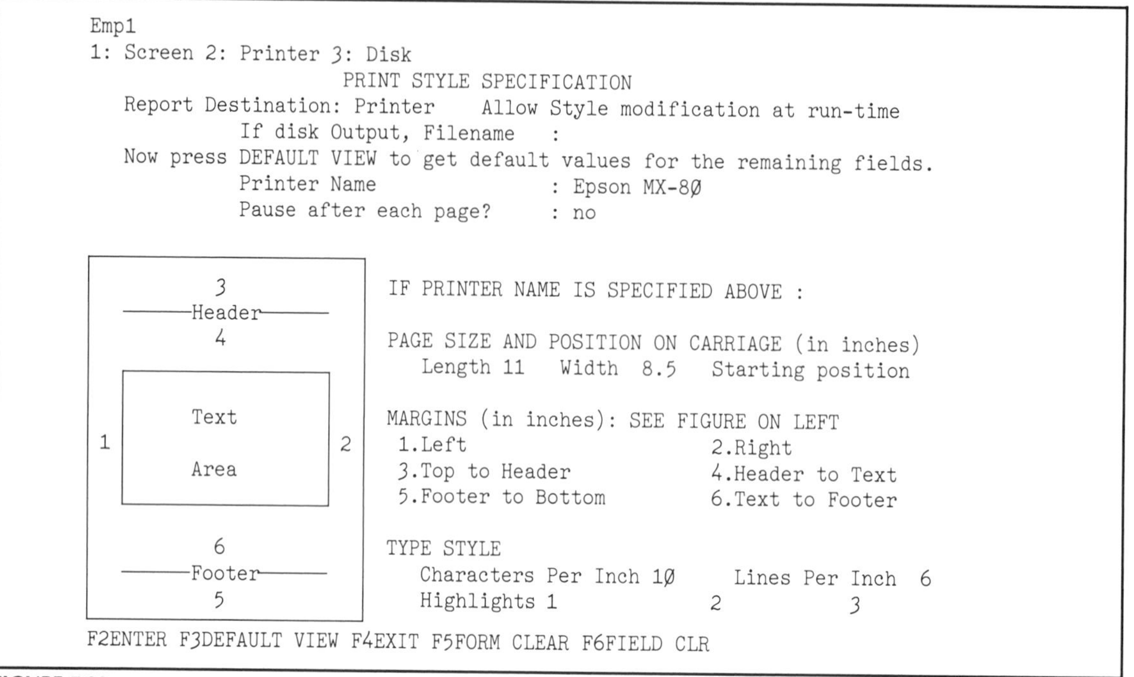

Emp1
1: Screen 2: Printer 3: Disk
PRINT STYLE SPECIFICATION
Report Destination: Printer Allow Style modification at run-time
If disk Output, Filename :
Now press DEFAULT VIEW to get default values for the remaining fields.
Printer Name : Epson MX-8Ø
Pause after each page? : no

3
Header
4
Text
1 2
Area
6
Footer
5

IF PRINTER NAME IS SPECIFIED ABOVE :

PAGE SIZE AND POSITION ON CARRIAGE (in inches)
Length 11 Width 8.5 Starting position

MARGINS (in inches): SEE FIGURE ON LEFT
1.Left 2.Right
3.Top to Header 4.Header to Text
5.Footer to Bottom 6.Text to Footer

TYPE STYLE
Characters Per Inch 1Ø Lines Per Inch 6
Highlights 1 2 3

F2ENTER F3DEFAULT VIEW F4EXIT F5FORM CLEAR F6FIELD CLR

FIGURE 7.23

If the report destination is the printer, you can specify **Yes** if the paper is to be changed after each page. Otherwise, specify **No**.

The page length and the page width should be specified in inches. Specify the page length as **0** for mailing labels and other continuous forms.

The starting position is usually left blank. Specify a starting position if the form-feed mechanism does not line up with the left edge of the printer's roller. This distance is indicated in inches.

Margins allow you to specify the positioning of the text within the page. If left blank, they are assumed to be **0**. The **left margin** measures the distance between the left edge of the paper and the first column of text. The **right margin** measures the distance between the last column of text and the right edge of the paper. The **top to header** margin measures the distance between the top edge of the page and the first line of header. If no header exists, it measures the distance between the top edge of the page and the first line of the text. The **header to text** margin measures the distance between the last line of the header and the first line of the text. If no header exists, leave it blank. The **text to footer** margin measures the distance between the last line of the text and the first line of the footer. If no footer exists, this should be left blank. The **footer to bottom** margin measures the distance between the last line of the footer and the bottom edge of the page. If no footer exists, it is the distance between the last line of the text and the bottom edge of the page.

The type style fields allow you to specify the typeface of the report by letting you control the character density and highlighting. Normal printing is 10 characters per inch. Condensed printing must have a value higher then 10. See your printer manual for exact specifications. For normal printing, specify 6 lines per inch. Otherwise, specify another value available for your printer. You may specify up to three highlights: **1** for **boldface**, **2** for **underline**, and **3** for **italicize**. Special effects 1 and 2 are used to change from correspondence and draft quality modes. The entire report will be printed in the specified manner.

After filling in the form, press the F2 ENTER key. The system will check to see if all the required fields are filled in. If a required field is left blank, it will position the cursor in that field and ask you to enter data into that particular field.

When you run the modified report by pressing **1**, **Run Report**, the output appears as Figure 7.24. Notice that each individual salary is not printed. Compare Figures 7.20 and 7.24.

DEFINING FORMAT

Choice **5**, **Define Format** on the Full Reports Menu enables you to change the format by adding headings, trailers, etc. You will now modify the query one more time and change the headings. Select **4**, **Modify Query** and change the query to match Figure 7.25. All you are doing is removing some statistics to make the output more meaningful.

When you select **5**, **Modify Format**, press **2** for **Yes** to indicate that you want group headers and trailers, as shown in Figure 7.26.

The output format that appears is shown in Figure 7.27.

```
================================================================================
      Position               Last             First              Salary
                             Name              Name
--------------------------------------------------------------------------------
 Ass't Manager          DeTrinis          Joan
 Manager                DeTrinis          Vincent
 Salesperson            Braun             Sheila
                        Comforto          Anthony
                        DiToro            Hank
                        Duke              Joan
                        Krawiec           Agnes
                        Talamo            Louis
                        Wasniewski        Joann
 Secretary              Caravan           Peggy
--------------------------------------------------------------------------------
sum                                                                 347,750.00
min                                                                  27,500.00
max                                                                  56,000.00
mean                                                                 34,775.00
variance                                                        87034027.77778
std.dev.                                                              9,329.20
std.err.                                                              2,950.15
================================================================================
```

FIGURE 7.24

```
FR2                          R  7 C  27

for Employees
;
list records
  Position in groups ;
  Last Name in order ;
  First Name ;
  Salary :  item sum mean.

F1INTERACTIVE F2ENTER F3CUT F4EXIT F5COPY F6PASTE F7DEL LINE F8INS LINE F9LEVEL
```

FIGURE 7.25

```
FR2
1: no 2: yes

        Minimum line length for a columnar report is 76
        What type of report format do you want? : columnar
        Do you want Group Headers and Trailers?










F9 QUICK  F4 EXIT DATABASE A PROG.A: DATA B: DATE          TIME
```

FIGURE 7.26

```
FR2                        R  1 C   2

=======================================================================
              Last              First                Salary
              Name               Name
-----------------------------------------------------------------------
.Group Header
Position
.items

.Group Trailer
sum
mean
.end
-----------------------------------------------------------------------
sum
mean
=======================================================================



F2ENTER F3CUT F4EXIT F5COPY F6PASTE F7DEL LINE F8INS LINE F9PRINT F1ØFIELD
```

FIGURE 7.27

Edit the output format so that it appears as in Figure 7.28. The bottom of the screen contains a menu that enables you to insert and delete lines, and copy and erase fields and text. You can also insert group headers and group trailers (by responding yes to the third question in columnar format). You can label the statistics as the **mean** and the **sum** by typing in the information wherever you want. To delete any line, press F7 DEL LINE. To delete single characters, press the DELETE key. To insert any text, just type while in the Insert mode. To discover the capabilities of the system, you should experiment with it. Press F2 ENTER when you have completed the new format.

When you press **1**, **Run Report**, the output should look like Figure 7.29. Notice that this report is much more readable than the previous one.

You can print the report definition by pressing **10**, **Print Report Definition** from the Full Reports Menu. It is shown in Figure 7.30.

You will now change one item to see how it will affect the output. Figure 7.31 shows that **group totals** has been added to the **Position** field. Now, **Position** will be printed in groups with group-totals.

Figure 7.32 shows the output format.

Figure 7.33 shows the output if the query in Figure 7.31 is run. As you can see, the statistics—the sum and average—are computed and printed for each group, as well as for all salaries in the report.

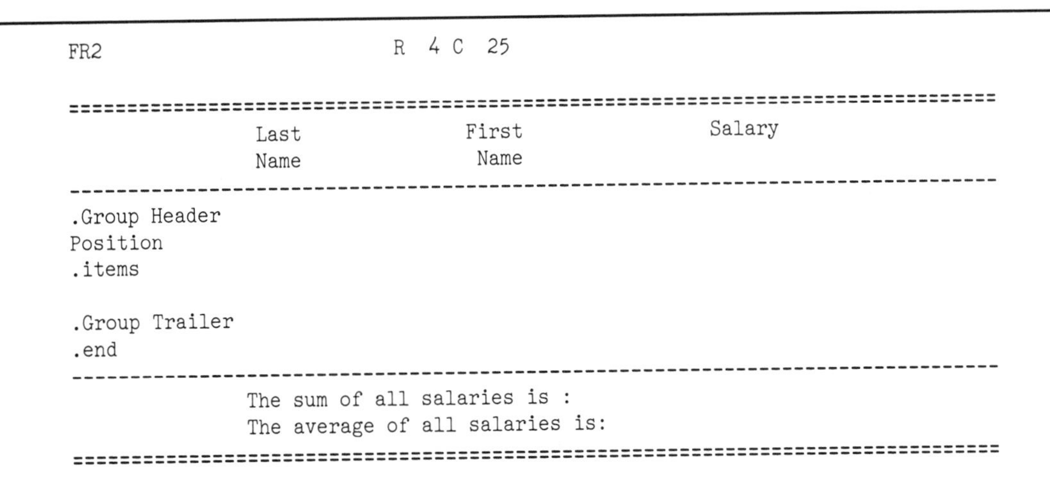

```
FR2                        R  4 C  25

===============================================================================
                Last              First                  Salary
                Name               Name
-------------------------------------------------------------------------------
.Group Header
Position
.items

.Group Trailer
.end
-------------------------------------------------------------------------------
               The sum of all salaries is :
               The average of all salaries is:
===============================================================================




F2ENTER F3CUT F4EXIT F5COPY F6PASTE F7DEL LINE F8INS LINE F9PRINT F10FIELD
```

FIGURE 7.28

```
===============================================================================
                Last              First                  Salary
                Name               Name
-------------------------------------------------------------------------------
Position Ass't Manager
          DeTrinis          Joan                           45,000.00
Position Manager
          DeTrinis          Vincent                        56,000.00
Position Salesperson
          Braun             Sheila                         33,000.00
          Comforto          Anthony                        31,000.00
          DiToro            Hank                           39,000.00
          Duke              Joan                           28,000.00
          Krawiec           Agnes                          27,500.00
          Talamo            Louis                          29,250.00
          Wasniewski        Joann                          31,500.00
Position Secretary
          Caravan           Peggy                          27,500.00
-------------------------------------------------------------------------------
               The sum of all salaries is :             347,750.00
               The average of all salaries is :          34,775.00
===============================================================================
```

FIGURE 7.29

```
REPORT FR2
------------------------------

       REPORT QUERY
       ------------

for Employees
;
list records
  Position in groups ;
  Last Name in order ;
  First Name ;
  Salary :  item sum mean

       REPORT FORMAT
       -------------

1       10        20        30        40        50        60        70        80
----+----+----+----+----+----+----+----+----+----+----+----+----+----+----+----+

================================================================================
                Last              First                 Salary
                Name              Name
--------------------------------------------------------------------------------
.Group Header
Position ____________________
.items
          _______________   _______________     ________________
.Group Trailer
.end
--------------------------------------------------------------------------------
               The sum of all salaries is :   ____________________
               The average of all salaries is:    ________________
================================================================================
----+----+----+----+----+----+----+----+----+----+----+----+----+----+----+----+
1       10        20        30        40        50        60        70        80

        FIELD DESCRIPTIONS
        ------------------

No. Name                     Type             Length  Remove
                                                      Spaces?
--- ------------------------ ---------------- ------  -------
  1 Position                 Text               20     No
  2 Last Name                Text               15     No
  3 First Name               Text               15     No
  4 Salary                   Number             16     No
     Number Type : Fixed point
     Digits to left of decimal = 13
  5 Salary                   Number             20     No
     Number Type : Fixed point
     Digits to left of decimal = 17
  6 Salary                   Number             16     No
     Number Type : Fixed point
     Digits to left of decimal = 13

Memory required:
  Report Definition:       1208
```

FIGURE 7.30

```
FR2                          R  7 C  27

for Employees
;
list records
  Position in groups with group-totals ;
  Last Name in order ;
  First Name ;
  Salary : item sum mean.









 F1INTERACTIVE F2ENTER F3CUT F4EXIT F5COPY F6PASTE F7DEL LINE F8INS LINE F9LEVEL
```

FIGURE 7.31

```
FR2                          R  1 C   1

================================================================================
                Last              First                 Salary
                Name               Name
--------------------------------------------------------------------------------
.Group Header
Position
.items

.Group Trailer
sum
mean
.end
--------------------------------------------------------------------------------
sum
mean
================================================================================



 F2ENTER F3CUT F4EXIT F5COPY F6PASTE F7DEL LINE F8INS LINE F9PRINT F1ØFIELD
```

FIGURE 7.32

```
==============================================================================
                Last               First               Salary
                Name                Name
------------------------------------------------------------------------------
Position Ass't Manager
          DeTrinis          Joan                       45,000.00
sum                                                   45,000.00
mean                                             45,000.00
Position Manager
          DeTrinis          Vincent                    56,000.00
sum                                                   56,000.00
mean                                             56,000.00
Position Salesperson
          Braun             Sheila                     33,000.00
          Comforto          Anthony                    31,000.00
          DiToro            Hank                       39,000.00
          Duke              Joan                       28,000.00
          Krawiec           Agnes                      27,500.00
          Talamo            Louis                      29,250.00
          Wasniewski        Joann                      31,500.00
sum                                                  219,250.00
mean                                             31,321.43
Position Secretary
          Caravan           Peggy                      27,500.00
sum                                                   27,500.00
mean                                             27,500.00
------------------------------------------------------------------------------
sum                                                   347,750.00
mean                                                   34,775.00
==============================================================================
```

FIGURE 7.33

FULL REPORTS—STATISTICS—FUNCTIONS—QUERY LANGUAGE

In this chapter you will learn how to create full reports whose fields have satisfied certain conditions. You will learn how to perform selected statistics on numeric fields. You will learn how to do date, text string, power, and financial functions on certain fields. You will learn how to use the Data-entry Form for transaction processing. You will learn how to use the query language to modify and delete records. You will become familiar with the relationships and terms used to initiate queries.

THE QUERY LEVELS

As mentioned in Chapter 7, queries can be entered in the Interactive mode by selecting choices from the DataEase Menu or by answering questions. In this mode, DataEase will check the syntax of the query. After you become proficient in creating queries, you may type the query in the Edit mode without any prompts from DataEase. A combination of the two modes can be used to create the query.

All queries start in the Interactive mode. For the most part, DataEase will ask you multiple choice questions and you will select an answer by typing the number of that choice. DataEase will place the word or phrase that corresponds to that number in the query in the question that is being constructed. Many of the questions that are asked are optional and may be skipped by pressing the ESC key or selecting **0** from the menu.

The Edit mode is entered by moving the cursor backwards (to the left) or up from the current phrase. This will happen automatically when you move the cursor to correct a previous character or you can intentionally do it to enter the Edit mode. There are *no prompts* in the Edit mode. You can use the cursor keys and other editing function keys to edit the query. The query is not checked for correctness in the Edit mode but will be checked when you return to the Interactive mode or when you save the query. In the Edit mode, the query may be typed in upper or lower case and spacing is up to you. You may format the query in any manner you choose.

When you are finished typing the query in the Edit mode, press the F2 ENTER key. The syntax of the query is now checked by DataEase. At the Low query level, DataEase exits the query if no errors are found. At the High query level, if no errors are found, DataEase places the cursor at the end of the query and asks you to choose the next action. Press ESC or **0** to exit the query.

To return to the Interactive mode, place the cursor where you want to resume, and press the F1 INTERACTIVE key. The query is checked up to the cursor. If an error message is found, the cursor is placed at the word or phrase that has an error, and an error message is displayed on the screen.

There are two query levels available in the Interactive mode. The Interactive mode starts at the Low level. This level gives the prompts for the more commonly used commands. To use commands that contain calculations, functions, batch update functions, nested record selection criteria, and renaming of relationships, you must change to the High query level. To change to the High query level, press the F9 LEVEL key. You can change from the High to the Low level and back again as many times as you wish.

SELECTING CERTAIN RECORDS

In the last chapter you did not select any records that met certain criteria. For example, records can be selected for all people who live in Massapequa or whose salary is greater than a certain amount. In this section you will list or print out records that will meet these conditions. Look at the beginning of a query that is shown in Figure 8.1.

After you select the file that you wish to query, (in this case, **EMPLOYEES**) DataEase responds with:

```
Any record selection criteria?
```

Press **1 with** to indicate to DataEase that you wish to select certain records. DataEase responds with the names of the fields that you can select. If you press the F1 MORE key, the window box at the right of Figure 8.2 displays all the possible fields that you can select.

In your query, you would like all the people who hold the position of Salesperson. Press **2** followed by the RETURN key to select **Position**. DataEase now responds with a selection of the comparison symbols as shown in Figure 8.3.

The **with** statement, which is on the next line after the **for** statement, selects the records from the file and specifies the selection criteria. Here you wish to find the statistics on the salaries of only the people who hold the position of Salesperson. Press **1** for = and Figure 8.4 appears.

```
                              R  2 C   1
Any record selection criteria?

Ø: NONE 1: with
for Employees











F1 MORE F4EXIT F9LEVEL QUERY LEVEL LOW    MODE Interactive
```

FIGURE 8.1

```
                              R 2 C   4

Select field name
                                                  Ø: NONE
Ø: NONE 1: Employee # 2: Position 3: Last Name 4: Fir 1: Employee #
for Employees                                      2: Position
with                                               3: Last Name
                                                   4: First Name
                                                   5: Address
                                                   6: City
                                                   7: State
                                                   8: Zip
                                                   9: Date of Birth
                                                   1Ø: Date Hired
                                                   11: Phone #
                                                   12: Social Security Numb
                                                   13: Salary
                                                   14: Marital Status



                                                    Ø to 14 UP DOWN RETURN
F1 MORE F4EXIT F9LEVEL QUERY LEVEL Low    MODE Interactive
```

FIGURE 8.2

```
                              R  2 C  15

Select a comparison symbol or the 'not' operator

1:  = 2: > 3: < 4: <= 5: >= 6: between 7: not
for Employees
with Position



F1 MORE F4EXIT F9LEVEL QUERY LEVEL LOW    MODE Interactive
```

FIGURE 8.3

```
                              R  2 C  17

Define comparison value
Specify a constant value
Enter a text string, enclosed in "". To skip hit ESC.
for Employees
with Position  =



F1 MORE F4EXIT F9LEVEL QUERY LEVEL Low    MODE Interactive
```

FIGURE 8.4

```
                              R  1 C   1

for Employees
with Position  =  "Salesperson";
list records
  Last Name in order ;
  First Name ;
  Salary in reverse :  item sum mean .









F1INTERACTIVE F2ENTER F3CUT F4EXIT F5COPY F6PASTE F7DEL LINE F8INS LINE F9LEVEL
```

FIGURE 8.5

As shown in Figure 8.4, you are now asked to type in a text string enclosed in quotes. Type in **Salesperson** as shown in Figure 8.5. Continue typing in the rest of the query as shown in Figure 8.5. The **Last Name** field will be printed in alphabetical order. As an additional note, you want the **Salary** field to be printed in reverse numerical order. This is an impossible task; you have only last names with no duplicates. In your situation, simultaneously placing the last names in alphabetical order and the salaries in reverse alphabetical order is impossible. DataEase would display salaries listed in reverse, provided there were more than one occurrence of the field you are grouping on, in this case, Last Name.

If you look at the output shown in Figure 8.6, you will notice that DataEase realizes it is impossible to print out the names of people in alphabetical order and, at the same time, print out the salaries in reverse numerical order. DataEase will not give you output that cannot be printed so it takes the first condition, printing out the names in alphabetical order. Notice the complete statistics shown at the bottom of Figure 8.6.

```
================================================================
       Last               First                Salary
       Name                Name
----------------------------------------------------------------
  Braun              Sheila                           33,000.00
  Comforto           Anthony                          31,000.00
  DiToro             Hank                             39,000.00
  Duke               Joan                             28,000.00
  Krawiec            Agnes                            27,500.00
  Talamo             Louis                            29,250.00
  Wasniewski         Joann                            31,500.00
----------------------------------------------------------------
sum                                                  219,250.00
mean                                                  31,321.43
================================================================
```

FIGURE 8.6

After the **with** statement, you can use any of several arithmetic operators that can perform comparison. Here are some with an illustration of each.

```
with Salary = 30000
with Salary > 30000
with Salary >= 30000
with Salary < 30000
with Salary <= 30000
with Salary between 20000 to 30000
with Salary no > 30000
```

You can also use the operators **and** and **or** to specify multiple conditions. If the field can have more than one value, specify each value with the operator **or** between each value. For example,

```
"John" or "Mary"
```

If you have multiple ranges, you can use the operators **or** and **and** between criteria. If you need to use both operators in the same sentence, be sure to use the parentheses to indicate the order of evaluation. Without parentheses, the default order of evaluation is: first the multiplications and divisions are performed, then addition and subtraction operations, and, finally, **and** and **or** operations. If several operations of equal priority are performed (as several multiplication and division operations), the one on the left is performed first. Always type parentheses at the appropriate place in a query to save time. For example,

```
>198Ø and <199Ø
(>95 and <1ØØ) or (>2ØØ and <2Ø5)
```

In the last example, parentheses are needed because you want to perform the two **and** statements before the **or**.

Figure 8.7 shows a query that will list a Salesperson who is married. Notice that as soon as the **Marital Status** field is shown, the choices are shown at the menu prompt.

```
                              R  3 C  2Ø

Define comparison value
Specify a constant value
Ø: NONE 1: Married 2: Single 3: Divorced 4: Separated
for Employees
with Position = "Salesperson" and
  Marital Status =

F1 MORE F4EXIT F9LEVEL QUERY LEVEL Low    MODE Interactive
```

FIGURE 8.7

The completed query is shown in Figure 8.8.

The output or run of the report is shown in Figure 8.9.

USING WILDCARDS IN SEARCHES

Even wildcard characters can be used in searches. Figure 8.10 searches for any customer who lives in Deer Park and whose last name begins with the letters *Her*. This could print out Herd, Herry, or Herbold as in our example. The * means that there can be any number of characters following the letters *Her*. The * can also be used to specify an undefined number of leading characters. For example, ***ler** will select any field ending with *ler*. The * wildcard can be used to match an undefined number of characters between a prefix and a suffix. For example, **R*A** will match all fields beginning with a *R*.

The output of the query is shown in Figure 8.11.

The **?** can be used in a comparison where only one character does not match. For example, if you specified a search for **D??K**, you might get Duck, Dock, Deek, etc.

Another example of using the selection criteria is selecting all the orders on a certain date. Figure 8.12 shows a query that will list all the orders that occurred today. "Current Date" is a reserved DataEase word.

SEARCHING FOR BLANK FIELDS

In the previous examples you do not want to perform statistics or calculations on fields that are blank. Figure 8.13 shows a query that will list the names of all people where the Salary field is omitted or left blank. Any type of field that has not been filled in is considered to be BLANK, which is another DataEase reserve word. This is a good way of checking input errors in transaction processing or data entry.

CALCULATIONS ON FIELDS

DataEase can also do calculations on numeric fields. Figure 8.14 shows what it would cost if you wanted to give to each Salesperson a 9% raise. Notice in Figure 8.15 that the statistics are shown for the totals.

The output is shown in Figure 8.15.

```
                              R  1 C   1

      for Employees
      with Position = "Salesperson" and
        Marital Status = Married ;
      list records
        Last Name in order ;
        First Name ;
        Salary .









      F1INTERACTIVE F2ENTER F3CUT F4EXIT F5COPY F6PASTE F7DEL LINE F8INS LINE F9LEVEL
```

FIGURE 8.8

```
                                         Running report
     END OF REPORT.  SPACE: Return to Menu

     ============================================================
             Last              First               Salary
             Name               Name
     ------------------------------------------------------------
       Comforto            Anthony                   31,ØØØ.ØØ
       DiToro              Hank                      39,ØØØ.ØØ
       Krawiec             Agnes                     27,5ØØ.ØØ
       Talamo              Louis                     29,25Ø.ØØ
     ============================================================








          F4 EXIT     DATABASE A PROG.A: DATA B: DATE          TIME
```

FIGURE 8.9

```
                              R  1 C   1

      for Customer
      with City  =  "Deer Park" and
        Last Name  =  "Her*";
      list records
        Last Name ;
        First Name .

      F1INTERACTIVE F2ENTER F3CUT F4EXIT F5COPY F6PASTE F7DEL LINE F8INS LINE F9LEVEL
```

FIGURE 8.10

```
                                            Running report
      END OF REPORT.  SPACE: Return to Menu

      ========================================

              Last              First
              Name               Name
      ----------------------------------------
        Herbold             Mary Ellen
      ========================================

            F4 EXIT     DATABASE A PROG.A: DATA B: DATE          TIME
```

FIGURE 8.11

```
                              R  1 C   1

      for Orders
      with Date  =  current date ;
      list records
        Order # in order ;
        Cust ID ;
        Emp # .

      F1INTERACTIVE F2ENTER F3CUT F4EXIT F5COPY F6PASTE F7DEL LINE F8INS LINE F9LEVEL
```

FIGURE 8.12

```
                              R  1 C   1

      for Employees
      with Salary  =  BLANK ;
      list records
        Last Name ;
        First Name .

      F1INTERACTIVE F2ENTER F3CUT F4EXIT F5COPY F6PASTE F7DEL LINE F8INS LINE F9LEVEL
```

FIGURE 8.13

```
                    R  1 C   1

for Employees
with Position = "Salesperson";
list records
  Last Name in order ;
  Salary :  item sum max mean min;
  Salary * 1.Ø9 : item sum mean max min ;
  Salary * 1.Ø9 - Salary : item sum mean max min .

F1INTERACTIVE F2ENTER F3CUT F4EXIT F5COPY F6PASTE F7DEL LINE F8INS LINE F9LEVEL
```

FIGURE 8.14

```
================================================================================
=
     Last             Salary              Salary *          Salary * 1.Ø9 -
     Name                                   1.Ø9                Salary
--------------------------------------------------------------------------------
-
 Braun                       33,ØØØ.ØØ           35,97Ø.ØØ              2,97Ø.ØØ
 Comforto                    31,ØØØ.ØØ           33,79Ø.ØØ              2,79Ø.ØØ
 DiToro                      39,ØØØ.ØØ           42,51Ø.ØØ              3,51Ø.ØØ
 Duke                        28,ØØØ.ØØ           3Ø,52Ø.ØØ              2,52Ø.ØØ
 Krawiec                     27,5ØØ.ØØ           29,975.ØØ              2,475.ØØ
 Talamo                      29,25Ø.ØØ           31,882.5Ø              2,632.5Ø
 Wasniewski                  31,5ØØ.ØØ           34,335.ØØ              2,835.ØØ
--------------------------------------------------------------------------------
-
sum                         219,25Ø.ØØ          238,982.5Ø             19,732.5Ø
min                          27,5ØØ.ØØ           29,975.ØØ              2,475.ØØ
max                          39,ØØØ.ØØ           42,51Ø.ØØ              3,51Ø.ØØ
mean                         31,321.43           34,14Ø.36              2,818.93
================================================================================
=
```

FIGURE 8.15

STRING, POWER, AND FINANCIAL FUNCTIONS

DataEase possesses numerous functions that pertain to date, time, text string, exponential and power, trigonometric, and financial functions. However, you must be in High level to access these functions. Figure 8.16 shows a query that illustrates just a few of these functions. It also includes a wildcard search.

You will notice that as you are typing, DataEase shows you a list of the available functions. Figure 8.16 shows a list of the first nineteen of these.

Figures 8.17 and 8.18 display the rest of the function choices that are available. As you can see from the menu, there are fifty-four functions built into DataEase. The DataEase reference manual describes each of these. Try experimenting with those that are of interest to you. REMEMBER: if you need help on any of them, press the ALT F1 HELP key.

The completed query is shown in Figure 8.19. If you make a mistake, press the left arrow and correct it. To get back into the Interactive mode, press the F1 INTERACTIVE key. DataEase will then prompt you for

```
                       R  6 C  13
Select a Function or press ESC.                 ┌──────────────────┐
                                                │Ø: NONE           │
Ø: NONE 1: if 2: month 3: day 4: year 5: yearday 6: w│1: if        │
for Employees                                   │2: month          │
   with Last Name = "D??E";                     │3: day            │
   list records                                 │4: year           │
      Last Name ;                               │5: yearday        │
      First Name ;                              │6: weekday        │
      firstc                                    │7: yearweek       │
                                                │8: date           │
                                                │9: julian         │
                                                │1Ø: spellmonth    │
                                                │11: spellweekday  │
                                                │12: spelldate     │
                                                │13: spellnumber   │
                                                │14: spellcurrency │
                                                │15: hours         │
                                                │16: minutes       │
                                                │17: seconds       │
                                                │18: timeampm      │
                                                │19: ampm          │
                                                └─ Ø to 54 UP DOWN RETURN ─┘
F1 MORE F4EXIT F9LEVEL QUERY LEVEL High   MODE Interactive
```

FIGURE 8.16

```
                        R  6 C  13
Select a Function or press ESC.                          20: firstc
Ø: NONE 1: if 2: month 3: day 4: year 5: yearday 6: w   21: lastc
for Employees                                            22: midc
   with Last Name = "D??E";                              23: firstw
   list records                                          24: lastw
      Last Name ;                                        25: midw
      First Name ;                                       26: jointext
      firstc                                             27: length
                                                         28: lastfirst
                                                         29: firstlast
                                                         3Ø: presentvalue
                                                         31: futurevalue
                                                         32: installment
                                                         33: rate
                                                         34: periods
                                                         35: exp
                                                         36: log
                                                         37: log1Ø
                                                         38: power
                                                         39: sqrt
                                                          Ø to 54 UP DOWN RETURN
F1 MORE F4EXIT F9LEVEL QUERY LEVEL High   MODE Interactive
```

FIGURE 8.17

```
                        R  6 C  13
Select a Function or press ESC.                          4Ø: sin
Ø: NONE 1: if 2: month 3: day 4: year 5: yearday 6: w   41: cos
for Employees                                            42: tan
   with Last Name = "D??E";                              43: asin
   list records                                          44: acos
      Last Name ;                                        45: atan
      First Name ;                                       46: atan2
      firstc                                             47: sinh
                                                         48: cosh
                                                         49: tanh
                                                         5Ø: random
                                                         51: abs
                                                         52: ceil
                                                         53: floor
                                                         54: mod

                                                          Ø to 54 UP DOWN RETURN
F1 MORE F4EXIT F9LEVEL QUERY LEVEL High   MODE Interactive
```

FIGURE 8.18

```
                              R  1 C   1

for Employees
with Last Name  =  "D??E";
list records
  Last Name ;
  First Name ;
  firstc (Last Name, 2);
  lastc (Last Name, 2);
  midc (Last Name, 2, 2);
  firstw (Address, 2);
  lastw (Address, 2);
  length (Last Name);
  jointext (firstw(First Name,1),lastw(Last Name,1));
  sqrt(155);
  rate (5000,30000,100,15);
  presentvalue (30000,150,9,15);
  futurevalue (5000,200,9,15);
  installment (5000,3000,9,15);
  periods (5000,30000,250,9).


F1INTERACTIVE F2ENTER F3CUT F4EXIT F5COPY F6PASTE F7DEL LINE F8INS LINE F9LEVEL
```

FIGURE 8.19

your next selection. The query is checked up to the cursor. If any errors are found, the cursor is positioned at the word or phrase that has the error and gives you an error message. Use the Interactive mode when you are learning how to use the DataEase Query Language. You can use the Type Ahead mode of the Interactive mode to type in the punctuation marks and other special symbols.

Figure 8.20 shows the output which is being printed one field per line for ease of readability.

The first seven statements in the query are text string functions.

firstc (Last Name, 2) takes the first two characters of the **Last Name** field.

lastc (Last Name, 2) takes the last two characters of the **Last Name** field.

midc (Last Name, 2, 2) takes two characters starting with the second character of the **Last Name** field.

```
                                        Running report
END OF REPORT.  SPACE: Return to Menu    LEFT and RIGHT Arrows: Scroll

================================================================================
 Last Name                               Duke
 First Name                              Joan
 firstc (Last Name, 2)                   Du
 lastc (Last Name, 2)                    ke
 midc (Last Name, 2, 2)                  uk
 firstw (Address, 2)                     1313 Golden
 lastw (Address, 2)                      Golden Court
 length (Last Name)                        4
 jointext (firstw(First Name,1),last     JoanDuke
 sqrt(155)                               12.4498996
 rate (5ØØØ,3ØØØØ,1ØØ,15)                11.7188949
 presentvalue (3ØØØØ,15Ø,9,15)           7Ø27.Ø3797
 futurevalue (5ØØØ,2ØØ,9,15)             24Ø84.5955
 installment(5ØØØ,3ØØØØ,9,15)            4Ø1.472Ø66
 periods (5ØØØ,3ØØØØ,25Ø,9)              16.692Ø233
================================================================================


      F4 EXIT     DATABASE A PROG.A: DATA B: DATE          TIME
```

FIGURE 8.20

firstw (Address, 2) takes the first two words of the **Address** field.

lastw (Address, 2) takes the last two words of the **Address** field.

length tells how many characters are in the **Last Name** field.

jointext (firstw(First Name,1),last concatenates the **First** and **Last Names** together.

The following statement is an exponential or power function.

sqrt (155) computes the square root of 155.

The following statements are financial functions.

rate (5000,30000,100,15) computes the interest rate with a present value of $5,000, maturity value of $30,000, payments of $100 for fifteen years.

presentvalue (30000,150,9,15) computes the present value if the future value is $30,000, installments of $150, at 9% interest for fifteen years. The present value is the cash value, today, of future returns.

futurevalue (5000,200,9,15) computes the future value if the present value is $5,000, installments of $200, at 9% interest for fifteen years. The future value is the value of an initial investment after a specified period of time at a particular rate of interest.

installment (5000,30000,9,15) computes how much money to pay as an installment for the present value of $5,000, future value of $30,000, at 9% interest for fifteen years.

periods (5000,30000,250,9) computes the pay periods for a present value of $5,000, future value of $30,000, installment of $250 at a 9% interest rate.

DATE FUNCTIONS

DataEase has many functions that relate to dates. Figure 8.21 shows an example of a query that demonstrates the use of date functions.

Figure 8.22 shows the run of the report.

As you can see from Figure 8.21, the function **month** gives the number of the month of the year (a number from 1 through 12). The function **day** gives the day of the month (a number 1 through 31). The function **year** gives the year number (a number from 1 through 99). The function **weekday** gives the number of the day of the week (a number from 1 through 7). The function **yearday** gives the number of the day of the year (a number from 1 through 366). The function **yearweek** gives the number of the week of the year (a number from 1 through 52). These would be used if you needed certain statistical information for insurance or employment benefits where you would need the date broken down into its components of month, day, and year.

TIME FUNCTIONS

Very similar to the date functions are the time functions. The function **hours** gives the hour of the day (a number from 0 through 23). The function **minutes** gives the number of minutes of the hour (a number from 0 through 59). The function **seconds** gives the number of seconds (a number from 0 through 59). The function **ampm** give the test value of either AM or PM. The function **timeampm** gives the time with AM or PM attached.

```
                              R  1 C   1

      for Employees
      ;
      list records
        Date Hired in order ;
        month ( Date Hired ) :
        day ( Date Hired ) ;
        year ( Date Hired);
        weekday (Date Hired);
        yearday (Date Hired);
        yearweek (Date Hired).











      F1INTERACTIVE F2ENTER F3CUT F4EXIT F5COPY F6PASTE F7DEL LINE F8INS LINE F9LEVEL
```

FIGURE 8.21

```
                                      Running report
     END OF REPORT.  SPACE: Return to Menu

     ================================================================================
         Date      month (   day (    year (    weekday     yearday    yearweek
         Hired      Date     Date     Date      (Date       (Date       (Date
                    Hired    Hired    Hired)     Hired)      Hired)     Hired)
                      )        )
     --------------------------------------------------------------------------------
       Ø3/13/66       3       13       66          7          72         11
       Ø3/13/66       3       13       66          7          72         11
       Ø7/Ø1/69       7        1       69          2         182         26
       Ø4/Ø5/71       4        5       71          1          95         14
       11/22/71      11       22       71          1         326         47
       Ø5/3Ø/72       5       3Ø       72          2         151         22
       Ø4/17/73       4       17       73          2         1Ø7         16
       Ø6/23/74       6       23       74          7         174         25
       Ø2/13/75       2       13       75          4          44          7
       Ø9/18/77       9       18       77          7         261         38
     ================================================================================



           F4 EXIT     DATABASE A PROG.A: DATA B: DATE          TIME
```

FIGURE 8.22

SPELL IT OUT FUNCTIONS

Figure 8.23 shows a query that has several spell it out functions. These functions write out the date, day of the week, month, a number, or a dollar amount.

As you can see from Figure 8.24 (only the first page of output is shown), all the numbers or dates are written out in phrases that are easy to understand.

USE OF DATA-ENTRY FORM

If you look at the Full Reports Menu in Figure 7.2, you have covered every choice except **3**, **Data-entry Form**. This is one of the two choices that differs from the Quick Reports Menu. The Data-entry Form allows you to input one or more fields that will be used in the selection or computation of data, such as the information to be printed, or the information to be placed into files. The Data-entry Form is used to enter information into the report at the time the report is run. Before you create your form, DataEase will ask as shown in the window box of Figure 8.25:

```
After running the report, display data-entry form again?
```

```
                              R  1 C   1

for Employees
;
list records
  Date Hired in order ;
  Salary ;
  spellmonth(month ( ( Date Hired ) ) );
  spellweekday(weekday ( Date Hired )) ;
  spelldate ( Date Hired);
  spellnumber(year (Date Hired));
  spellcurrency (Salary).

F1INTERACTIVE F2ENTER F3CUT F4EXIT F5COPY F6PASTE F7DEL LINE F8INS LINE F9LEVEL
```

FIGURE 8.23

```
                                     Running report
SPACE: Continue Report  EXIT: Abort Report  LEFT and RIGHT Arrows: Scroll

==============================================================================
 Date Hired                           Ø3/13/66
 Salary                                      45,ØØØ.ØØ
 spellmonth(month ( ( Date Hired ) )  March
 spellweekday(weekday ( Date Hired )  Sunday
 spelldate ( Date Hired)              March 13, 1966
 spellnumber(year (Date Hired))       Sixty Six
 spellcurrency (Salary)               Forty Five Thousand Dollars and ØØ Cents

 Date Hired                           Ø3/13/66
 Salary                                      56,ØØØ.ØØ
 spellmonth(month ( ( Date Hired ) )  March
 spellweekday(weekday ( Date Hired )  Sunday
 spelldate ( Date Hired)              March 13, 1966
 spellnumber(year (Date Hired))       Sixty Six
 spellcurrency (Salary)               Fifty Six Thousand Dollars and ØØ Cents

 Date Hired                           Ø7/Ø1/69
 Salary                                      33,ØØØ.ØØ
 spellmonth(month ( ( Date Hired ) )  July
 spellweekday(weekday ( Date Hired )  Tuesday
      F4 EXIT     DATABASE A PROG.A: DATA B: DATE          TIME
```

FIGURE 8.24

```
Reports
1: no 2: yes

      F U L L   R E P O R T S   M E N U

   1. Run Report
   2. Start New Report
   3. Define Data-entry Form
   4. Define Query
   5. Define Format
   6. Define Print Style
   7. Save Report
   8. Load Report
   9. Delete Report
   1Ø. Print Report Definition

 —— 1 to 1Ø — UP — DOWN — RETURN — END ——

 After running the report, display data-entry form again?

F9 QUICK  F4 EXIT DATABASE A PROG.A: DATA B: DATE          TIME
```

FIGURE 8.25

You will answer yes to this question by pressing **2** for **yes**. This will enable you to run the report several times without returning to the menu. Here the Data-entry Form can be considered a transaction input form.

Figure 8.26 shows a very elementary Data-entry Form where the price of computer hardware is asked. With the Data-entry Form you can ask to input one or more fields to be used in the selection or computation of data, the information to be printed, or the information to be placed into files. Figure 8.26 asks the person to type in the price and DataEase will list all items greater than that price. Not shown in Figure 8.26 is the name and description of the field which is declared by pressing the F10 FIELD key and typing in the **Price** field with its field characteristics. You can do this right after the period in the sentence.

You can use this Data-entry Form to enter transactions into the database. You can also use any of the fields in the Data-entry Form as additional data for your report. When you have finished typing in the form, press F2 ENTER.

```
FORM                          R  3 C  21

    Type in the price and I will give you the name of the items that cost more
    than that price.











F2ENTER F3CUT F4EXIT F5COPY F6PASTE F7DEL LINE F8INS LINE F9PRINT F1ØFIELD
```

FIGURE 8.26

Figure 8.27 shows the beginning of your query. Notice that DataEase will prompt you with **data-entry** as one of the choices.

The complete query is shown in Figure 8.28.

When the report is run, the Data-entry screen where the program is displayed for the operator to type in the input price is shown in Figure 8.29.

When the price is entered, press F2 ENTER to enter the information. The price that is entered will generate a report that prints out the description of the product and the price that is greater than the price that is entered (in this case $1,000). This is shown in Figure 8.30.

When the F4 EXIT or SPACEBAR key is pressed again, the report is run again (see Figure 8.25). In this case the report operator has typed in 2,000.00 as shown in Figure 8.31. The report operator then presses F2 ENTER.

The output is shown in Figure 8.32.

As you can see, this is an extremely powerful feature of DataEase. This feature cannot be accomplished in the Quick Reports Menu. The complete report definition is printed in Figure 8.33. Notice the Data-entry Form at the beginning of the report. You can see the underline shows where the price is entered by the report operator. The field description of the **Price** field is given below the Data-entry field description.

After you have defined the DataEase form, it may be modified or deleted. If you wish to delete the DataEase form, press **3**, **Modify Data-entry**. DataEase asks:

```
Delete the data-entry form?
```

If you wish to delete it, type:

```
Yes
```

If you answer **No**, DataEase asks:

```
After running the report, display data-entry form again?
```

```
                              R  2 C  15
Any record selection criteria?
Define comparison value

Ø: NONE 1: current 2: data-entry
for Products
with Price >=

F1 MORE F4EXIT F9LEVEL QUERY LEVEL Low    MODE Interactive
```

FIGURE 8.27

```
                              R  1 C   1

for Products
with Price >=  data-entry Price ;
list records
  Description in order ;
  Price .

F1INTERACTIVE F2ENTER F3CUT F4EXIT F5COPY F6PASTE F7DEL LINE F8INS LINE F9LEVEL
```

FIGURE 8.28

```
Type in the price and I will give you the name of the items that cost more
than that price.   1,ØØØ.ØØ




F2ENTER F4EXIT F5FORM CLEAR F6FIELD CLR
```

FIGURE 8.29

```
                                Running report
END OF REPORT.  SPACE: Return to Menu

================================================================================
                 Description                          Price
--------------------------------------------------------------------------------
  IBM Personal Computer System - Color                 2,2ØØ.ØØ
  IBM Personal Computer System - Mono                  1,4ØØ.ØØ
  Laser Printer                                        5,432.ØØ
================================================================================




      F4 EXIT     DATABASE A PROG.A: DATA B: DATE          TIME
```

FIGURE 8.30

```
Type in the price and I will give you the name of the items that cost more
than that price.   2,000.00











F2ENTER F4EXIT F5FORM CLEAR F6FIELD CLR
```

FIGURE 8.31

```
                                 Running report
END OF REPORT.  SPACE: Return to Menu

=================================================================================
                  Description                             Price
---------------------------------------------------------------------------------
  IBM Personal Computer System - Color                     2,200.00
  Laser Printer                                            5,432.00
=================================================================================











      F4 EXIT     DATABASE A PROG.A: DATA B: DATE          TIME
```

FIGURE 8.32

```
REPORT Data-Entry
------------------------------

DATA-ENTRY FORM
---------------

1        1Ø        2Ø        3Ø        4Ø        5Ø        6Ø        7Ø        8Ø
----+----+----+----+----+----+----+----+----+----+----+----+----+----+----+----+


    Type in the price and I will give you the name of the items that cost more
    than that price. __________
----+----+----+----+----+----+----+----+----+----+----+----+----+----+----+----+
1        1Ø        2Ø        3Ø        4Ø        5Ø        6Ø        7Ø        8Ø

        FIELD DESCRIPTIONS
        ------------------
No.  Name                 Type       Long Reqd In- Uni- Der- Rng Pre-  Record
                                                dex que  ived Chk vent size offset
---  -------------------- ---------- ---- ---- --- ---- ---- --- ---- ---- ------
  1  Price                Number       1Ø Yes  No   No   No   No  No      8     3
       Number Type : Fixed point
       Digits to left of decimal = 7
---- -------------------- ---------- ---- ---- --- ---- ---- --- ---- ---- ------

Record size 11

Memory required for form: Text  1Ø7, Fields 39, Total 146 bytes.

       REPORT QUERY
       -----------
for Products
with Price >= data-entry Price ;
list records
  Description in order ;
  Price .

       REPORT FORMAT
       -------------

1        1Ø        2Ø        3Ø        4Ø        5Ø        6Ø        7Ø        8Ø
----+----+----+----+----+----+----+----+----+----+----+----+----+----+----+----+

================================================================================

                 Description                       Price
--------------------------------------------------------------------------------
.items
  ________________________________________   _______________

.end
================================================================================
```

FIGURE 8.33

```
1        10        20        30        40        50        60        70        80
----+----+----+----+----+----+----+----+----+----+----+----+----+----+----+----+


        FIELD DESCRIPTIONS
        ------------------

No.  Name                          Type              Length  Remove
                                                             Spaces?
---  ---------------------------  ---------------- ------  -------
  1  Description                   Type               40      No
  2  Price                         Number             13      No
       Number Type : Fixed point
       Digits to left of decimal = 10

Memory required:
  Report Definition:            777
  Data-entry Form:              146
```

FIGURE 8.33 (continued)

After answering the question, the Data-entry Form appears, and you may modify it, if needed. If you define, modify, or delete a Data-entry Form, the query should also be modified before the report can be saved.

MODIFYING RECORDS

Unlike Quick Reports, Full Reports can be used to change or modify the actual records. Figure 8.34 shows the beginning of a query that will be used to give each salesperson a 25% raise. If you look at the window box on the right-hand side of Figure 8.34, you notice that besides modifying records, you can also list, delete, or enter records if you are in the High Level Query mode. In your situation you will select **2: modify records**.

The rest of the query is shown in Figure 8.35. Notice that you can now list the last names in alphabetical order along with their first names and salaries. After you modify records, it is always a good idea to list all the records with the new changes to make sure that they have been actually performed. A hardcopy of the results is always useful for

```
                              R  3 C  13

                                                    Ø: NONE
Ø: NONE 1: list records 2: modify records 3: delete r 1: list records
for Employees                                       2: modify records
with Position =  "Salesperson";                     3: delete records
modify records                                      4: enter a record
                                                    5: if
                                                    6: else
                                                    7: end
                                                    8: while
                                                    9: for
                                                    1Ø: break
                                                    11: exit
                                                    12: define
                                                    13: assign
                                                    14: .

                                                    Ø to 14 UP DOWN RETURN
F1 MORE F4EXIT F9LEVEL QUERY LEVEL High   MODE Interactive
```

FIGURE 8.34

reference both before and after the changes have been made. It is also advisable to make a backup of the database before changes are made in case you change the wrong field or fields. Notice the period that appears before the **list records** in Figure 8.35. The period signifies the end of the modify records procedure.

In a similar manner you can change the query to delete or enter new records.
For example,

```
delete records in Orders
  with (date <Ø1/Ø1/88).
```

will delete all orders that were taken before January 1, 1988.

```
for Employees
  with Position =  "Vice-President";
  delete records.
```

```
                              R  1 C   1

for Employees
with Position = "Salesperson";
modify records
  Salary : = Salary * 1.25 .
list records
  Last Name in order ;
  First Name ;
  Salary .

F1INTERACTIVE F2ENTER F3CUT F4EXIT F5COPY F6PASTE F7DEL LINE F8INS LINE F9LEVEL
```

FIGURE 8.35

In this query, all employees that are vice-presidents are selected and their records deleted. It is also possible to delete records in other files through the use of the **Delete Records In** statement. The query above is rewritten to illustrate this.

```
for Employees
  with Position = "Vice-President";
  delete records .
  delete records in orders .
  delete records in customer .
```

NOTE: If there is not a relationship between Employee-Orders and Employee-Customer, then all records from **ORDERS** and **CUSTOMER** will be deleted. Be careful!

In this query, you select employees that are vice-presidents and delete them from the **EMPLOYEES** file. The corresponding records are also deleted from the **ORDERS** and **CUSTOMER** file.

The **enter a record** statement is used to enter a new record in a file. If this statement is used in combination with a **FOR** statement, one record is entered in the destination file for each record in the source file. The general form of the statement is:

```
ENTER A RECORD IN Form-Name Enter-Items.
```

For example, if you wish to take the orders that were taken before a given date (from the **ORDERS** file) and place them in an archive file called **OLDORDER**, you might write the query as:

```
for orders
    with date <Ø1/Ø1/88
    enter a record in oldorder
       Last Name := orders last name ;
       First Name := orders first name ;
       Date := orders date ;
       Amount := orders amount ;
       oldorder date := current date.
```

The := symbol means "to be replaced by". The primary file is **ORDERS**. You are placing all the records of the **ORDERS** file that were posted before January 1, 1988 in another file called **OLDORDER**. All the fields that are to be copied are now specified. The values that are entered are usually taken from the primary file (**ORDERS**). If all the fields from the primary file (**ORDERS**) have the same name as the destination file (**OLDORDER**), you may use the **copy all from Form-Name** option to specify that all fields with matching names be copied. The above query can be rewritten as:

```
for orders
    with date <Ø1/Ø1/88
    enter a record in oldorder
       copy all from orders ;
       oldorder date := current date.
```

The **copy all from Form-Name** option makes it easier to define the query by eliminating the need to type the name of each field to be transferred.

IF STATEMENTS IN FULL REPORTS

The above query can be written using an **IF** statement. Figure 8.36 shows that if a person holds the title of salesperson they will get a 25% raise. Everyone else in the company will get a 10% raise. Notice the period before the **else** of the **IF** statement. DataEase will give you an error if the semicolon is omitted.

Another variation of the same query is shown in Figure 8.37. This demonstrates the use of the **IF-THEN-ELSE** statement along with a nested **IF** statement. According to our query, all salespeople get a 25% raise, all secretaries a 20% raise, while all other employees get a 10% raise. Notice that there are two **end** statements. There is one for each of the two **IF** statements. DataEase will always give you an error if you are missing one or have one too many.

The **IF** statement tests a condition. If it is true, the statements in the **then** part are executed. If it is false, the statements in the **else** part are executed. As you can see from Figure 8.37, there is one IF statement contained in another **IF** statement. This is called nesting **IF** statements. Again, notice that there are two **end** statements, one for each of the

```
                         R  1 C   1

for Employees
if Position =  "Salesperson"then
  modify records
  Salary := Salary * 1.25.
else
  modify records
  Salary :=Salary * 1.1Ø.
end

F1INTERACTIVE F2ENTER F3CUT F4EXIT F5COPY F6PASTE F7DEL LINE F8INS LINE F9LEVEL
```

FIGURE 8.36

```
                         R  1 C   1

for Employees
;
if Position = "Salesperson" then
   modify records
   Salary := Salary * 1.25.
else
 if Position = "Secretary" then
   modify records
   Salary :=Salary * 1.2∅
else
   modify records
   Salary :=Salary * 1.1∅
end
end




F1INTERACTIVE F2ENTER F3CUT F4EXIT F5COPY F6PASTE F7DEL LINE F8INS LINE F9LEVEL
```

FIGURE 8.37

two **IF** statements. Don't forget to place the period at the end of the **IF** statement before the **else** statement, or DataEase will not save this.

THE WHILE STATEMENT

Another type of control statement is the **WHILE** statement. The general form of the **WHILE** statement is:

```
WHILE Condition DO Statements END
```

Suppose you wanted to count how many orders were placed in each of the twelve months of the year. Figure 8.38 shows a complete query that will accomplish this. Just like the **IF** statement, the **WHILE** statement has its own **end** statement. If you get an error after typing in the **1**, insert another space before typing in the next period. DataEase is very demanding of that space between the number and the period. Do not include a period after the word "do." DataEase will again give you an error for placing it in. You are creating a temporary variable month which will change from 1 to 12. The temporary variable month is

```
                          R  1 C   1

define "month" number .
temp month : = 1 .
while temp month <=  12 do
  list records
     count of orders with ( month (date)  =  (temp month)) .
temp month : =  month  + 1 .
end .

F1INTERACTIVE F2ENTER F3CUT F4EXIT F5COPY F6PASTE F7DEL LINE F8INS LINE F9LEVEL
```

FIGURE 8.38

initialized to 1 before the **WHILE** loop. It is then incremented by 1 until you get to the 12th month of the year.

THE DEFINE STATEMENT

DataEase will even allow you to define temporary variables which have temporary storage locations. The general form of the **Define** statement which defines a temporary variable of the given type is:

```
DEFINE "Variable-Name" Type<Length>
```

Looking at Figure 8.39, you see a temporary variable called **Bonus**. This temporary variable is of type number. Other variable types are text, numeric string, date, time, dollar, yes or no, or choice. If you define a temporary variable to be of type text or numeric string, then you may specify the length. The length of the string is optional and is twenty-five characters long by default. You can also initialize the value of this number. In your example you are setting the initial value of the number at zero as shown in the second line of Figure 8.39. Initializing the value

```
                         R  1 C   1

define "Bonus" Number .
assign temp Bonus : = Ø .
for Employees ;
      if (Position  =  "Salesperson")
            then Bonus : =  1ØØØ .
      else Bonus : =  3ØØ
      end
      list records
            Last Name in order ;
            First Name ;
            Bonus.

F1INTERACTIVE F2ENTER F3CUT F4EXIT F5COPY F6PASTE F7DEL LINE F8INS LINE F9LEVEL
```

FIGURE 8.39

to zero is not required by DataEase and in some situations will create bugs if inserted.

In this query, you are giving all employees who are salespeople a bonus of $1,000. All other employees will get a bonus of $300. Notice that you are using the **IF** statement in this query. Notice the space between the end of each of the numbers and the period. If you do not type in a space, DataEase assumes that you wish to type in the decimal part of the number and will give you an error. Be sure to include the space after you type in the numbers.

When you run the query, the output appears as Figure 8.40.

Notice that the secretary and the two managers get a bonus of $300 while all the salespeople get a bonus of $1,000. Notice that one of the title headings is **Bonus** even though **Bonus** is not one of the original fields in the file. Temporary fields can be listed as headings in Full Reports.

```
                                             Running report
END OF REPORT.  SPACE: Return to Menu

===========================================================
        Last                 First              Bonus
        Name                  Name
-----------------------------------------------------------
  Braun              Sheila            1000
  Caravan            Peggy             300
  Comforto           Anthony           1000
  DeTrinis           Joan              300
  DeTrinis           Vincent           300
  DiToro             Hank              1000
  Duke               Joan              1000
  Krawiec            Agnes             1000
  Talamo             Louis             1000
  Wasniewski         Joann             1000
===========================================================




      F4 EXIT     DATABASE A PROG.A: DATA B: DATE          TIME
```

FIGURE 8.40

In this query you did not modify any records. The original salaries are unchanged. When the query is erased, DataEase will no longer recognize the variable **Bonus**. Figure 8.41 shows the same query but shows the total accumulated bonuses.

Here two temporary variables—**Bonus** and **Total Bonus**—are defined and also initialized to zero. It is not necessary to initialize **Total Bonus** to zero as DataEase assumes all initial values to be zero. The statement:

```
Total Bonus := Total Bonus + Bonus.
```

would not cause confusion to DataEase as it assumes that the initial value of **Total Bonus** would be zero if you did not state it in the query.

Notice that there are two separate statements for the **IF** part and two separate statements for the **else** part. These statements are separated by a period. Since there is only one **IF** statement, there is only one **end** statement. Again notice the very important space between the end of

```
                         R  1 C   1

define "Bonus" Number .
define "Total Bonus" Number .
Bonus := Ø .
Total Bonus := Ø .
for Employees ;
    if (Position = "Salesperson")
       then Bonus := 1ØØØ . Total Bonus := Total Bonus + Bonus.
    else Bonus := 3ØØ .
    Total Bonus := Total Bonus + Bonus.
    end
    list records
       Last Name in order ;
       First Name ;
       Bonus;
       Total Bonus.




F1INTERACTIVE F2ENTER F3CUT F4EXIT F5COPY F6PASTE F7DEL LINE F8INS LINE F9LEVEL
```

FIGURE 8.41

each number and the period. If you omit the space, DataEase will give you an error by telling you to insert a period. The output of the query is shown in Figure 8.42.

You can see in Figure 8.42 that the two temporary variables are used as headings. The **Total Bonus** is shown in the last column as it accumulates through each of the employees. If you only want the final **Total Bonus**, you can change the report by changing the output format as shown in Figure 8.43.

When the query is run with these format changes, the output appears as in Figure 8.44. In this particular query only the sum of all the bonuses is printed.

ANY OPERATOR

The **any** operator processes only one matching record for a Referenced relationship. Simply put, the **any** operator tells DataEase to go to a particular file, find a particular piece of information, and list it. If there

```
                              Running report
END OF REPORT.  SPACE: Return to Menu

================================================================================
        Last              First               Bonus              Total
        Name              Name                                   Bonus
--------------------------------------------------------------------------------
  Braun              Sheila              1ØØØ              1ØØØ
  Caravan            Peggy               3ØØ               13ØØ
  Comforto           Anthony             1ØØØ              23ØØ
  DeTrinis           Joan                3ØØ               26ØØ
  DeTrinis           Vincent             3ØØ               29ØØ
  DiToro             Hank                1ØØØ              39ØØ
  Duke               Joan                1ØØØ              49ØØ
  Krawiec            Agnes               1ØØØ              59ØØ
  Talamo             Louis               1ØØØ              69ØØ
  Wasniewski         Joann               1ØØØ              79ØØ
================================================================================

      F4 EXIT     DATABASE A PROG.A: DATA B: DATE          TIME
```

FIGURE 8.42

```
                         R 12 C   1
                              Running
================================================================================
        Last              First              Bonus
        Name              Name
--------------------------------------------------------------------------------
.items

.end
================================================================================
The sum of all the bonuses is:

================================================================================

F2ENTER F3CUT F4EXIT F5COPY F6PAST F7DEL LINE F8INS LINE F9PRINT F1ØFIELD
```

FIGURE 8.43

```
Bonus                                       Running report Bonus
END OF REPORT.  SPACE: Return to Menu

================================================================================
        Last              First              Bonus
        Name               Name
--------------------------------------------------------------------------------
  Braun              Sheila            1ØØØ
  Caravan            Peggy             3ØØ
  Comforto           Anthony           1ØØØ
  DeTrinis           Joan              3ØØ
  DeTrinis           Vincent           3ØØ
  DiToro             Hank              1ØØØ
  Duke               Joan              1ØØØ
  Krawiec            Agnes             1ØØØ
  Talamo             Louis             1ØØØ
  Wasniewski         Joann             1ØØØ
================================================================================

The sum of all the bonuses is:  79ØØ

================================================================================


      F4 EXIT     DATABASE A PROG.A: DATA B: DATE          TIME
```

FIGURE 8.44

are several matching records, it is impossible to predict which one will be selected by DataEase. It selects a value from the first related record. If there is no relationship, then DataEase will choose the last record of the file. In your simulated computer store, suppose that, as owner, you wish to see which employees are making the most sales. You wish to write a query that will obtain the first and last names of any employee who made a sale of over $2,000, along with the first and last names with phone numbers of the customer who made the purchase. This information is contained in several files: **ORDERS**, **EMPLOYEES**, and **CUSTOMER**. In your query you will use the **any** statement, which will select a value from the **ORDERS** file and select the corresponding information from the **CUSTOMER** and **EMPLOYEES** files. Figure 8.45 shows the beginning of the query.

You are initially accessing the **ORDERS** file to find all **Total Orders** over $2,000. After pressing **5** for **Total Order**, Figure 8.46 appears.

```
                          R 2 C   6

Select field name
                                                      Ø: NONE
Ø: NONE 1: Order # 2: Cust ID 3: Stock # 4: Quantity  1: Order #
for orders                                            2: Cust ID
with                                                  3: Stock #
                                                      4: Quantity Ordered
                                                      5: Total Order
                                                      6: Date
                                                      7: Emp #

                                                  — Ø to 7 UP DOWN RETURN —
F1 MORE F4EXIT F9LEVEL QUERY LEVEL Low    MODE Interactive
```

FIGURE 8.45

```
                          R  2 C  18

Select a comparison symbol or the 'not' operator

1:  =  2: > 3: < 4: <=  5: >=  6: between 7: not
for orders
with Total Order

F1 MORE F4EXIT F9LEVEL QUERY LEVEL Low    MODE Interactive
```

FIGURE 8.46

```
                          R  2 C  24

Define comparison value
Specify a constant value
Enter a number.  To skip hit ESC.
for orders
with Total Order > 2000









F1 MORE F4EXIT F9LEVEL QUERY LEVEL High    MODE Interactive
```

FIGURE 8.47

Press **2** for > and Figure 8.47 appears. Type in **2000** with no commas or dollar signs. When you are using relational operators, you should switch to the High level query.

Figure 8.48 shows that you want to list the order numbers in increasing numeric order.

Figure 8.49 shows the window with all choices available. Press **2** for **any**. The **any** statement is used in conjunction with many-to-one relationships. It provides the name of each customer and of each employee related to all **Total Orders** over $2,000.

As soon as the word **any** appears on the screen, DataEase provides a list of the predefined relationships as shown in Figure 8.50.

Since you want to access the **CUSTOMER** file, press **1** for **CUSTOMER** file. A list of all the fields that you can access is shown in Figure 8.51.

```
                              R  6 C   3

Select field name                                            Ø: NONE
                                                             1: Order #
Ø: NONE 1: Order # 2: Cust ID 3: Stock # 4: Quantity         2: Cust ID
for orders                                                   3: Stock #
with Total Order > 2ØØØ                                      4: Quantity Ordered
;                                                            5: Total Order
list records                                                 6: Date
  Order # in order ;                                         7: Emp #

                                                        — Ø to 7 UP DOWN RETURN —
F1 MORE F4EXIT F9LEVEL QUERY LEVEL Low    MODE Interactive
```

FIGURE 8.48

```
                              R  6 C   3

Select relationship summary operation                        Ø: NONE
                                                             1: all
Ø: NONE 1: all 2: any 3: count of 4: highest of 5: lo        2: any
for orders                                                   3: count of
with Total Order > 2ØØØ                                      4: highest of
;                                                            5: lowest of
list records                                                 6: sum of
  Order # in order ;                                         7: mean of

                                                        — Ø to 7 UP DOWN RETURN —
F1 MORE F4EXIT F9LEVEL QUERY LEVEL Low    MODE Interactive
```

FIGURE 8.49

```
                          R  9 C   7

Predefined relationship?

Ø: NONE 1: Customer 2: Products 3: Employees
for orders
with Total Order > 2ØØØ
;
list records
  Order # in order ;
  any





F1 MORE F4EXIT F9LEVEL QUERY LEVEL Low    MODE Interactive
```

FIGURE 8.50

```
                          R  6 C  16

Select field name
                                                     Ø: NONE
Ø: NONE 1: Cust ID 2: Last Name 3: First Name 4: Stre 1: Cust ID
for orders                                           2: Last Name
with Total Order > 2ØØØ                              3: First Name
;                                                    4: Street
list records                                         5: City
  Order # in order ;                                 6: State
  any Customer                                       7: Zip
                                                     8: Phone #



                                                 — Ø to 8 UP DOWN RETURN —
F1 MORE F4EXIT F9LEVEL QUERY LEVEL Low    MODE Interactive
```

FIGURE 8.51

```
                          R  6 C  26

Select any ordering, grouping, or group-totals for this item?

Ø: NONE 1: in order 2: in reverse 3: in groups 4: in groups with group-totals
for orders
with Total Order > 2ØØØ
;
list records
  Order # in order ;
  any Customer Last Name ;










F1 MORE F4EXIT F9LEVEL QUERY LEVEL Low    MODE Interactive
```

FIGURE 8.52

Type **2** for **Last Name**. Figure 8.52 will appear.

Continue with the query by pressing **3** for **First Name** and **8** for **Phone #** as shown in Figure 8.53. Be sure to specify **any Customer** for each field from **CUSTOMER** that you wish to list.

You will now press **3** to access the **EMPLOYEES** file and **3** for **Last Name** as shown in Figure 8.54. Be sure to repeat **Any Formname** before the second field.

Figure 8.55 shows the final query. Remember that you are accessing information that is contained in three files: **ORDERS**, **CUSTOMER**, and **EMPLOYEES**.

Since the report is eighty-eight columns long and will not fit across one screen, you will type **2 field per line** as the output format as shown in Figure 8.56.

```
                              R  9 C   7

Predefined relationship?

Ø: NONE 1: Customer 2: Products 3: Employees
for orders
with Total Order > 2ØØØ
;
list records
  Order # in order ;
  any Customer Last Name ;
  any Customer First Name ;
  any Customer Phone # ;
  any









F1 MORE F4EXIT F9LEVEL QUERY LEVEL Low    MODE Interactive
```

FIGURE 8.53

```
                              R  9 C  17

Select field name
                                                    Ø: NONE
Ø: NONE 1: Employee # 2: Position 3: Last Name 4: Fir 1: Employee #
for orders                                          2: Position
with Total Order > 2ØØØ                             3: Last Name
;                                                   4: First Name
list records                                        5: Address
  Order # in order ;                                6: City
  any Customer Last Name ;                          7: State
  any Customer First Name ;                         8: Zip
  any Customer Phone # ;                            9: Date of Birth
  any Employees                                     1Ø: Date Hired
                                                    11: Phone #
                                                    12: Social Security Numb
                                                    13: Salary
                                                    14: Marital Status




                                                    Ø to 14 UP DOWN RETURN
F1 MORE F4EXIT F9LEVEL QUERY LEVEL Low    MODE Interactive
```

FIGURE 8.54

```
                              R  1 C   1

      for orders
      with Total Order > 2ØØØ
      ;
      list records
        Order # in order ;
        any Customer Last Name ;
        any Customer First Name ;
        any Customer Phone # ;
        any Employees Last Name ;
        any Employees First Name .

      F1INTERACTIVE F2ENTER F3CUT F4EXIT F5COPY F6PASTE F7DEL LINE F8INS LINE F9LEVEL
```

FIGURE 8.55

```
   1: columnar 2: field per line 3: export 4: special 5: Record Entry 6: Template

         Minimum line length for a columnar report is 88
         What type of report format do you wnat? : field per line

   F9 QUICK  F4 EXIT DATABASE A PROG.A: DATA B: DATE          TIME
```

FIGURE 8.56

When the report is run the output appears as shown in Figure 8.57.

The report can be saved on the disk by pressing **7 Save Report** and typing in a name as shown in Figure 8.58. This report will be called FR3 for full report #3.

To print out the report definition as shown in Figure 8.59, press **10 Print Report Definition**.

Another example of the **any** statement is shown in Figure 8.60.

The output that this report generates is shown in Figure 8.61.

ALL OPERATOR

Another operator that may be used is the **all** operator. It gives a set of values from all related records. It differs from the **any** operator in that it is used where a one-to-many relationship exists. The **all** operator may be used in place of the **any** operator if several records are known to exist in a Referenced relationship. The **all** operator is the only operator that produces a set of values. It can only be used in a list item and cannot be used as part of a formula. Figure 8.62 shows an example that demonstrates the use of a query with the **all** statement.

It then lists each **Employee #**, **Total Order**, and the corresponding **Cust ID**. If an employee made several sales, it would list them all.

COPY ALL FUNCTION

The **all** operator and the **copy all** function are in no way related. The **copy all** function was previously discussed. Fields may be copied from one file (the source file) to another file (the destination file) through the use of the **copy all** option. The field names have to be the same in each of the two files. You may also combine information from several files into a single file. Figure 8.63 demonstrates an example that uses this option. In this example, all the fields that have the same name in the files **EMPLOYEES** and **INCREMENTS** are combined into a new file called **EMP-ORDERS** if they are salespersons whose total orders are over $1,000.

Figure 8.63 also illustrates the use of the nested **FOR** statement. If one **FOR** statement is nested inside another **FOR** statement, then for every record selected in the outer **FOR** statement, one or more related record

```
                                          Running report
SPACE: Continue Report  EXIT: Abort Report  LEFT and RIGHT Arrows: Scroll

=================================================================================
 Order #                                  O-ØØ3
 any Customer Last Name                   Vultaggio
 any Customer First Name                  Brema
 any Customer Phone #                     (516)-795-7914
 any Employees Last Name                  Krawiec
 any Employees First Name                 Agnes

 Order #                                  O-ØØ7
 any Customer Last Name                   Mena
 any Customer First Name                  Paul
 any Customer Phone #                     (8Ø3)-556-1336
 any Employees Last Name                  Comforto
 any Employees First Name                 Anthony

 Order #                                  O-ØØ8
 any Customer Last Name                   Herbold
 any Customer First Name                  Mary ELlen
 any Customer Phone #                     (516)-243-23Ø8
 any Employees Last Name                  Talamo
 any Employees First Name                 Louis
      F4 EXIT     DATABASE A PROG.A: DATA B: DATE          TIME
```

FIGURE 8.57

```
                               R 11 C   1



 for orders
 with Total Order > 2ØØØ
 ;
 list records
   Order # in order ;
   any Customer Last Name ;
   any Customer First Name ;
   any Customer Phone # ;
   any Employees Last Name ;
   any Employees First Name .


  Please enter the report name: FR3

 F1 MORE F4EXIT F9LEVEL QUERY LEVEL Low    MODE Interactive
```

FIGURE 8.58

```
REPORT FR3
------------------------------

       REPORT QUERY
       ------------
for orders
with Total Order > 2ØØØ
;
list records
  Order # in order ;
  any Customer Last Name ;
  any Customer First Name ;
  any Customer Phone # ;
  any Employees Last Name ;
  any Employees First Name .

       REPORT FORMAT
       -------------

1       1Ø        2Ø        3Ø        4Ø        5Ø        6Ø        7Ø        8Ø
----+----+----+----+----+----+----+----+----+----+----+----+----+----+----+----+

================================================================================
.items
 Order #                                  _____
 any Customer Last Name                   _______________
 any Customer First Name                  _______________
 any Customer Phone #                     ______________
 any Employees Last Name                  _______________
 any Employees First Name                 _______________

.end
================================================================================
1       1Ø        2Ø        3Ø        4Ø        5Ø        6Ø        7Ø        8Ø
----+----+----+----+----+----+----+----+----+----+----+----+----+----+----+----+


         FIELD DESCRIPTIONS
         ------------------

No.  Name                    Type              Length  Remove
                                                       Spaces?
___  _______________________ ________________  ______  _______
  1  Order #                 Text                6       No
  2  any Customer Last Na    Text               15       No
  3  any Customer First N    Text               15       No
  4  any Customer Phone #    Numeric String     14       No
  5  any Employees Last N    Text               15       No
  6  any Employees First     Text               15       No

Memory required:
 Report Definition         1646
```

FIGURE 8.59

```
                              R  1 C   1

for Orders
;
list records
  any Customer Last Name ;
  any Products Description ;
  any Employees Last Name .




F1INTERACTIVE F2ENTER F3CUT F4EXIT F5COPY F6PASTE F7DEL LINE F8INS LINE F9LEVEL
```

FIGURE 8.60

```
                                        Running report
END OF REPORT.  SPACE: Return to Menu

================================================================================
  any Customer                 any Products                 any Employees
      Last                     Description                      Last
      Name                                                      Name
--------------------------------------------------------------------------------
 Willoughby      IBM Personal Computer System - Mono      Braun
 Herbold         20 Megabyte Hard Card                    Duke
 Vultaggio       IBM Personal Computer System - Color     Krawiec
 Bergen          Six Pak Multifunction Board              Caravan
 Vultaggio       Epson FX-85 Printer                      Braun
 Tabone          EGA Monitor                              Talamo
 Mena            Laser Printer                            Comforto
 Herbold         IBM Personal Computer System - Mono      Talamo
 Willoughby      IBM Personal Computer System - Color     Duke
================================================================================



      F4 EXIT     DATABASE A PROG.A: DATA B: DATE          TIME
```

FIGURE 8.61

```
                              R  1 C   1

      for Employees
      ;
      list records
        Employee # in order ;
        all orders Total Order ;
        all orders Cust ID .






      F1INTERACTIVE F2ENTER F3CUT F4EXIT F5COPY F6PASTE F7DEL LINE F8INS LINE F9LEVEL
```

FIGURE 8.62

```
      for Employees
             with Position  =  "Salesperson" ;
        for Orders
               with ( Total Order > 1000 )
          enter a record in Emp-Orders
               copy all from Employees ;
               copy all from Increments
        end
      end .






      F1INTERACTIVE F2ENTER F3CUT F4EXIT F5COPY F6PASTE F7DEL LINE F8INS LINE F9LEVEL
```

FIGURE 8.63

are selected in the inner **FOR** statement. In Figure 8.63, this means that for each person in the **EMPLOYEES** file with the position of "Salesperson" (outer **FOR** statement), one or more records that have total orders over $1,000 will be written to a new file (inner **FOR** statement). Those records in **ORDERS** that meet the criteria of position = salesperson and orders > 1000 will be selected.

COUNT OF

Figure 8.64 shows an example of a query that illustrates the **count of** operator.

In this example, the report is counting how many orders were taken by each salesperson. It will count how many records in the **ORDERS** file match the **Employee #** in the **EMPLOYEE** file. As you can see from the output shown in Figure 8.65, next to each salesperson is the number of orders placed.

```
                         R 1 C  1

for Employees
with Position = "Salesperson";
list records
   Employee # in order ;
   Last Name ;
   First Name ;
   count of orders.

F1INTERACTIVE F2ENTER F3CUT F4EXIT F5COPY F6PASTE F7DEL LINE F8INS LINE F9LEVEL
```

FIGURE 8.64

```
                                               Running report
END OF REPORT.  SPACE: Return to Menu

====================================================
 Emplo       Last            First        count of
  yee        Name            Name          orders
   #
----------------------------------------------------
 Ø3999 Comforto        Anthony          1
 Ø4545 Krawiec         Agnes            1
 29952 DiToro          Hank             Ø
 34343 Duke            Joan             2
 76723 Wasniewski      Joann            Ø
 87698 Talamo          Louis            2
 98798 Braun           Sheila           2
====================================================




      F4 EXIT     DATABASE A PROG.A: DATA B: DATE          TIME
```

FIGURE 8.65

SUM OF

Just as the operator **count of** shows the count of all related records, the operator **sum of** provides the total of all related records. Figure 8.66 shows that you would like the sum of all orders taken by each salesperson.

Notice in parentheses:

```
Emp # = Employees Employee #
```

This says to find the sum of the orders where the field **Emp #** of the **ORDERS** file is equal to the field **Employee #** of the **EMPLOYEES** file. This was defined in the Relationships form. However, if you did not declare the relationship there, you could state it for just that query. The DataEase reference manual calls this an ad-hoc relationship. Again, if you did not declare relationships in the relations form, you could declare it temporarily within a query. This is another extremely powerful feature of the Full Report. It enables you to link files together as needed during a query. This relationship is only available for that particular

```
                              R  1 C   1

     for Employees
     with Position = "Salesperson";
     list records
       Last Name in reverse ;
       First Name ;
       sum of Orders with ( Emp # = Employees Employee # ) Total Order .

     F1INTERACTIVE F2ENTER F3CUT F4EXIT F5COPY F6PASTE F7DEL LINE F8INS LINE F9LEVEL
```

FIGURE 8.66

query. The query does not have to be based on fields that are the same in two separate files. All the other relationship criteria that were available to generate reports can be used. This enables you to link two files together that you never originally intended to relate. The output of this report is shown in Figure 8.67. The salespeople with no orders next to their names did not make any sales for that particular time period.

DEFINE AND ASSIGN STATEMENTS

The **Define** and **Assign** statements were used previously in several examples. As shown through the many examples in this chapter, there are many ways to initiate a query. Figure 8.68 shows a temporary variable, **Increase**, which is assigned a temporary value. The general form of the **Assign** statement is:

```
ASSIGN Variable := Value.
```

The **Assign** statement is used to initialize temporary variables and can also be used to initialize variables in a Data-entry Form. The word "ASSIGN" is optional in the query.

```
                                      Running report
     END OF REPORT.  SPACE: Return to Menu

     ===============================================
          Last            First          sum of
          Name            Name        Orders with
                                       ( Emp # =
                                       Employees
                                      Employee # )
                                         Total
                                         Order
     -----------------------------------------------
      Wasniewski      Joann
      Talamo          Louis                3,320.00
      Krawiec         Agnes                8,800.00
      Duke            Joan                 4,100.00
      DiToro          Hank
      Comforto        Anthony              5,432.00
      Braun           Sheila               2,300.00
     ===============================================


          F4 EXIT     DATABASE A PROG.A: DATA B: DATE          TIME
```

FIGURE 8.67

```
                               R 12 C   3
     Select the desired action.


     0: NONE 1: list records 2: modify records 3: delete records              F1MORE
     Define "Increase" number .
     for Products
     ;
     if Price < 1000 then Increase := 0
                     else Increase : = Price * 0.08.
     end
     list records
       Description ;
       Price : item ;
       Increase : item .


     F1 MORE F4EXIT F9LEVEL QUERY LEVEL Low    MODE Interactive
```

FIGURE 8.68

```
                                      Running report
END OF REPORT.  SPACE: Return to Menu   LEFT and RIGHT Arrows: Scroll

================================================================================
                 Description                            Price          Increase
--------------------------------------------------------------------------------
  IBM Personal Computer System - Mono                1,400.00     112
  IBM Personal Computer System - Color               2,200.00     176
  20 Megabyte Hard Disk Drive                          725.00     0
  20 Megabyte Hard Card                                950.00     0
  Epson FX-85 Printer                                  450.00     0
  Epson LQ-800 Printer                                 620.00     0
  EGA Monitor                                          520.00     0
  Laser Printer                                      5,432.00     434.56
  Six Pak Multifunction Board                          380.00     0
  2400 Baud Modem                                      535.00     0




      F4 EXIT     DATABASE A PROG.A: DATA B: DATE          TIME
```

FIGURE 8.69

The output of the query is shown in Figure 8.69.

Another powerful operator that can be used for relational operators is the **named** operator. Suppose you wish to count the number of employees who live in the same city. First, you must change the query level to High (press the F9 LEVEL key). You are defining multiple relationships within the same form. Figure 8.70 shows a query that uses the **named** operator.

Same City can be called any name at all. It is good to use a name that represents what is taking place. What the next phrase of the sentence does (City = Employees City) is check each city with all the other cities in the **EMPLOYEES** file and count them if an identical city is found. It will also find the sum of the salaries of the people that live in that city. For example, if you run this you will get a count of three for the first city and a sum of the salaries as $132,000. This means that there are three people living in the same town of Massapequa, the sum of whose salaries is $132,000. This information is printed three times in the output as shown in Figure 8.71.

```
                         R  1 C   1

for Employees
;
list records
  City ;
  count of Employees named "Same City" with (City = Employees City);
  sum of Same city salary.




F1INTERACTIVE F2ENTER F3CUT F4EXIT F5COPY F6PASTE F7DEL LINE F8INS LINE F9LEVEL
```

FIGURE 8.70

```
                                    Running report
END OF REPORT.  SPACE: Return to Menu

===============================================================================
          City              count of      sum of Same city
                            Employees          salary
                           named "Same
                           City" with
                             (City =
                            Employees
                              City)
-------------------------------------------------------------------------------
  Massapequa                  3                 132,000.00
  Massapequa                  3                 132,000.00
  Bethpage                    1                  39,000.00
  Massapequa                  3                 132,000.00
  Brooklyn                    2                  59,000.00
  Queens                      1                  29,250.00
  Farmingdale                 1                  28,000.00
  Keansburg                   1                  27,500.00
  Wantagh                     1                  33,000.00
  Brooklyn                    2                  59,000.00
===============================================================================
      F4 EXIT     DATABASE A PROG.A: DATA B: DATE          TIME
```

FIGURE 8.71

Another example of the **named** operator is shown in Figure 8.72. Here you wish to list all the people in the file and count how many have duplicate last names. This is very useful in checking the file to see if the same name has been entered more than once.

Figure 8.73 shows the output of this query.

The reference manual of DataEase illustrates many ways to make a query and their various forms. Above all experiment. Write a query several different ways and see what happens. DataEase will always check the syntax or grammar of the query before it will execute the query itself. If you have an error, DataEase will tell you what it is. You can always switch back and forth from the Interactive mode as needed. As you become more proficient in the use of query language, you can turn off the Interactive mode.

PARENT RELATIONSHIP FIELD

It was previously mentioned that relationships connect files that keep related information. This is useful so that information from multiple files can be used simultaneously. A field from one record may be obtained by specifying the relationships name and the field name. In our example, if there are two files, **EMPLOYEES** and **DEPENDENTS**, you could calculate the age difference between each employee and his or her spouse by the following statement:

```
All Dependents (Employees Age - SpouseAge)
```

In this example, the **EMPLOYEES** file would be the parent file and Employees Age is a Parent Relationship field.

```
                          R  1 C   1

     for Employees
     ;
     list records
       Last Name ;
       First Name ;
       count of Employees named "Same Name" with (Last Name =  Employees Last Name )










     F1INTERACTIVE F2ENTER F3CUT F4EXIT F5COPY F6PASTE F7DEL LINE F8INS LINE F9LEVEL
```

FIGURE 8.72

```
                                     Running report
    SPACE: Continue Report  EXIT: Abort Report
    ================================================
            Last              First          count of
            Name               Name          Employees
                                            named "Same
                                            Name" with
                                            (Last Name =
                                             Employees
                                             Last Name
                                                 )
    ------------------------------------------------------
      DeTrinis          Vincent             2
      DeTrinis          Joan                2
      DiToro            Hank                1
      Comforto          Anthony             1
      Krawiec           Agnes               1
      Talamo            Louis               1
      Duke              Joan                1
      Caravan           Peggy               1
      Braun             Sheila              1
      Wasniewski        Joann               1
    ======================================================
          F4 EXIT     DATABASE A PROG.A: DATA B: DATE          TIME
```

FIGURE 8.73

MENUS

In this chapter you learn how to create menus that will be assigned to users that have certain security levels. You will learn how to run these menus and what to do if you get errors.

CREATING A CUSTOM MENU

DataEase allows you to customize a menu so that entering data into the database, modifying data, viewing data, running reports, etc., will be less threatening to the user. The menus provided by DataEase can be very confusing to a person who is just doing data entry or printing reports. You can have a different menu for each user depending on his/her security clearance and his/her need to know certain information in the database. The first thing that you will do is create a menu and then tell DataEase who can access that particular menu. You, as owner of this simulated computer store, have a "high" security clearance. You can access all the menus that are created with this database, but you must have a "high" security clearance. To define or create menus you must also have a high security clearance.

To design a menu, press **6** from DataEase's Main Menu. This will give you the Menus and Relationships Menu as shown in Figure 9.1.

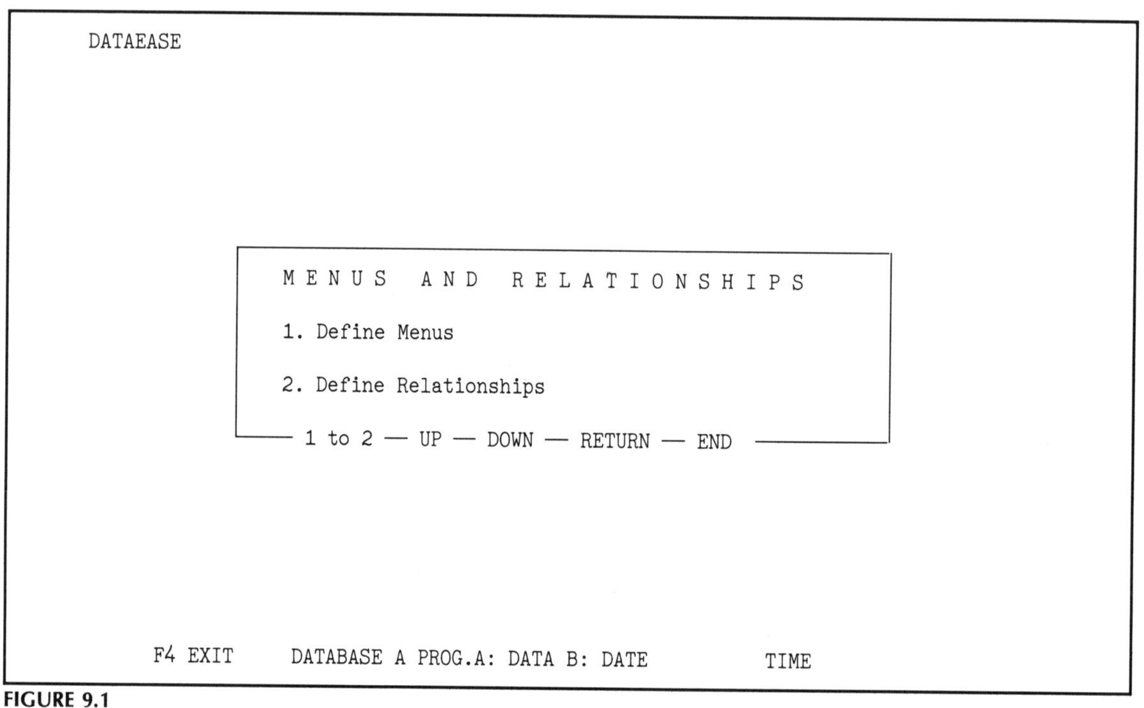

FIGURE 9.1

```
menus
No record on screen
                          MENU DEFINITION
         MENU NAME                              SECURITY LEVEL

You can define upto 9 choices per menu, selected by digits 1 to 9.
Choice Ø always returns to the previous menu.

For each choice, provide the Choice Description and the Function Type.
Function  Name is required for "user menu", "record entry", and "run report"
functions, and optional for "Data Import" and "Program Call" functions.
For "Program Call", Function Name may be continued into the next Description.

   MENU TITLE
NO.          CHOICE DESCRIPTION                 FUNCTION TYPE    FUNCTION NAME
1.
2.
3.
4.
5.
6.
7.
8.
9.
F2ENTER F3VIEW F4EXIT F5FORM CLR F6FLD CLR F7DELETE F8MODIFY F9REPORT F1ØMULTI
```

FIGURE 9.2

Press **1 Define Menus** and Figure 9.2 now appears.

This blank form enables you to create a menu. There is a single form for each menu. You will create a menu form that will enable the manager of your computer store to perform certain functions. You would like him to enter, view, or modify data; print out various reports as customer mailing labels and form letters; backup the database files; import data from a dBase III program; and perform various other maintenance functions on the database. If you want to, you can create separate menus for the assistant manager, the secretary, and the salespeople.

Figure 9.2 shows that the first item that DataEase would like is the name of the menu. This name must be unique—two menus cannot have the same name. This name will not appear on the screen when the program is run. You will call this menu **Manager** as shown in Figure 9.3.

```
menus

                              MENU DEFINITION
          MENU NAME  Manager                 SECURITY LEVEL Medium1

You can define upto 9 choices per menu, selected by digits 1 to 9.
Choice Ø always returns to the previous menu.

For each choice, provide the Choice Description and the Function Type.
Function  Name is required for "user menu", "record entry", and "run report"
functions, and optional for "Data Import" and "Program Call" functions.
For "Program Call", Function Name may be continued into the next Description.

   MENU TITLE  Manager's Menu
NO.          CHOICE DESCRIPTION                  FUNCTION TYPE    FUNCTION NAME
1.Enter, View, or Modify Data
2.
3.
4.
5.
6.
7.
8.
9.
F2ENTER F3VIEW F4EXIT F5FORM CLR F6FLD CLR F7DELETE F8MODIFY F9REPORT F1ØMULTI
```

FIGURE 9.3

Press the RETURN or TAB key to advance to the next entry, the security level. As you do this you will notice that the list of security levels appears at the top of the screen. Press the **2 Medium1** key. This means that the person who can access this particular menu must have a security level that is at least medium1. If you want any person to access this menu, you can type in the lowest security level, low3. If a person tries to access a menu without the proper security level, DataEase will tell them that the menu does not exist. If you press the RETURN or TAB key again, you will be asked for the Menu Title. Type:

```
Manager's Menu
```

This title will appear on the screen when the program is run. It cannot be longer than sixty characters. After typing in the Menu Title, you will be asked for the description of choice 1. There are nine menu lines. You can have any number of choices up to nine. Type:

```
Enter, View, or Modify Data
```

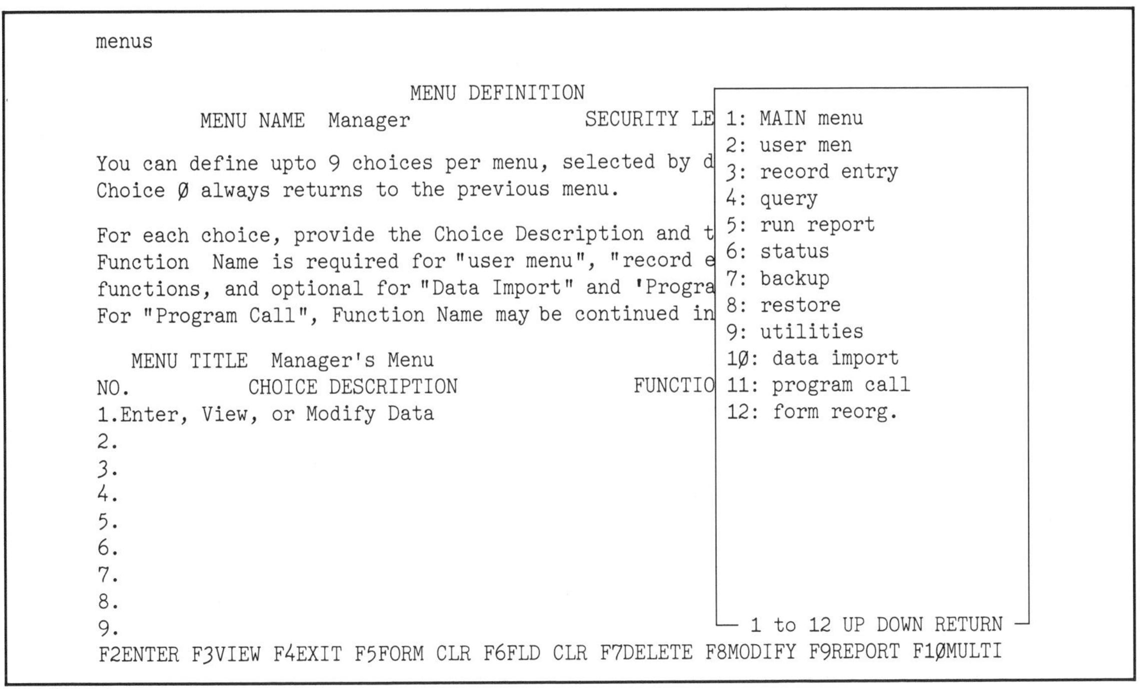

FIGURE 9.4

This tells the manager that he can enter, see, or change data in any one of the four files that you would like him to see. The Choice Description can be up to forty-four characters in length. When you move over to Function Type, you can press any one of the twelve choices as shown in Figure 9.4.

A short description of each of the choices is shown in Figure 9.5.

You will now press **2 user menu**. This means that when the manager chooses **1**, it will access another menu. Figure 9.6 shows the complete menu for the manager.

For choice **1**, the Function Name is Manager Data Entry. This will be the name of the next menu if the manager chooses to enter, view, or modify data. As you can see, one menu can access another menu.

The Function Name is required only if you are using User Menu, Record Entry, or Form Reorganization. In our first menu, only choices **1**,

CHOICE	NAME	USE IF FUNCTION NAME IS ENTERED	USE IF NO FUNCTION NAME IS ENTERED
1	MAIN MENU	Calls DataEase Main Menu (Function Name is ignored).	Same
2	User Menu	Calls the user menu listed here	Invalid
3	Record Entry	Lets the user enter, change or view data in the form listed here	Invalid
4	Query	Displays the report menu and the user to view or run any report, but NOT modify; also, lets the user create and run a new report but not save it. (Function name is ignored).	Same
5	Run Report	Runs the report listed here.	Displays the report menu & allows the user to view or run any report, but NOT modify; also, run a report but not save it (Same as Query)
6	Status	Displays status of the database (Function name is ignored).	Same
7	Backup	Backups the database (Function name is ignored).	Same
8	Restore	Restores the database (Function name is ignored).	Same
9	Utilities	Displays Utilities menu (Function name is ignored).	Same
10	Import	Runs the Import listed here (Function name is ignored).	Allows the user to define & run a 1-time import.
11	Program Call	Calls the DOS program	Allows the user to enter a DOS program call.
12	Form Reorg.	Reorganizes form listed here.	Invalid

FIGURE 9.5

```
menus

                         MENU DEFINITION
     MENU NAME  Manager                SECURITY LEVEL Medium1

You can define upto 9 choices per menu, selected by digits 1 to 9.
Choice Ø always returns to the previous menu.

For each choice, provide the Choice Description and the Function Type.
Function  Name is required for "user menu", "record entry", and "run report"
functions, and optional for "Data Import" and "Program Call" functions.
For "Program Call", Function Name may be continued into the next Description.

   MENU TITLE  Manager's Menu
NO.          CHOICE DESCRIPTION                FUNCTION TYPE    FUNCTION NAME
1.Enter, View, or Modify Data                   user menu    Manager Data Entry
2.Reports                                       user menu    Manager Reports
3.Backup Files                                  backup       Manager Backup
4.dBase III Interface                           user menu    dBase Access
5.System Utilities                              utilities    Database Utilities
6.Database Status                               status       Database Status
7.
8.
9.
F2ENTER F3VIEW F4EXIT F5FORM CLR F6FLD CLR F7DELETE F8MODIFY F9REPORT F1ØMULTI
```

FIGURE 9.6

2, and **4** require a Function Name. All the others are optional. As you can see from Figure 9.6, your manager can enter, view, or modify data; print out various reports such as customer mailing labels and form letters; backup the database files; import data from a dBase III program; and perform various other maintenance functions on the database. Three of the menus to be accessed have not been created yet. When you are finished typing Figure 9.6, press the F2 ENTER key to save the menu.

The screen will not display another blank menu form. To start your next menu on a cleared screen, press the F5 CLEAR key. You will now enter the information onto the menu screen that is shown in Figure 9.7.

The name of this new menu, Manager Data Entry, must be the same name entered as the Function Name in Choice **1** in Figure 9.6. When the manager selects **1**, DataEase will access the menu listed under Function Name, which, in this case, is Manager Data Entry. One menu may call another menu which, in turn, may call another menu, etc. Figure 9.7 shows the same Menu Title as shown in Figure 9.6's Choice

```
menus                                      Record found
Record 5 on screen
                               MENU DEFINITION
         MENU NAME  Manager Data Entry    SECURITY LEVEL Medium1

You can define upto 9 choices per menu, selected by digits 1 to 9.
Choice Ø always returns to the previous menu.

For each choice, provide the Choice Description and the Function Type.
Function  Name is required for "user menu", "record entry", and "run report"
functions, and optional for "Data Import" and "Program Call" functions.
For "Program Call", Function Name may be continued into the next Description.

   MENU TITLE  Enter, View, or Modify Data
NO.          CHOICE DESCRIPTION               FUNCTION TYPE    FUNCTION NAME
1.Employees                                    record entry EMPLOYEES
2.Products                                     record entry PRODUCTS
3.
4.
5.
6.
7.
8.
9.
F2ENTER F3VIEW F4EXIT F5FORM CLR F6FLD CLR F7DELETE F8MODIFY F9REPORT F1ØMULTI
```

FIGURE 9.7

Description of Choice 1. This is not necessary but it may be helpful to your user. In Figure 9.7, you are letting the manager of the computer store enter, view, and change information in the **EMPLOYEES** and **PRODUCTS** files. If you wanted, you could have allowed access to the other two files—**ORDERS** and **CUSTOMER**—as well. When you have completed Figure 9.7, press the F2 ENTER key to save the second menu. Then press the F5 CLEAR key to clear the screen.

You now want to create a menu to generate reports that the manager will need. Figure 9.8 displays the menu for the manager's reports.

Notice that the Menu Name Manager Reports is the same as the Function Name for choice **2** shown in Figure 9.6. When the manager selects choice **2**, the Manager Reports menu is accessed. Also, notice that the Menu Title Reports is the same as the Choice Description of choice **2** in Figure 9.6; this is not necessary, but helpful to your user.

```
menus                                   Record found
Record 3 on screen
                              MENU DEFINITION
         MENU NAME  Manager Reports        SECURITY LEVEL Medium1

You can define upto 9 choices per menu, selected by digits 1 to 9.
Choice Ø always returns to the previous menu.

For each choice, provide the Choice Description and the Function Type.
Function  Name is required for "user menu", "record entry", and "run report"
functions, and optional for "Data Import" and "Program Call" functions.
For "Program Call", Function Name may be continued into the next Description.

   MENU TITLE  Reports
NO.          CHOICE DESCRIPTION                FUNCTION TYPE    FUNCTION NAME
1.Customer Mailing List                         run report   Mail
2.Customer Letters                              run report   Letter
3.Product List                                  run report   QR1
4.Orders List                                   run report   FR1
5.
6.
7.
8.
9.
F2ENTER F3VIEW F4EXIT F5FORM CLR F6FLD CLR F7DELETE F8MODIFY F9REPORT F1ØMULTI
```

FIGURE 9.8

Figure 9.8 shows that there is a possibility of four different reports that can be run. There is a customer mailing list, form letters for customers, a products list, and an orders list. The report names might be different from the ones shown if you called them something else. The Function Name is required here to specify the name of the report you want to run. If you have more than nine reports, you can break the reports down into groups of nine so they can be accessed by different menus. When you are finished typing in that menu, press F2 ENTER to save the menu.

The last sub-menu that you want to create will import data from a dBase III program. In a later chapter you will see all the different types of data that DataEase can accept from other programs and how to implement them. Figure 9.9 shows how that menu can be created.

Notice that the Menu Name dBase Access is the same name as the Function Name in choice 4 of Figure 9.6. Also, the Menu Title dbase III Interface is the same as the Choice Description. One menu is again calling another menu. To save this menu, press the F2 ENTER key.

```
menus
No record on screen
                          MENU DEFINITION
         MENU NAME  dBase Access          SECURITY LEVEL Medium1

You can define upto 9 choices per menu, selected by digits 1 to 9.
Choice Ø always returns to the previous menu.

For each choice, provide the Choice Description and the Function Type.
Function  Name is required for "user menu", "record entry", and "run report"
functions, and optional for "Data Import" and "Program Call" functions.
For "Program Call", Function Name may be continued into the next Description.

   MENU TITLE  dBase III Interface
NO.          CHOICE DESCRIPTION               FUNCTION TYPE    FUNCTION NAME
1.Import data from dBase III                   data import  dbaseimp
2.
3.
4.
5.
6.
7.
8.
9.
F2ENTER F3VIEW F4EXIT F5FORM CLR F6FLD CLR F7DELETE F8MODIFY F9REPORT F1ØMULTI
```

FIGURE 9.9

If you want to view all the menus that you have created, press F3 VIEW. DataEase will scroll through the menus one at a time allowing you to check the information. If you see an error, change it and press the F8 MODIFY key. If you want to delete a menu, press F7 DELETE. You have created several menus for just the manager of the store. You can create separate menus for any one person or group of people. DataEase will allow you to create as many menus as you desire. However, all menus are stored in memory and take up space. The more menus you have the less space you have for other functions.

ASSIGNING USERS TO MENUS

You have just created several menus that will be used by the manager of the computer store, but you have not told DataEase how the manager will access these menus. Return to the Main Menu by pressing F4 EXIT. You must access the Users Form to assign the menus. When you are in the Main Menu, select **7 System Administration**. To access the Users Form, select **1**. The user information is now filled in. Figure 9.10 shows a filled in User Form for the manager of the company.

```
users                                    Record found
Record 3 on screen

                         USER INFORMATION
                         ----------------

          Name           : Vincent

          Password       : menu

          Level          : medium1

          Screen Style   :
                           Leave blank for system provided default styles.

          Start-up Menu  : Manager
                           Leave blank to use system provided menus.

          Help Level     :
                           Leave blank to provide help on demand.


F2ENTER F3VIEW F4EXIT F5FORM CLR F6FLD CLR F7DELETE F8MODIFY F9REPORT F10MULTI
```

FIGURE 9.10

You have given him a password. DataEase checks the password when he signs on to see if he is the right person. The start-up menu in this situation is Manager. When the manager of the computer store enters DataEase, the computer will check the name and password against the name and password stored in the user file. If they do not match, the program will deny access to the person and ask him to try again.

RUNNING THE CUSTOM MENU

When the manager of the store logs on to the system with the correct password, the manager's menu is automatically shown as in Figure 9.11.

As you can see, this menu is clearer than the system menu, especially if the person using the system need only access several parts of the database. When the manager presses **1 Enter, View,** or **Modify Data** the next sub-menu appears as shown in Figure 9.12.

```
DATAEASE

                    Manager's Menu

   1. Enter, View, or Modify Data

   2. Reports

   3. Backup Files

   4. dBase III Interface

   5. System Utilities

   6. Database Status

 ---- 1 to 6 — UP — DOWN — RETURN — END ----

F4 EXIT   DATABASE A PROG.A: DATA B: DATE        TIME
```

FIGURE 9.11

```
DATAEASE

            Enter, View, or Modify Data

   1. Employees

   2. Products

 ---- 1 to 2 — UP — DOWN — RETURN — END ----

F4 EXIT   DATABASE A PROG.A: DATA B: DATE        TIME
```

FIGURE 9.12

```
Employees
No record on screen

   Employee #:                        Position:

   Last Name:                         First Name:

   Address:                           City:

   State:                             Zip:

   Date of Birth:     / /             Date Hired:     / /

   Phone #:  (   )-   -               Social Security Number:      - -

   Salary:

   Marital Status:



F2ENTER F3VIEW F4EXIT F5FORM CLR F6FLD CLR F7DELETE F8MODIFY F9REPORT F10MULTI
```

FIGURE 9.13

This figure shows that the manager may enter, view, or modify data in either the **EMPLOYEES** or **PRODUCTS** file. If he presses **1** to access the **EMPLOYEES** file, a blank **EMPLOYEES** form appears on the screen as shown in Figure 9.13.

The manager of the store can now view, edit, or enter data into the file, facilitated by the use of menus. The manager does not have to go through any programming or possess an in-depth knowledge of computers to use the menus.

If the manager presses **2** for the Reports as shown in Figure 9.12, the user menu called Reports appears as shown in Figure 9.14.

He can now print a customer mailing list, print customer letters, produce a product list, and produce an orders list with just the stroke of a key. Here is a good place to put the most commonly produced reports.

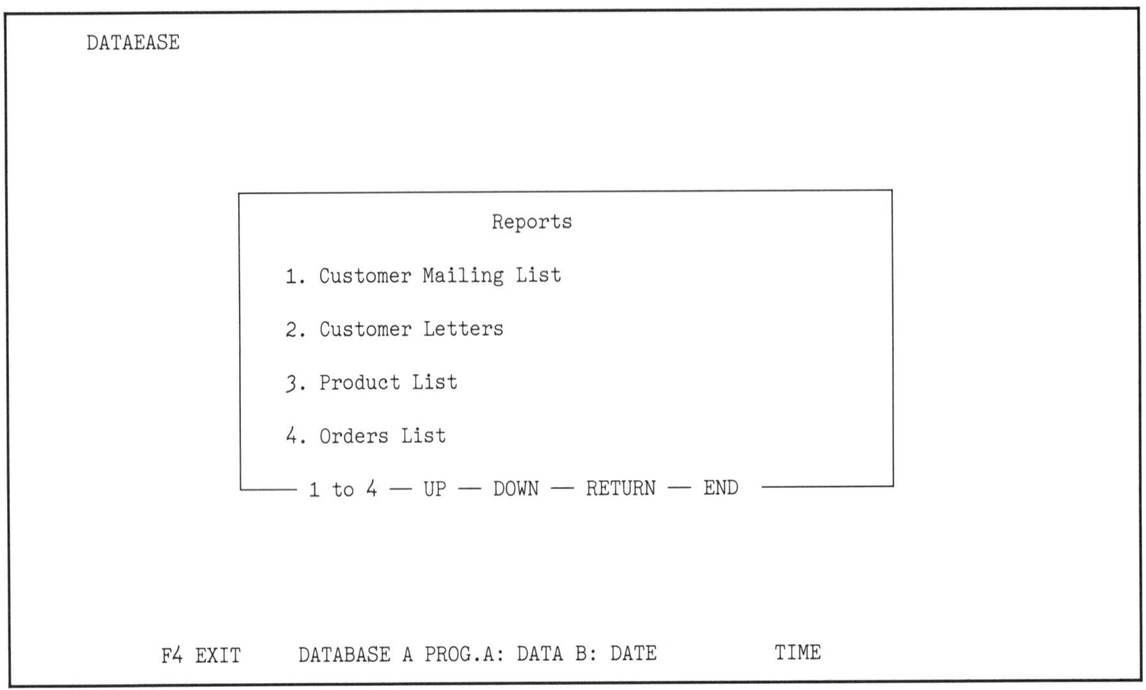

FIGURE 9.14

If the manager wants to make a backup of the database, all he has to do is press **3** for **Backup Files** from the Manager Menu in Figure 9.11. When he does that, Figure 9.15 appears. All the manager has to do is specify the disk drive that the backup will be made on and press RETURN.

If the manager presses **4 dBASE III Interface** as shown in Figure 9.11, Figure 9.16 appears. Here, the previously defined import **dbaseimp** will be run, bringing data written in dBase III into DataEase. In a later chapter you will see how to import and export DataEase data files for a variety of programs.

If the manager presses **5 System Utilities** in his Manager Menu as shown in Figure 9.12, Figure 9.17 will appear. This menu will be discussed in a later chapter.

The last item, **6 DataBase Status**, gives the manager a list of all the forms, reports, and imports that are in his database. This will be discussed in the next chapter.

```
DATAEASE

                    Manager's Menu

           1. Enter, View, or Modify Data

           2. Reports

           3. Backup Files

           4. dBase III Interface

           5. System Utilities

  Specify the Drive to use for Backup disketts and press RETURN :



      F4 EXIT    DATABASE A PROG.A: DATA B: DATE          TIME
```

FIGURE 9.15

```
DATAEASE




                    dBase III Interface

           1. Import data from dBase III

     — 1 to 1 — UP — DOWN — RETURN — END —




      F4 EXIT    DATABASE A PROG.A: DATA B: DATE          TIME
```

FIGURE 9.16

```
DATABASE UTILITIES

            U T I L I T I E S   M E N U

        1. Import

        2. Transfer Data

        3. Install Form

        4. Install Report

        5. Remove Data Base

        6. Install an Application

     —— 1 to 6 — UP — DOWN — RETURN — END ——

Alt-F1HELP F4EXIT DATABASE A PROG.A: DATA B: DATE        TIME
```

FIGURE 9.17

ERRORS IN MENUS

As you are creating Custom Menus, DataEase will not give you an error if you have entered an improper instruction. Errors are given when the menu is accessed. For example, if you try to run a report that doesn't exist or import a file that has the wrong name, DataEase will give you an error message. If you run a menu and you get an error message, check the menu to see if there are any misspellings. See if you are calling a nonexistent file or report.

It is always a good idea to test each selection of the menu and sub-menus after you have finished creating them.

CHAIN MENUS

DataEase allows you to link several menu selections together through the use of the Chain Menu. Suppose the manager of the store wants to always print out a customer list for mailing labels followed by printing out the necessary form letters. He could then chain the two functions together. Figure 9.18 shows an example of a Chain Function.

```
menus

                          MENU DEFINITION
         MENU NAME  MAILINGS              SECURITY LEVEL Medium1

You can define upto 9 choices per menu, selected by digits 1 to 9.
Choice Ø always returns to the previous menu.

For each choice, provide the Choice Description and the Function Type.
Function  Name is required for "user menu", "record entry", and "run report"
functions, and optional for "Data Import" and "Program Call" functions.
For "Program Call", Function Name may be continued into the next Description.

   MENU TITLE  CHAIN
NO.          CHOICE DESCRIPTION                FUNCTION TYPE    FUNCTION NAME
1.Customer Mailing List                         run report   Mail
2.Customer Letter                               run report   Letter
3.
4.
5.
6.
7.
8.
9.
F2ENTER F3VIEW F4EXIT F5FORM CLR F6FLD CLR F7DELETE F8MODIFY F9REPORT F1ØMULTI
```

FIGURE 9.18

The menu with the name Mailings is composed of two functions: Run Report Mail and Run Report Letter. The Menu Title must be Chain to indicate that each choice in this menu is to be performed in the order listed without user intervention. If you need to chain more than nine functions, you can call another menu which has in it several functions that are chained together. A Chain menu can be called from a start-up menu or can be called from another menu. When you call a Chain menu, it is not displayed on the screen. Instead, the functions are executed automatically in the order shown on the menu. If a report uses up too much memory, you can break it up into multiple reports and run it as a chain so that the user thinks just one report was run.

MAINTENANCE

In this chapter you will learn how to check the database status, how to backup a database, how to restore a database, and how to use DOS functions from within DataEase.

MAINTENANCE MENU

To access the Maintenance Menu, choose **4** from the Main Menu of DataEase. Figure 10.1 appears. If you want to return to the Main Menu, press F4 EXIT.

If you press **1 Database Status**, Figure 10.2 appears.

DATABASE STATUS

If you press **1 Forms**, DataEase asks:

```
    Press PRINT key to print status, else press any other
key.
```

If you want the forms status printed to a printer and displayed on the screen, press the F9 PRINT key. Pressing any other key will display the information only on the screen. Figure 10.3 appears.

```
DATABASE MAINTENANCE

    M A I N T E N A N C E   M E N U

  1. Database Status

  2. Backup Database

  3. Restore Database

  4. DOS Functions

  1 to 4 — UP — DOWN — RETURN — END

   F4 EXIT    DATABASE A PROG.A: DATA B: DATE         TIME
```

FIGURE 10.1

```
DATABASE STATUS
1: Forms 2: Reports 3: Import Specifications
Status of :









F9 PRINT  F4 EXIT DATABASE A PROG.A: DATA B: DATE          TIME
```

FIGURE 10.2

Figure 10.3 displays the total number of forms at the top of the page. This includes both the user defined and the system defined forms. Below these totals are the name of each form, the number of existing and deleted records, and the DOS file names for the form definition file, the data file, and any index files. It also shows the number of bytes in each file.

To print the Reports Status, press **2 Reports** in the Maintenance Menu. If you want the reports status to be printed, press F9 PRINT, otherwise, hit any other key. Figure 10.4 will now appear.

Figure 10.4 tells you that there are twelve reports, what the report names are, their DOS file names, and the number of bytes in each report file.

If you press **3 Import Specifications** from Status Menu, you will see the defined import name, its DOS file name, and the number of bytes in each import specification. You do not have any import specifications here, but you will look at importing and exporting DataEase files in the next chapter.

Number of forms: User defined : 5 System defined : 6 Total forms : 11

No.	FORM NAME	NO. OF RECORDS EXISTING	DELETED	DISK FILE NAMES	FILE SIZE Bytes
1.	users	3	0	B:USERAAAA.DBM	189
2.	configuration	1	0	B:CONFAAAA.DBM	96
3.	printers	17	0	B:PRINAAAA.DBM	5117
4.	screen styles	3	0	B:SCREAAAA.DBM	201
5.	relationships	3	0	B:RELAAAAA.DBM	612
6.	menus	6	1	B:MENUAAAA.DBM	4704
7.	Employee	0	0	B:EMPLAAAA.DBM	0
	Index File			B:EMPLAAAA.I01	512
	Index File			B:EMPLAAAA.I0B	512
	Form Definition File			B:EMPLAAAA.DBA	722
8.	Employees	10	0	B:EMPLAAAB.DBM	1460
	Index File			B:EMPLAAAB.I01	1024
	Index File			B:EMPLAAAB.I0C	1024
	Form Definition File			B:EMPLAAAB.DBA	776
9.	Customer	11	14	B:CUSTAAAA.DBM	2400
	Form Definition File			B.CUSTAAAA.DBA	363
10.	Products	10	0	B:PRODAAAA.DBM	590
	Index File			B.PRODAAAA.I01	1024
	Form Definition File			B.PRODAAAA.DBA	247
11.	Orders	9	2	B.ORDEAAAA.DBM	374
	Form Definition File			B:ORDEAAAA.DBA	535

FIGURE 10.3

BACKING UP THE DATABASE

It is always a good idea to backup a database periodically. A database, with all of its data, can be lost or destroyed by computer error, power failure, or human error. A backup can be performed on floppy disks which can then be placed in a safe place away from where you are working. It is strongly suggested that you make several backup copies and place them in different places. A backup should be made at the end of each session at the computer, at the end of each day, or when a large quantity of information has been entered into the machine.

Always make a backup before you import data into a DataEase program.

```
No of reports 12
No.    REPORT NAME          DISK FILE NAME  FILE SIZE Bytes
--- -------------------- -------------- ---------------
 1. Emp1                 B.EmpAAAAA.DBR      1Ø42
 2. Emp2                 B:EmpAAAAB.DBR      1266
 3. mail                 B:mailAAAA.DBR       656
 4. letter               B:lettAAAA.DBR       899
 5. Cust1                B:CustAAAA.DBR       759
 6. Cust2                B:CustAAAB.DBR       815
 7. qr1                  B:qrAAAAAA.DBR      1425
 8. FR1                  B:FRAAAAAA.DBR       929
 9. FR2                  B:FRAAAAAB.DBR      1633
1Ø. FR3                  B:FRAAAAAC.DBR      2993
11. Data-Entry           B:DataAAAA.DBR       764
    Data-entry Form      B:DataAAAA.DBF       183
12. Bonus                B:BonuAAAA.DBR      1727
--- -------------------- -------------- ---------------
```

FIGURE 10.4

Before you backup database disks, you should have several formatted blank diskettes. They can easily be formatted with the DOS format command. If the disks are already formatted but contain some files, DataEase will erase information on them before it performs a backup. To backup a disk, press **2 Backup Database** from the Maintenance Menu. The box at the bottom of Figure 10.5 appears.

DataEase will ask you to specify the drive on which the backup is to be made. In this situation the database will be backed up on Drive A. Normally all backups are placed on floppy disks.

The system will then ask you what you want to do if a system error occurs. Notice the menu that appears on the top of the screen. If you press **1 Ignore Error and Continue**, DataEase will ignore any errors and continue with the backup. If you press **2 Cancel**, DataEase will stop the backup. If you press **3 Decide upon error**, DataEase will ask you to decide what to do when the error occurs.

```
DATABASE MAINTENANCE
1: Ignore Error and Continue 2: Cancel 3: Decide upon Error

        M A I N T E N A N C E   M E N U

    1. Database Status

    2. Backup Database

    3. Restore Database

    4. DOS Functions

    1 to 4 — UP — DOWN — RETURN — END

  Specify the Drive to use for Backup diskettes and press RETURN :a

  If a Backup Error occurs, what do you want to do ?

    F4 EXIT     DATABASE A PROG.A: DATA B: DATE          TIME
```

FIGURE 10.5

When you select one of the choices, Figure 10.5 appears. This is a safeguard measure to make sure that you put the backup disk in Drive A and do not accidentally erase the DataEase system disk. You have two choices at this point—press the RETURN key to start the backup or press F4 EXIT to exit. When you press RETURN, DataEase tells you that the backup is progressing as shown in Figure 10.6. It will tell you the name of each file that it is backing up. If there are any errors, it will tell you.

When the backup is complete, press RETURN as shown in Figure 10.7 to return to the Maintenance Menu. Figure 10.7 tells you that the backup is complete with no errors found.

RESTORING THE DATABASE

The Restore utility returns the database to the way it was at the time of the last backup. It recreates your database from the backup diskettes. It is used if there was any type of data loss. The Restore function also removes all deleted information from a database. When a record is

```
BACKUP DATABASE

STARTING BACKUP
PLEASE INSERT FIRST BACKUP DISK IN DRIVE A:
PRESS 'RETURN' WHEN READY OR 'EXIT' TO ABORT

backup in progress...

Backing up form "REPORT DIRECTORY"
Backing up form "users"
Backing up form "configuration"
Backing up form "printers"
Backing up form "screen styles"
Backing up form "relationships"
Backing up form "menus"
Backing up form "Employee"
Backing up form "Employees"
Backing up form "Customer"
Backing up form "Products"
Backing up form "Orders"

Backing up report "Emp1"
Backing up report "Emp2"
Backing up report "mail"
```

FIGURE 10.6

```
Backing up form "Products"
Backing up form "Orders"

Backing up report "Emp1"
Backing up report "Emp2"
Backing up report "mail"
Backing up report "letter"
Backing up report "Cust1"
Backing up report "Cust2"
Backing up report "qr1"
Backing up report "FR1"
Backing up report "FR2"
Backing up report "FR3"
Backing up report "Data-Entry"
Backing up report "Bonus"


BACKUP COMPLETE: PLEASE REMOVE DISK AND LABEL IT:
    BACKUP DISK NUMBER: 1
    DATE: 03/13/88    TIME: 22:27:21

PRESS 'RETURN' WHEN READY
**B A C K U P   C O M P L E T E D  -  N O   E R R O R S**
PRESS 'RETURN' TO EXIT BACKUP
```

FIGURE 10.7

deleted, the space that this record occupied is not deleted from the records file. If you have a lot of unused space in your records file, the Restore command physically removes the deleted records so you have more free space on your disk. The Restore command can also be used to return a database to a previous state if an Import or Batch Update is terminated while data are being transferred.

If you wish to consolidate disk space, log on to the existing database and start the Restore operation.

If you cannot log on to your database because it has been damaged, erase all your data files. If you are restoring data onto a floppy disk, erase all the files on the disk or re-format the disk. If you are restoring data onto a hard disk, erase all the files by using the DOS command:

```
ERASE ????"Data Base Name"A??.*
```

or

```
ERASE ????(insert database letter from A-Z)*.*
```

followed by recopying the System and Utilities files.

Do not type in the quotes in the above command; just substitute the name of the database. Create a database with the same name used on the backup disks or hard disk. When the main menu appears, begin the Restore operation.

To begin the Restore operation, select **3** from the Maintenance Menu. You will notice by looking at Figure 10.8 that the instructions in the window box are very similar to the instructions for creating backup disks, shown in Figure 10.5.

You again type in the drive letter and press RETURN.

DataEase then asks:

```
If a Restore error occurs, what do you want to do?
```

Notice the menu in the command line on the top of Figure 10.8. If you choose **1**, DataEase will ignore any errors in Restore. If you choose **2**, the Restore operation will terminate when it encounters an error. If you choose **3**, you can decide what to do when the error occurs. After

```
DATABASE MAINTENANCE
1: Ignore Error and Continue 2: Cancel 3: Decide upon Error

        M A I N T E N A N C E   M E N U

     1. Database Status

     2. Backup Database

     3. Restore Database

     4. DOS Functions

  --- 1 to 4 — UP — DOWN — RETURN — END ---

  Specify the Drive to use for Backup diskettes and press RETURN :a

  If a Restore Error occurs, what do you want to do ?

     F4 EXIT     DATABASE A PROG.A: DATA B: DATE          TIME
```

FIGURE 10.8

you make your selection, the Restore operation will begin. DataEase will ask you to:

```
PLEASE INSERT FIRST BACKUP DISK IN DRIVE A:
PRESS 'RETURN' WHEN READY OR 'EXIT' TO ABORT
```

If you want to stop the operation, press the F4 EXIT key. Make sure that the backup disk is in Drive A before you press the RETURN key. DataEase responds:

```
CURRENT BACKUP DISK INSERTED IS:
 DISK NUMBER: 1
 DATE: 03/13/88 TIME: 21:13:11
IS THIS THE DESIRED BACKUP DISK? (y/n):
```

If this is correct, type **Y**. DataEase responds with the message:

```
restore in progress...
```

The information on the existing database is restored. DataEase recreates the database by reading the information from the backup disks. Just as in the backup procedure, it lists the name of each form that it is restoring. If there is an error, the error message will be displayed on the screen. DataEase will prompt you for subsequent disks in this set of backup disks. When DataEase is finished reading the final disk, it responds:

```
PLEASE REMOVE BACKUP DISK FROM DRIVE A
PRESS 'RETURN' WHEN READY
```

When you press RETURN, the following message is displayed:

```
* * RESTORE  COMPLETED - NO ERRORS * *
PRESS 'RETURN' TO EXIT RESTORE
```

If there are any errors, instead of 'NO ERRORS', DataEase will display the actual number of errors. Notice the similarity between the Backup procedure and the Restore procedure.

When you press RETURN, DataEase responds:

```
Database Restored. Exiting DataEase. Please sign-on again.
```

You will now be returned to DOS and must now log on again.

DOS FUNCTIONS

If you want to call a DOS function from most database management products you have to exit the product and return to DOS. DataEase allows you to access the DOS functions without leaving DataEase. From the Maintenance Menu, select **4** to reach the DOS functions. The DOS functions are shown in Figure 10.9.

If you choose **1**, the DOS command **DIR** is executed as shown in Figure 10.10. This gives a list of all files on the data disk.

If you choose **2**, the **CHKDSK** DOS command is executed (assuming it is on your floppy or hard disk). It lists the total space on the data drive, the number of files, the space taken up by all your files, and the free space available on the disk. It also gives similar statistics for the computer memory.

```
DOS Functions                              Invalid key, ignored

          D O S   F U N C T I O N S

     1. Data Disk Directory

     2. Check Data Disk

     3. Format New Disk

     4. DOS Backup

     5. DOS Restore

     6. Other

    1 to 6 — UP — DOWN — RETURN — END

     F4 EXIT    DATABASE A PROG.A: DATA B: DATE          TIME
```

FIGURE 10.9

```
RDRRAAAA DBM      663  3-13-87    9:ØØp
REPOAAAA DBM      468  3-Ø2-87    4:48p
USERAAAA DBM      189  3-11-87   11:48p
CONFAAAA DBM       96  2-15-87    5:55p
PRINAAAA DBM     5117  2-15-87    5:55p
SCREAAAA DBM      2Ø1  2-15-87    5:55p
RELAAAAA DBM      612  2-22-87    8:4Øp
MENUAAAA DBM     47Ø4  3-13-87    9:ØØp
EMPLAAAA DBM        Ø  2-15-87    7:ØØp
EMPLAAAA IØ1      512  2-15-87    7:ØØp
EMPLAAAA IØB      512  2-15-87    7:ØØp
EMPLAAAA DBA      722  2-15-87    7:ØØp
EMPLAAAA DBM     146Ø  2-22-87    9:1Øp
EMPLAAAB IØ1     1Ø24  2-22-87    9:1Øp
EMPLAAAB IØC     1Ø24  2-22-87    9:1Øp
EMPLAAAB DBA      776  2-15-87    7:Ø4p
CUSTAAAA DBM     24ØØ  2-27-87    2:Ø8p
CUSTAAAA DBA      363  2-27-87    9:Ø2p
PRODAAAA DBM      59Ø  2-22-87   1Ø:13p
PRODAAAA IØ1     1Ø24  2-22-87   1Ø:12p
PRODAAAA DBA      247  2-15-87    8:27p
ORDEAAAA DBM      374  2-27-87    3:21p
ORDEAAAA DBA      535  2-15-87    8:41p
Strike a key when ready . . .
```

FIGURE 10.10

If you choose **3**, the **FORMAT** DOS command is executed (assuming it is on your floppy or hard disk). Before it executes it, it asks for the disk drive where the disk will be formatted. You are asked to insert a disk in the appropriate drive and press the RETURN key.

Choice **4** is used to perform a DOS backup of your data files. Figure 10.11 shows what happens if Choice **4** is selected. You are asked to enter the name of the drive for the backup disks and then to press RETURN.

This DOS backup command differs from the previously mentioned DataEase backup command in several ways. The DataEase backup checks each record before writing it to disk, in order to physically remove the deleted records and consolidate space. The DOS backup does not perform this check but is faster than the DataEase backup. Also, the DataEase backup does not store the index files. These files are reconstructed when performing a DataEase Restore. Finally, the DataEase backup will store the import files; the DOS backup will not. Remember that the backup disk must be a formatted disk.

```
DOS Functions

          D O S   F U N C T I O N S

   1. Data Disk Directory

   2. Check Data Disk

   3. Format New Disk

   4. DOS Backup

   5. DOS Restore

   6. Other

 ---- 1 to 6 — UP — DOWN — RETURN — END ----

 Specify the Drive to use for Backup diskettes and press RETURN :

     F4 EXIT     DATABASE A PROG.A: DATA B: DATE          TIME
```

FIGURE 10.11

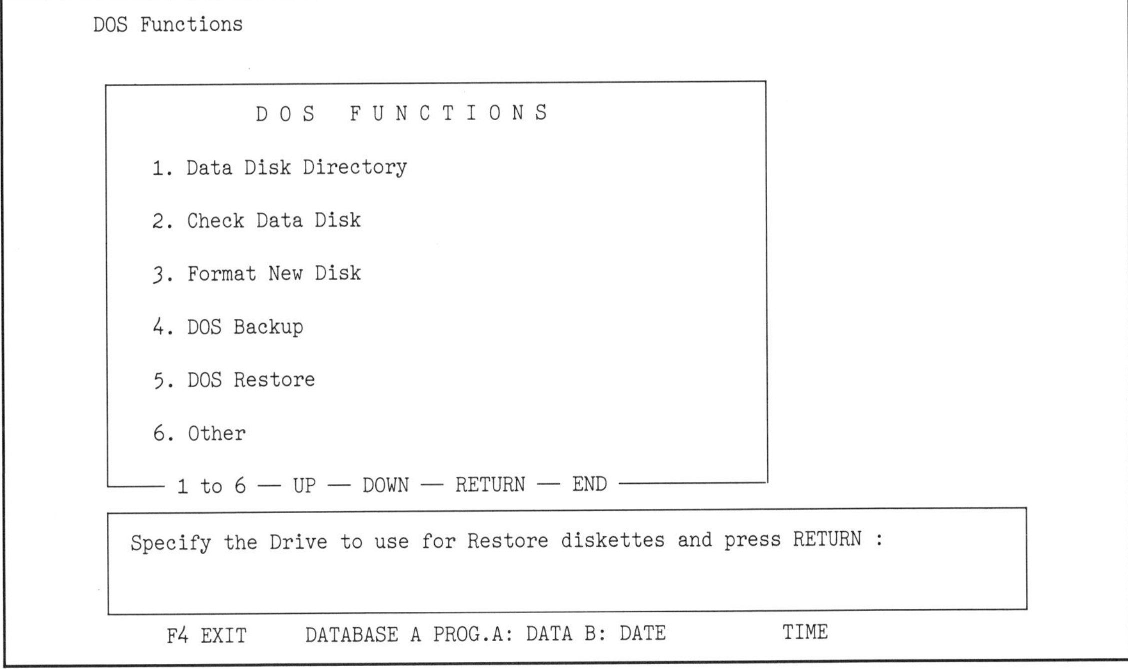

FIGURE 10.12

Choice **5** is used to restore your DOS backup disks. When you call this function, Figure 10.12 appears. It asks you for the disk drive from which you wish the restored copy to take place (assuming you are using a dual floppy system).

If you select choice **6 Other**, you can type in any DOS command that you wish.

Exporting and Importing Data Utilities

In this chapter you will learn how to export data to other programs through the use of the Define Format option of the Quick and Full Reports Menus. You will learn how to import data into a DataEase database through the Utilities Menu. You will learn how to install forms and reports, remove a database, and install an application.

EXPORT FORMATS

In the chapters on quick and full reports, many defined formats were discussed including columnar, field per line, special, and record entry. All of these are found in the Define Report Format option, choice **5** of both the Quick Reports and the Full Reports Menus. One of the formats that was omitted was the export format as shown in Figure 11.1.

When you do an export do not include a printer name when doing print style configurations as that will put control strings in your file and give an undesired export. To access the export format, type **3** in answer to the second question:

```
What type of format do you want?
```

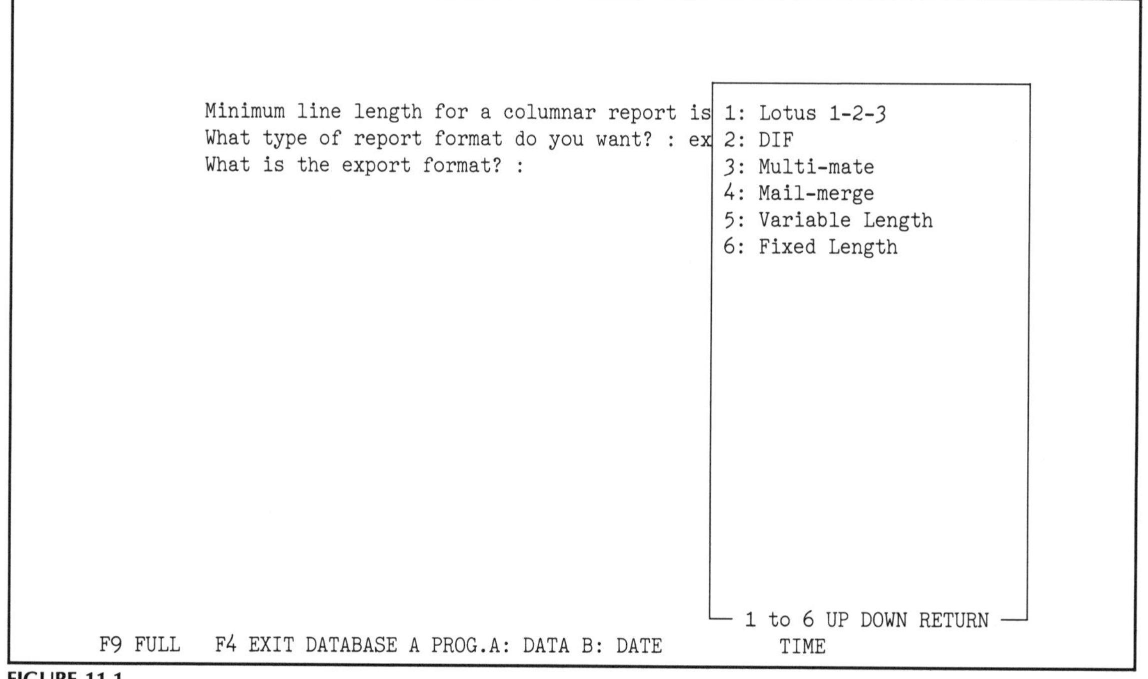

FIGURE 11.1

As you can see in the window box at the right hand side of Figure 11.1, there are six export formats that DataEase can create.

Choice **1** allows you to export data to Lotus 1-2-3 or Lotus Symphony. Each exported field will be a column on the Lotus spreadsheet while each exported record will be a row on the spreadsheet. Remember not to group fields when exporting. When you choose to export to Lotus, DataEase responds with:

```
export Lotus 1-2-3
```

When you select choice **2**, the DIF (Data Interchange Format) format is chosen. This allows DataEase to export the data to other spreadsheets or graphics programs that use this format. When you choose this option, you will be asked if you want to include field names in the format as shown in Figure 11.2.

A portion of the output is shown in Figure 11.3 when you choose the exporting DIF format.

```
1: no 2: yes

        Minimum line length for a columnar report is 186
        What type of report format do you want? : export
        What is the export format? : DIF
        Include field names in the format :




F9 FULL   F4 EXIT DATABASE A PROG.A: DATA B: DATE          TIME
```

FIGURE 11.2

```
                              R  1 C   1
TABLE
Ø,1
""
VECTORS
Ø,1ØØ
""
TUPLES
Ø,14
""
DATA
Ø,Ø
""
-1,Ø
BOT
1,Ø
"Employee #"
1,Ø
"Position"
1,Ø
"Last Name"
1,Ø
"First Name"
F2ENTER F3CUT F4EXIT F5COPY F6PASTE F7DEL LINE F8INS LINE F9PRINT F1ØFIELD
```

FIGURE 11.3

If you select choice **3**, you will select the Multimate option. This allows you to export your data to the Multimate word processing program. A portion of the output is shown in Figure 11.4.

If there are commas in the fields and you are delimiting by commas, the Mail-merge would be the choice. If you select choice **4**, you select the Mail-merge option, as shown in Figure 11.5. This feature is used if you wish to merge data with the Mail-merge feature of the Wordstar word processor. Again, it asks you if you want the field names in the format.

When the output is run, it appears as shown in Figure 11.6.

If you select choice **5**, you select the variable length export format, as shown in Figure 11.7. The variable length format is used if you want to export data to other microcomputers. Variable length format is useful because it contains a general format for files that contain ASCII variable length records. It is more flexible than the other formats. Fixed

```
                                   R  1 C   1
.items
├Employee #├
     ├
├Position├
                     ├
├Last Name├
                ├
├First Name├
                ├
├Address├
                     ├
├City├
                     ├
├State├
  ├
├Zip├
     ├
├Date of Birth├
        ├
├Date Hired├
        ├
├Phone #├
F2ENTER F3CUT F4EXIT F5COPY F6PASTE F7DEL LINE F8INS LINE F9PRINT F1ØFIELD
```

FIGURE 11.4

```
1: no 2: yes

         Minimum line length for a columnar report is 186
         What type of report format do you want? : export
         What is the export format? : Mail-merge
         Include field names in the format :


F9 FULL   F4 EXIT DATABASE A PROG.A: DATA B: DATE          TIME
```

FIGURE 11.5

```
                              R  1 C   1

"Employee #","Position","Last Name","First Name","Address","City","State","Zip",
.items
     ,"                      ","                ","                 ","
.end







F2ENTER F3CUT F4EXIT F5COPY F6PASTE F7DEL LINE F8INS LINE F9PRINT F1ØFIELD
```

FIGURE 11.6

```
1: no 2: yes

         Minimum line length for a columnar report is 186
         What type of report format do you want? : export
         What is the export format? : Variable Length
         FIELD  SEPARATOR character (If new line, press RETURN):
         Include field names in the format :







F9 FULL   F4 EXIT DATABASE A PROG.A: DATA B: DATE          TIME
```

FIGURE 11.7

length format is usually from mainframes. DataEase will ask:

```
FIELD SEPARATOR character (if new line, press RETURN):
```

Type in the field separator character and press the RETURN key.

It asks you if you wish to include field names in the format.

The output shown on the screen is in Figure 11.8.

The last selection, choice **6**, is also used to export data to a mainframe. This format exports information that is of fixed length. If you are using Release 3 of DataEase, the last choice is Graftalk.

IMPORT FORMAT

Just as you can export data to other programs, you can also import data from these programs by using the import feature of the Utilities Menu. To access the Utilities Menu, choose **5** on the Main Menu. The Utilities Menu now appears, as shown in Figure 11.9. If you want to exit this menu, press F4 EXIT.

```
                              R 1 C  1

     Employee #
     Position
     Last Name
     First Name
     Address
     City
     State
     Zip
     Date of Birth
     Date Hired
     Phone #
     Social Security Numb
     Salary
     Marital Status
     .items




     F2ENTER F3CUT F4EXIT F5COPY F6PASTE F7DEL LINE F8INS LINE F9PRINT F10FIELD
```

FIGURE 11.8

```
DATABASE UTILITIES

        U T I L I T I E S   M E N U

     1. Import

     2. Transfer Data

     3. Install Form

     4. Install Report

     5. Remove Data Base

     6. Install an Application

   1 to 6 — UP — DOWN — RETURN — END

Alt-F1HELP F4EXIT DATABASE A PROG.A: DATA B: DATE          TIME
```

FIGURE 11.9

If you select **1** from the Utilities Menu, you will select the import feature, and the Data Import Menu will appear, as shown in Figure 11.10. This feature allows you to import data into all fields or selected fields of specific forms. The data can be used to create new records or update existing records.

If you press **1** of the Data Import Menu, you are requesting a One-time import. The system will ask:

```
Please select destination form name:
```

This is shown in Figure 11.11.

Notice in the window box on the right-hand side of Figure 11.11 that DataEase gives you a list of all the forms into which you can import data. You would like to import data into the **EMPLOYEES** file so select **3**. This is the file that data will be entering.

```
DATA IMPORT

        D A T A   I M P O R T   M E N U

    1. One-time Import

    2. Run Defined Import

    3. Define an Import

    4. View of Modify an Import

    5. Delete an Import

    1 to 5 — UP — DOWN — RETURN — END

Alt-F1HELP F4EXIT DATABASE A PROG.A: DATA B: DATE          TIME
```

FIGURE 11.10

```
IMPORT DATA

     D A T A E A S E - D A T A   I M P O R T   F A

Please select the destination form name :          Ø: NONE
                                                    1: System
                                                    2: Employee
                                                    3: Employees
                                                    4: Customer
                                                    5: Products
                                                    6: Orders

                                                    Ø to 6 UP DOWN RETURN
      F4 EXIT    DATABASE A PROG.A: DATA B: DATE          TIME
```

FIGURE 11.11

DataEase will now ask:

```
Please enter the source data file name:
```

Type in the name of the source file, in this case Lotus.WK1, as shown in Figure 11.12. Be sure to include the extension **.WK1.** If the Lotus file is not on the data drive, you must specify the drive name with the file name. This menu also imports relationships, users, menus, printers, etc., by importing files menubaaa.dma, relabaaa.dbm, etc., which are in DataEase format.

DataEase will now ask:

```
What is the source data file format?
```

Figure 11.13 in the window box on the right gives a list of the file formats that DataEase recognizes. You would like to have data come from Lotus 1-2-3 so type **7**. The data will be transferred from your Lotus file into your DataEase database. Each column in the spreadsheet of Lotus is a field in a record of DataEase. Each row in the spreadsheet of Lotus is a record in DataEase.

DataEase will now ask about the source file organization as shown in Figure 11.14.

As seen in Figure 11.14, the first row of a Lotus spreadsheet must consist of the Source Field Names. In your situation, you will select **1** by Field Order. In Field Order the number and order of the fields of the source (sending) file must match the number and order of the fields in the destination (receiving) form. If you select **2 by Field Name**, data is sent from the source file to the destination form if the fields have the same name.

DataEase will now ask:

```
How should the matching records be processed?
```

Notice the menu at the top of Figure 11.15.

```
IMPORT DATA

     D A T A E A S E  - D A T A   I M P O R T   F A C I L I T Y

Please select the destination form name :               Employees

Please enter the source data file name  :               Lotus.WK1



     F4 EXIT     DATABASE A PROG.A: DATA B: DATE          TIME
```

FIGURE 11.12

```
IMPORT DATA

     D A T A E A S E  - D A T A   I M P O R T   F A
                                                      1: DATAEASE
Please select the destination form name :             2: DIF
                                                      3: dBASE II
Please enter the source data file name  :             4: MAIL-MERGE
What is the data file format ? :                      5: VARIABLE LENGTH
                                                      6: FIXED LENGTH
                                                      7: LOTUS 1-2-3
                                                      8: dBASE III

                                                       1 to 8 UP DOWN RETURN
     F4 EXIT     DATABASE A PROG.A: DATA B: DATE          TIME
```

FIGURE 11.13

```
IMPORT DATA
1: BY FIELD ORDER 2: BY FIELD NAME
     D A T A E A S E  - D A T A   I M P O R T   F A C I L I T Y

Please select the destination form name :                Employees

Please enter the source data file name  :                Lotus.WK1
What is the data file format ? :                         LOTUS 1-2-3
The FIELDS in the source file can be organized in two ways:
1. FIELD ORDER matches the DATAEASE form, ALL fields are transferred.
2. FIELD NAMES match DATAEASE field names,  MATCHING fields are transferred.
   For LOTUS files, The FIRST ROW must consist of SOURCE FIELD NAMES.
How is the source file organized ?:










     F4 EXIT    DATABASE A PROG.A: DATA B: DATE         TIME
```

FIGURE 11.14

```
IMPORT DATA                            data in the field is required
1: ADD NON-MATCHING 2: UPDATE MATCHING 3: ADD OR UPDATE 4: DO NOT MATCH
     D A T A E A S E  - D A T A   I M P O R T   F A C I L I T Y

Please select the destination form name :                Employees

Please enter the source data file name  :                Lotus.WK1
What is the data file format ? :                         LOTUS 1-2-3
The FIELDS in the source file can be organized in two ways:
1. FIELD ORDER matches the DATAEASE form, ALL fields are transferred.
2. FIELD NAMES match DATAEASE field names,  MATCHING fields are transferred.
   For LOTUS files, The FIRST ROW must consist of SOURCE FIELD NAMES.
How is the source file organized ?:                      BY FIELD ORDER
Processing can be based on MATCH between existing and new records.
How should the matching records be processed ?








     F4 EXIT    DATABASE A PROG.A: DATA B: DATE         TIME
```

FIGURE 11.15

If you choose option **1 Add Non-Matching**, only the new records from the Lotus file will be added. Any duplicate records will not be used.

If you choose option **2 Update Matching**, only the records in the Lotus file that match records in the DataEase file will be used to update the DataEase file. If there are any records in the Lotus file that have no corresponding records in the DataEase file, they will not be added.

If you choose option **3 Add or Update**, records that are both in the Lotus file and the DataEase file will cause the DataEase file to be updated. Records that are in the Lotus file but not in the DataEase file will cause a new record to be added to the DataEase file.

If you choose option **4 Do Not Match**, all the records of the Lotus file are added to the DataEase file without checking for duplicate records. This is used if you do not want to spend time checking for duplicates. This should be used only sparingly. The amount of time spent in checking records is well worth it.

In your example you want to update, so press **2 Update Matching**, as shown in Figure 11.16.

DataEase now asks you to:

```
Press ENTER to Proceed, EXIT to Abort, or Modify to Modify
```

If you press F2 ENTER, the one-time import will begin.

In a similar manner, you may import data from other programs, including DataEase itself. If you choose option **1 DataEase** as the data file format, you can combine several DataEase databases into one. If, for example, several departments of a company merged, this feature could be used to merge their databases as well. This is shown in Figure 11.17. The source file comes from the source data diskette of database B (assuming you are in database A and merging data from B). The name of the data file can be obtained from accessing the Maintenance Menu and checking the Database Status function when in database B, as mentioned in the last chapter.

If you decide to import data into DataEase using the DIF (Data Interchange Format), you would select **2 DIF** for the data file format. This

```
IMPORT DATA

     D A T A E A S E  - D A T A   I M P O R T   F A C I L I T Y

Please select the destination form name :                Employees

Please enter the source data file name  :                Lotus.WK1
What is the data file format ? :                         LOTUS 1-2-3
The FIELDS in the source file can be organized in two ways:
1. FIELD ORDER matches the DATAEASE form, ALL fields are transferred.
2. FIELD NAMES match DATAEASE field names,  MATCHING fields are transferred.
   For LOTUS files, The FIRST ROW must consist of SOURCE FIELD NAMES.
How is the source file organized ?:                      BY FIELD ORDER
Processing can be based on MATCH between existing and new records.
How should the matching records be processed ?           UPDATE MATCHING
Press ENTER to Proceed, EXIT to Abort, or MODIFY to Modify





F2 ENTER F4 EXIT F8MODIFY
```

FIGURE 11.16

```
IMPORT DATA

     D A T A E A S E  - D A T A   I M P O R T   F A C I L I T Y

Please select the destination form name :                Employees

Please enter the source data file name  :                EMPLBAAB.DBM
What is the data file format ? :                         DATAEASE
Is the source form same as the destination form ?        yes

Processing can be based on MATCH between existing and new records.
How should the matching records be processed ?           UPDATE MATCHING
Press ENTER to Proceed, EXIT to Abort, or MODIFY to Modify





F2 ENTER F4 EXIT F8MODIFY
```

FIGURE 11.17

would be used to enter data from most spreadsheets into DataEase. If you are importing information from a spreadsheet, the field names should be typed in the top row of the spreadsheet. The field names could also be typed in the first column but the spreadsheet data must be saved by column.

If you decide to import data into DataEase using the dBase II program, you would select **3 dBase II** as the data file format. The data import facility would appear to look like Figure 11.18. If the source file organization is selected "By Field Name," limit the DataEase field name to ten characters or less because that is the restriction placed on field names by dBase II.

If you decide to import data into DataEase using the Mail-Merge format, you would select **4 Mail-merge** as the data file format. This is a very useful format if you are importing from a program such as Wordstar as shown in Figure 11.19. All the fields in the Wordstar file would be separated by commas. Each record would be started on a new line.

```
IMPORT DATA

      D A T A E A S E  - D A T A   I M P O R T   F A C I L I T Y

Please select the destination form name :              Employees

Please enter the source data file name  :              Sample.DBF
What is the data file format ? :                       dBASE II
The FIELDS in the source file can be organized in two ways:
1. FIELD ORDER matches the DATAEASE form, ALL fields are transferred.
2. FIELD NAMES match DATAEASE field names,  MATCHING fields are transferred.
   For dBASE II/III files, the SOURCE FIELD NAMES are taken from the file header
How is the source file organized ?:                    BY FIELD ORDER
Processing can be based on MATCH between existing and new records.
How should the matching records be processed ?         UPDATE MATCHING
Press ENTER to Proceed, EXIT to Abort, or MODIFY to Modify





F2 ENTER F4 EXIT F8MODIFY
```

FIGURE 11.18

```
IMPORT DATA

     D A T A E A S E  - D A T A   I M P O R T   F A C I L I T Y

Please select the destination form name :                Employees

Please enter the source data file name  :                Wordstar.DAT
What is the data file format ? :                         MAIL-MERGE
The FIELDS in the source file can be organized in two ways:
1. FIELD ORDER matches the DATAEASE form, ALL fields are transferred.
2. FIELD NAMES match DATAEASE field names,  MATCHING fields are transferred.
   The FIRST RECORD must consist of SOURCE FIELD NAMES.
How is the source file organized ?:                      BY FIELD NAME
Processing can be based on MATCH between existing and new records.
How should the matching records be processed ?           UPDATE MATCHING
Press ENTER to Proceed, EXIT to Abort, or MODIFY to Modify







F2 ENTER F4 EXIT F8MODIFY
```

FIGURE 11.19

If you decide to import data into DataEase using the variable length format, you would select **5 Variable Length** as the data file format as shown in Figure 11.20. This is used if you are working with files with an ASCII variable length format. This is used in most applications.

Notice something different in this format compared with some of the previous ones. DataEase asks:

```
FIELD SEPARATOR character (If new line, press RETURN):
```

Type in the symbol that separates the various fields. Here it is the comma but it could be the semicolon or any other symbol.

DataEase then asks:

```
RECORD SEPARATOR character (If new line, press RETURN):
```

```
IMPORT DATA

     D A T A E A S E  - D A T A   I M P O R T   F A C I L I T Y

Please select the destination form name :                Employees

Please enter the source data file name  :                Main.DAT
What is the data file format ? :                         VARIABLE LENGTH
FIELD  SEPARATOR character (If new line, press RETURN):  ,
RECORD SEPARATOR character (If new line, press RETURN):

For fixed point fields, should the decimal be automatically inserted? :yes
The FIELDS in the source file can be organized in two ways:
1. FIELD ORDER matches the DATAEASE form, ALL fields are transferred.
2. FIELD NAMES match DATAEASE field names,  MATCHING fields are transferred.
   For VAR. LENGTH files, the FIRST RECORD must consist of SOURCE FIELD NAMES.
How is the source file organized ?:                      BY FIELD ORDER
Processing can be based on MATCH between existing and new records.
How should the matching records be processed ?           ADD OR UPDATE
Press ENTER to Proceed, EXIT to Abort, or MODIFY to Modify



F2 ENTER F4 EXIT F8MODIFY
```

FIGURE 11.20

Here you are specifying a simple carriage return as the record separator. Press the RETURN key to signify this. DataEase asks:

```
For fixed point fields, should the decimal be
automatically inserted?
```

You will answer **Yes** to indicate that the source file does not have decimal points in its numeric fields.

If you decide to import data into DataEase using the fixed length format, you would select **6 Fixed Length** as the data file format as shown in Figure 11.21.

This is a format that would be very useful in importing information from mainframe computers. The ordering of the fields is of the utmost importance. The order of the source and the destination fields must match exactly. The number of fields in both the source and destination files must match exactly. The source file should not have any field or

```
IMPORT DATA

     D A T A E A S E  - D A T A   I M P O R T   F A C I L I T Y

Please select the destination form name :              Employees

Please enter the source data file name  :              Main.DAT
What is the data file format ? :                       FIXED LENGTH
Is the file in a FIXED LENGTH format with NO SEPARATORS? yes
Do the field ORDER and LENGTHS match the DATAEASE form ? yes

For fixed point fields, should the decimal be automatically inserted? :yes
Processing can be based on MATCH between existing and new records.
How should the matching records be processed ?         UPDATE MATCHING
Press ENTER to Proceed, EXIT to Abort, or MODIFY to Modify









F2 ENTER F4 EXIT F8MODIFY
```

FIGURE 11.21

record separators. If you import onto a formatted field such as telephone number or date, this field must be formatted on the mainframe as well as the microcomputer.

As you can see, fixed length format is quite limited. The reference manual of DataEase says that it is inflexible and error prone. Therefore, it should be used only when necessary.

If you decide to import data into DataEase using the dBase III format, you would select **8 dBase III** as the data file format as shown in Figure 11.22. As you can see, the data import facility for dBase III and dBase II are very similar but you must use the correct specification.

You can also run defined imports by selecting **2 Run Defined Import** from the Data Import Menu. DataEase asks for the Import Specification Name as shown in Figure 11.23.

```
IMPORT DATA

     D A T A E A S E - D A T A  I M P O R T  F A C I L I T Y

Please select the destination form name :              Employees

Please enter the source data file name  :              Main.DAT
What is the data file format ? :                       dBASE III
The FIELDS in the source file can be organized in two ways:
1. FIELD ORDER matches the DATAEASE form, ALL fields are transferred.
2. FIELD NAMES match DATAEASE field names,  MATCHING fields are transferred.
   For dBASE II/III files, the SOURCE FIELD NAMES are taken from the file header
How is the source file organized ?:                    BY FIELD ORDER
Processing can be based on MATCH between existing and new records.
How should the matching records be processed ?         UPDATE MATCHING
Press ENTER to Proceed, EXIT to Abort, or MODIFY to Modify




F2 ENTER F4 EXIT F8MODIFY
```

FIGURE 11.22

```
DATA IMPORT

        D A T A  I M P O R T  M E N U

    1. One-time Import

    2. Run Defined Import

    3. Define an Import

    4. View of Modify an Import

    5. Delete an Import

     1 to 5 — UP — DOWN — RETURN — END

  Import Specification Name :

Alt-FIHELP F4EXIT DATABASE A PROG.A: DATA B: DATE         TIME
```

FIGURE 11.23

You will be given a list of imports. Select one of them and press RETURN. You will then be asked to press RETURN to start the import or to press EXIT to abort.

If you press **3 Define an Import** in the Data Import Menu, you will be asked for an Import Specification Name. The name can be up to eight characters long. Type a name followed by pressing the RETURN key. You will then be asked the Import Specification questions. Press F2 ENTER after answering them.

If you press **4 View or Modify an Import**, you will get a list of imports. Choose the import name. You may make any modifications by pressing the F8 MODIFY key. Press the F2 ENTER key to save any changes in the import specification.

If you press **5 Delete an Import**, you will be given a list of import specifications to delete. Select the one you want deleted.

TRANSFERRING DATA

This feature of DataEase allows you to transfer data between forms in the database that you are currently using. All the information from the source form is sent to the destination form. There is no check for duplicate information. To transfer data, choose **2** from the Utilities Menu, as shown in Figure 11.24. The menu at the top of the screen lists all the files in your present database.

DataEase now responds:

```
Please select the source form:
```

Type **3 Employees** to select the **EMPLOYEES** file.

DataEase now responds:

```
Please select the destination form:
```

You can select the destination form, for example, **EMPLOYEE**. As soon as you choose a file, the transfer of information begins. The fields are transferred based on field name. When the transfer is completed, you are returned to the Utilities Menu.

```
FORM DATA TRANSFER
Ø: NONE 1: System 2: Employee 3: Employees 4: Customer 5: Products 6: Orders

     D A T A E A S E   F O R M   T R A N S F E R

    Please select the source form :                    Employees

    Please enter the destination form :




Alt-F1HELP F4EXIT DATABASE A PROG.A: DATA B: DATE         TIME
```

FIGURE 11.24

INSTALLING A FORM

When you want to install a form, choose **3** on the Utilities Menu. This function installs a form from one database to another database. The data associated with that form may be transferred also. When you enter this form name, you must use the DOS file associated with the form. Figure 11.25 shows a copy of the DataEase Form Installation.

DataEase responds:

```
Please enter the new form name:
```

Type in the new form name (in your case Pay) then press RETURN. DataEase will now ask:

```
Please enter the form (DBA) file name:
```

Type the form name (in your case Payabaaa) then press RETURN. The form file has an extension **DBA**. DataEase now asks:

```
INSTALL FORM


    D A T A E A S E   F O R M   I N S T A L L A T I O N

  Please enter the new form name to be defined :      Pay

  Please enter the Form (DBA) filename:               Payabaaa

  Please enter any data (DBM) filename :              Payabaaa









Alt-F1HELP F4EXIT DATABASE A PROG.A: DATA B: DATE         TIME
```

FIGURE 11.25

```
Please enter any data (DBM) file name:
```

Since you want the data, along with the form, to be transferred, type the file name (Payabaaa) then press RETURN. The data file has an extension **DBM**. If you don't want any data, just press RETURN to bypass this menu.

INSTALLING A REPORT

Besides transferring a form with/without its data, you can also install a report from one database to another database. Choose **4 Install Report** from the Utilities Menu. Figure 11.26 shows a report installation.

As shown in Figure 11.26, enter the new report name and the Report Filename (which has an extension of **DBR** by default). DataEase will also ask you if the report has a Data-entry form—the **.DBF** associated with **.DBR**. Answer **Yes** if it did have one and **No** if it didn't. The report will now be installed.

```
INSTALL REPORT
1: no 2: yes

   D A T A E A S E   R E P O R T   I N S T A L L A T I O N

  Please enter the new report name to be defined :     Payroll List

  Please enter the Report (DBR) Filename:              Payabaaa

  Does the Report have a Data-entry Form ?       :

Alt-F1HELP F4EXIT DATABASE A PROG.A: DATA B: DATE          TIME
```

FIGURE 11.26

REMOVING A DATABASE

When a database is removed, so are its form definitions, data, and report definitions. If a database is removed, it cannot be recovered.

If you want to remove a database, press **5 Remove Database** on the Utilities Menu. Figure 11.27 now appears.

DataEase will now ask you to state your name and your password as a security check. After you type in your name and password, DataEase responds:

```
Are you sure you want to remove the ENTIRE DATA BASE?
```

DataEase is giving you a chance to back out of erasing the database. Type in **Yes** to erase it and **No** if you change your mind. Don't forget—when you erase a database it is gone forever.

APPLICATION INSTALLATION

If you choose **6 Install an Application** from the Utilities Menu, DataEase will ask you to enter the name of the Installation file as shown in Figure 11.28. Install an application if you want to execute commands to install forms, replace forms, install reports, replace reports, or import data into a file. New forms can be created with or without data. New data can be installed into an existing form. Old forms can be replaced with updated versions. These command lines may be created by using a word processor or DOS's EDLIN facility, since your application file is just an ASCII file with DataEase commands in it.

It will then ask you to insert the installation disk to start the installation.

Figure 11.29 shows a list of the commands that can be used.

```
REMOVE DATA BASE
1: no 2: yes

     D A T A E A S E   - R E M O V E   T H E   D A T A B A S E

*** ALL the data base information will be Removed from the disk ***

What is your name :                                    Paul
What is your password :

Are you sure you want to remove the ENTIRE DATA BASE ?











Alt-F1HELP F4EXIT DATABASE A PROG.A: DATA B: DATE         TIME
```

FIGURE 11.27

```
Application Installation


         D A T A E A S E   A P P L I C A T I O N   I N S T A L L A T I O N

   Please enter the name of the Installation file :     MeritPay
Insert the Installation diskette.
Press EXIT to abort, or any other key to start installation.















Alt-F1HELP F4EXIT DATABASE A PROG.A: DATA B: DATE         TIME
```

FIGURE 11.28

```
                        INSTALLATION COMMANDS
INSTALL FORM
    Used to install a new form, install a new form with data, or to
install new data into an existing form. The general format of the
command are:

    install form <form name> from: <dba name>;

    install form <form name> from <dba name> data: <dbm name>;

    install form <form name> data: <dbm name>

REPLACE FORM
    Used to replace an existing form with a revised version. The data
in the existing form is reorganized to reflect the revision in the
form. The format for the command is:

    Replace form <form name> from : <dba name>;

INSTALL REPORT
    Used to install a new report. The format of the command is:

    Install report <report name> from: <dbr name>;

REPLACE REPORT
    Used to replace an existing report. The format of the command is:

    Replace report <report name> from: <dbr name>;

IMPORT
    Imports data according to an already defined import specification.
The format of the command is:

    Import from <Import spec name>;

NAME FORMATS
    <form name>    The form name may be several words long. If the name
                   conflicts with a keyword (any, all, data), it must
                   be enclosed in double quotes.

    <report name>  The report may be several words long. If the
                   name conflicts with a keyword (any, all, data), it
                   must be enclosed in double quotes.

    <dba name>     This is the name of the form definition file. If the
                   file is in the same disk drive as the command file,
                   then the disk drive name may be omitted as the
                   extension .DBA.

    <dbr name>     This is the name of the Report Definition file. If
                   the file is in the same disk drive as the command
                   file, then the disk drive name may also be omitted
                   as the file extension .DBR.

    <Import spec name> This is the name of Import Specification file.
                       If the file is in the same disk drive as the
                       command file, then the disk drive name may be
                       omitted as the file extension .DBI.
```

FIGURE 11.29

CREATING AND ACCESSING TEMPLATES

A template is a prewritten form that guides a person step-by-step through a particular application. For example, standard formats may be provided for analyzing forecast trends, income and expenses, preparing financial statements, establishing budgets, and so on. A template simplifies processing. A user displays a standard format, enters data into appropriate places, and initiates processing with a simple command. The user does not have to spend time designing formats or entering standard formulas. In this chapter you will learn what a template is, how to create a simple Template file, and how to call a Template file to print out a report.

DEFINITION OF A TEMPLATE

A form with no entries or data is called a template. Any file with a **.DBA** extension is a template. All the labels and fields are present but there is no data entered into the form. A template can be used to format predefined mailing labels, form letters, or special reports. All of these templates or special forms can be stored in a separate database and can be accessed from any other database. If you had special business forms that were required on a periodic basis, you could make a template of these forms which could be called by anyone with minimal knowledge. One advantage of using a template is you do not have to define the format for a report.

When templates are used in business there may be a large number of templates in common among the various divisions and departments in the company. A template which has the headings and formulas already filled in can be created so that the user only has to put in the numbers to complete a form.

A template can be viewed as an application program with three functional parts: input, processing, and output. A good template should require the user to input the data to be processed in a structured format. It should process the data correctly. Finally, it should provide some way to get the results to the user easily.

A good template will have one or more input screens that allow easy entry of the data. An input area should have a lot of label entries to provide this formlike appearance. Making a good input screen is similar to designing a good form. Information is entered from the top downward and from left to right. Numeric and alphanumeric information should not be indiscriminately mixed. The input and output screen(s) should be completely separate from the processing area of the template.

CREATING A TEMPLATE

In your computer store, you would like to create a simple template that can give the names and addresses of all employees with their salaries and social security numbers. The first thing that you must do is create the template. You will create the template in a separate database so this information can be accessed by many computer stores, if needed. By placing the template in a separate file, they will not get confused with the forms that are already in that database.

You will create a new database and call it **b**, as shown in Figure 12.1.

You can use your own name and password. If you do not want to give your database a password, press the RETURN key. If you do give your database a password, be sure to remember it or write it down. From the DataEase Main Menu, choose **1 Form Definition** to create the template file. From the Forms Definition Menu, choose **1 Define a Form** to create the Template file. As shown in Figure 12.2, when DataEase asks for the template name, type **Template1** or any other appropriate name.

```
DATAEASE 2.5 Release 2
Copyright Software Solutions Inc, USA. 1986
                                        Serial Number   AØ-ØØØ8Ø15

        D A T A E A S E  - S I G N   O N

      Data base Name ( A to Z ) : b
      Data Base does not exist on drive B:
      Create a new data base (y/n) ?:  y
      New data base will be created on drive B:

      What is your name            :  Paul

Alt-F1HELP F4EXIT DATABASE   PROG.A: DATA B: DATE          TIME
```

FIGURE 12.1

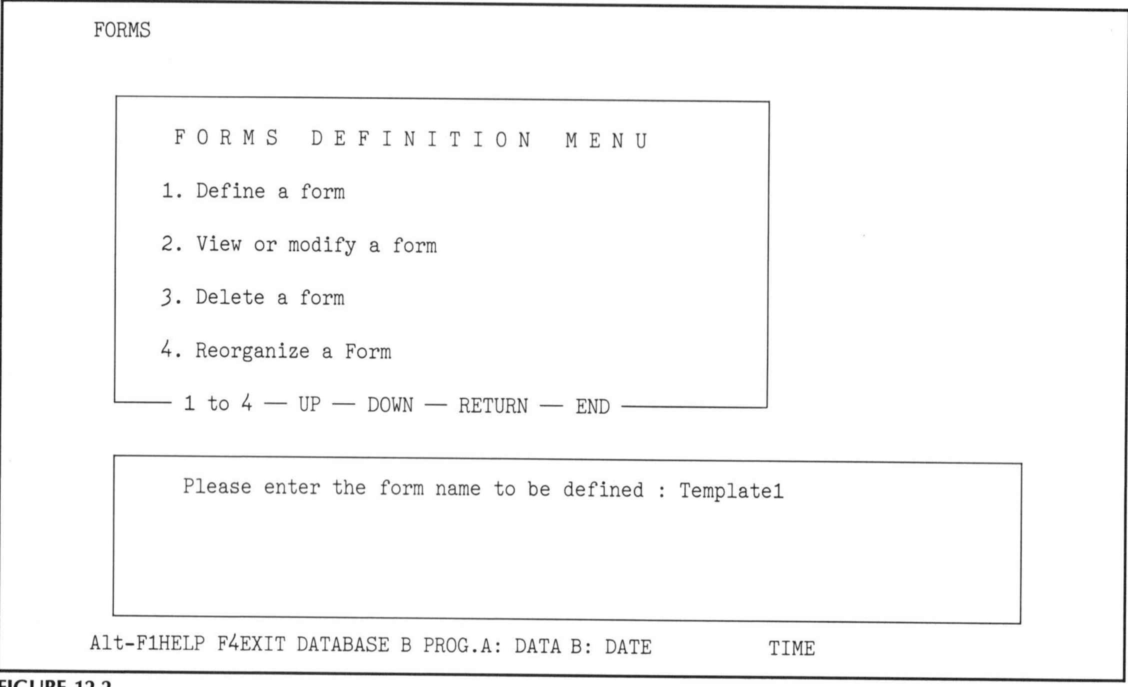

FIGURE 12.2

A template file is created just like any other form. The text and field lines are placed wherever you would like them. The fields can be placed anywhere you would like. Figure 12.3 shows the form that we will use as our template.

If you decided to open up several different computer stores, this template could be accessed by any or all of them. Looking at Figure 12.6, there are some field names that have asterisks around them and some that do not. You will later access the template instead of creating a report format for a report in the **EMPLOYEES** file. For the report format to display a field name as shown in the template, the field name in the report must match. The fields First Name, Last Name, Address, City, State, and Zip must be identical in both the sending and receiving fields. The salary and security fields both have asterisks around them in the field descriptions to indicate that there doesn't have to be exact matches, as shown in Figure 12.4. This means that any fields that contain the words salary and security will match as yearly salary and social security number.

```
FORM template 1             R  1 C   1

First Name:                    Last Name:

Address:

City:                        State:      Zip:

Salary:

Security:






F2ENTER F3CUT F4EXIT F5COPY F6PASTE F7DEL LINE F8INS LINE F9PRINT F10FIELD
```

FIGURE 12.3

```
FORM Template1
Please hit Enter, Delete or Modify key
     Field name :                                 *Salary*
     Field type :                                 Number
     Number Type :                                Fixed point
     Maximum digits to the left of decimal? :      6
     Digits to the right of decimal :              2
     Press ENTER, MODIFY or DELETE any time to skip the remaining questions
     Is this field REQUIRED to be entered? :                     no
     Does this field require fast (INDEXED) access ?:            no
     Is it one of the UNIQUE fields? :                           no
     Does the field require a RANGE CHECK? :                     no
     Is the field DERIVED (calculate/lookup/sequence/default)? :no
     PREVENT data-entry in the field? :           no
     Minimum Security Level to View the Field:
     Minimum Security Level to Write the Field:
     Field Help


     Field display attribute:



F2 ENTER F7 DELETE F8 MODIFY
```

FIGURE 12.4

The template can handle different queries with similar field names and provide a "Predefined" report format for those queries. For example, the salary field in the template can match annual salary, yearly salary, or just plain salary. If you had several computer stores that used different names for a field, this would be a way of overcoming this. The last field, security, would accept social security number, soc. security number, social security, or any field that contained the word security. This allows the template to be more flexible in the acceptance of data. The field descriptions are also entered for each data field, as shown in Figure 12.5.

The field name, field type, and length of field are specified in Figure 12.5. All the other questions must be omitted or answered **NO**. If, when you run the report to access the template, you get wrong or omitted data, check the field description to make sure that all the resulting questions have an answer of **NO**. The complete Form Definition for the template is shown in Figure 12.6.

```
FORM Template1
Please hit Enter, Delete or Modify key
     Field name :                                  *Security*
     Field type :                                  Numeric String
     Is it a formatted string ?                    soc.sec.no.
     Press ENTER, MODIFY or DELETE any time to skip the remaining questions
     Is this field REQUIRED to be entered? :                      no
     Does this field require fast (INDEXED) access ?:             no
     Is it one of the UNIQUE fields? :                            no
     Does the field require a RANGE CHECK? :                      no
     Is the field DERIVED (calculate/lookup/sequence/default)? :no
     PREVENT data-entry in the field? :            no
     Minimum Security Level to View the Field:
     Minimum Security Level to Write the Field:
     Field Help


     Field display attribute:




F2 ENTER F7 DELETE F8 MODIFY
```

FIGURE 12.5

```
FORM   Template1
----------------------------

1       10        20        30        40        50        60        70        80
----+----+----+----+----+----+----+----+----+----+----+----+----+----+----+----+

================================================================================

First Name: _______________    Last Name: _______________

Address: ____________________

City: ____________________   State: __   Zip: _____

Salary: __________

Security: __________
----+----+----+----+----+----+----+----+----+----+----+----+----+----+----+----+
1       10        20        30        40        50        60        70        80
```

FIELD DESCRIPTIONS

No.	Name	Type	Long	Reqd	In-dex	Uni-que	Der-ived	Rng Chk	Pre-vent	Record size	offset
1	First Name	Text	15	No	No	No	No	No	No	15	3
2	Last Name	Text	15	No	No	No	No	No	No	15	18
3	Address	Text	20	No	No	No	No	No	No	20	33
4	City	Text	20	No	No	No	No	No	No	20	53
5	State	Text	2	No	No	No	No	No	No	2	73
6	Zip	Num.String	5	No	No	No	No	No	No	5	75
7	*Salary*	Number	10	No	No	No	No	No	No	8	80
	Number Type : Fixed point Digits to left of decimal = 7										
8	*Security*	Num.String	11	No	No	No	No	No	No	9	88

Record size 97

Memory required for form: Text 111, Fields 209, Total 320 bytes.

FIGURE 12.6

To access this form you must know the DOS name of the file. That is, the eight letter file name with the **.dba** extension. If you access the file by using its report name **Template1**, it will give you an error message and say "report not found." To find the DOS name of the template, exit to the DataEase Main Menu, and choose **4 Data Base Maintenance**. This will give you the Maintenance Menu which was discussed in the last chapter. Since you would like to know the name of the form, choose **1 Database Status**. DataEase will now respond:

```
DATABASE STATUS
1: Forms 2: Reports 3: Import Specifications
Status of:
```

Since you want the status of the forms, choose **1 Forms** to have them shown on the screen or printed out. The status of the forms will now be printed out, as shown in Figure 12.7.

As you can see at the bottom of Figure 12.7, the DOS name of the file is **TEMPBAAA**. Make a note of it so you can use it later when you want

```
Number of forms: User defined : 1  System defined : 6  Total forms : 7
--------------------------------------------------------------------------------
No.    FORM NAME              NO. OF RECORDS      DISK FILE NAMES  FILE SIZE Bytes
                            EXISTING DELETED
--- -----------------     ------- --------    ---------------  ---------------
 1. users                       1        Ø    B:USERBAAA.DBM          63
 2. configuration               1        Ø    B:CONFBAAA.DBM          96
 3. printers                   17        Ø    B:PRINBAAA.DBM        5117
 4. screen styles               3        Ø    B:SCREBAAA.DBM         2Ø1
 5. relationships               Ø        Ø    B:RELABAAA.DBM           Ø
 6. menus                       Ø        Ø    B:MENUBAAA.DBM           Ø
 7. Template1                   Ø        Ø    B:TEMPBAAA.DBM           Ø
        Form Definition File                  B:TEMPBAAA.DBA         358
--------------------------------------------------------------------------------
```

FIGURE 12.7

to access the template. You would now like to exit from this database **b** and enter database **a** where your computer store files are located. As stated before, it is a good idea to store all templates in a separate file so that they can be accessed by other databases and don't get mixed in with the other reports located within each database.

ACCESSING A TEMPLATE

The template is now stored in database **b** and you now want to access it by using the **EMPLOYEES** file located in database **a**. If you have not done so already, exit to the DOS A> prompt by pressing the F4 EXIT key. Enter DataEase by typing **DEASE**, your database letter, and typing your name and password. From the Main Menu, type **2 Record Entry and Quick Reports**. This will give you the Records Menu, as shown in Figure 12.8.

Notice that a list of all the files in your current database is presented in the window box at the right-hand side of Figure 12.8. Since you want the **EMPLOYEES** file to access the template, type **3 Employees**. The

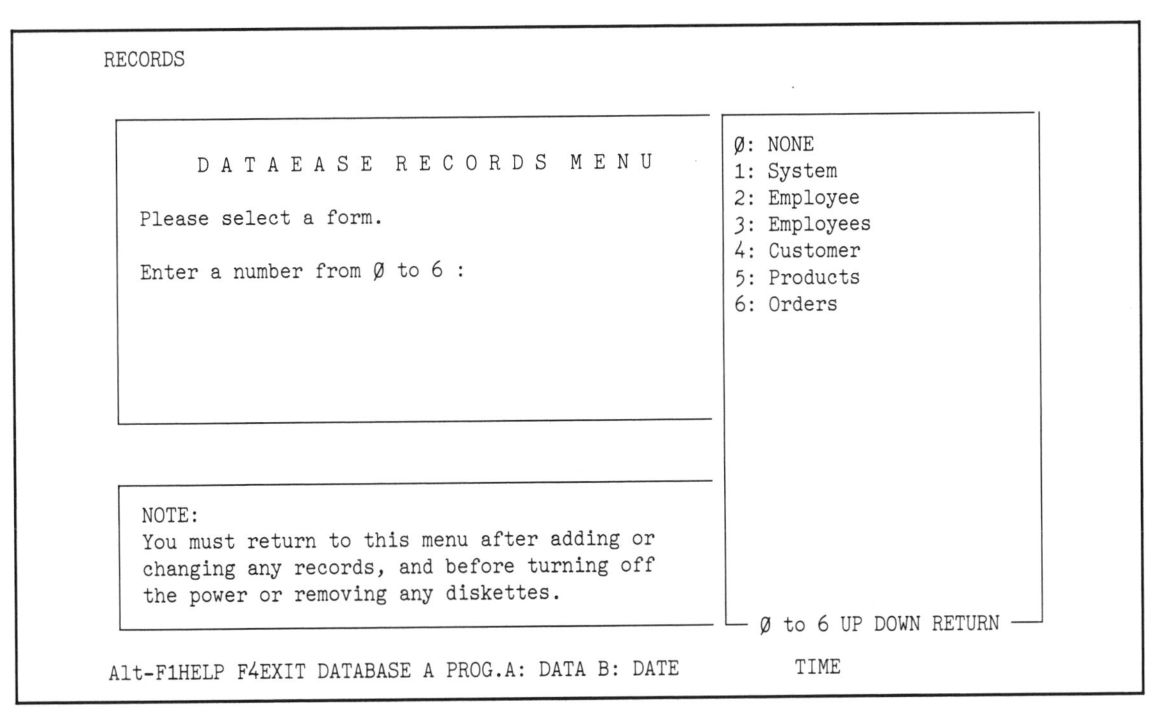

FIGURE 12.8

blank form for the **EMPLOYEES** file will appear on the screen, as shown in Figure 12.9.

You will access the template through the Quick Reports Menu by pressing the F9 REPORT key. This will give you the Quick Reports Menu. Since you want to start a new report, press **2 Start New Report**. Since you want the report to contain all the records, you will omit **3 Define Record Selection** and **4 Define List Fields**. When you press **5 Define Format**, Figure 12.10 will appear.

Since you would like the report format to be template, press the **6 Template** key. When you press **6**, Figure 12.11 will appear.

DataEase will ask you for the name of the Template file that you wish to use. Type:

```
b:Tempbaaa
```

The **b:** indicates the name of the drive followed by the DOS file name. That is why you had to get the status of database **b** to write down the template DOS name. If you typed in the name that you gave the template **Template1**, DataEase will give the message that the file was not found. As soon as you type in the template name and press RETURN, DataEase will give you the Template form, as shown in Figure 12.12.

Here, if you wish, you can edit the template form to your liking. If you wanted to delete the salary and social security field from your report you could easily do so. The Report Definition is printed out and shown in Figure 12.13.

When you press **1 Run Report**, the report is run using the template. Figure 12.14 shows a screen dump of the first page of output. Remember that the fields and labels could easily be edited before the report is run.

As you can see, only the fields that are listed in the template are listed in the run. Templates are very useful for reports or forms that are recurring or periodical. If there are changes to the report or form letter, all you have to do is make a change to the template, which would be stored in a single database. If you had five different computer stores, you would only need one set of reports stored as templates for billings, mailing labels, form letters, etc.

```
Employees
No record on screen

   Employee #:                       Position:

   Last Name:                        First Name:

   Address:                          City:

   State:                            Zip:

   Date of Birth:    / /             Date Hired:     / /

   Phone #:  (    )-    -            Social Security Number:     - -

   Salary:

   Marital Status:



F2ENTER F3VIEW F4EXIT F5FORM CLR F6FLD CLR F7DELETE F8MODIFY F9REPORT F10MULTI
```

FIGURE 12.9

```
 1: columnar 2: field per line 3: export 4: special 5: Record Entry 6: Template

          Minimum line length for a columnar report is 186
          What type of report format do you want? : columnar



F9 FULL   F4 EXIT DATABASE A PROG.A: DATA B: DATE          TIME
```

FIGURE 12.10

```
Minimum line length for a columnar report is 186
What type of report format do you want? : Template
Name of the Template file : b:Tempbaaa




F9 FULL   F4 EXIT DATABASE A PROG.A: DATA B: DATE          TIME
```

FIGURE 12.11

```
                          R  1 C   1

First Name:                    Last Name:

Address:

City:                        State:      Zip:

Salary:

Security:




F2ENTER F3CUT F4EXIT F5COPY F6PASTE F7DEL LINE F8INS LINE F9PRINT F1ØFIELD
```

FIGURE 12.12

```
REPORT

------------------------------

       REPORT FORMAT
       -------------

1       10        20        30        40        50        60        70        80
----+----+----+----+----+----+----+----+----+----+----+----+----+----+----+----+

================================================================================

First Name: _______________    Last Name: _______________

Address: ____________________

City: ____________________    State: __    Zip: _____

Salary: __________

Security: __________
----+----+----+----+----+----+----+----+----+----+----+----+----+----+----+----+
1       10        20        30        40        50        60        70        80

        FIELD DESCRIPTIONS
        ------------------

No.  Name                     Type              Length  Remove
                                                        Spaces?
---  -----------------------  ----------------  ------  -------
  1  First Name               Text               15      No
  2  Last Name                Text               15      No
  3  Address                  Text               20      No
  4  City                     Text               20      No
  5  State                    Text                2      No
  6  Zip                      Numeric String      5      No
  7  Salary                   Number             10      No
      Number Type : Fixed point
      Digits to left of decimal = 7
  8  Social Security Numb     Numeric String     11      No

Memory required:
  Report Definition:        1117
```

FIGURE 12.13

```
                                   Running report
SPACE: Continue Report  EXIT: Abort Report

First Name: Vincent          Last Name: DeTrinis

Address: 11 Oxford Avenue

City: Massapequa           State: NY   Zip: 11758

Salary:  56,ØØØ.ØØ

Security: Ø35-66-5234

First Name: Joan             Last Name: DeTrinis

Address: 11 Oxford Avenue

City: Massapequa           State: NY   Zip: 11758

Salary: 45,ØØØ.ØØ

Security: Ø42-71-723Ø

First Name: Hank             Last Name: DiToro
      F4 EXIT    DATABASE A PROG.A: DATA B: DATE          TIME
```

FIGURE 12.14

Enhancing DataEase—Software Options

This chapter will examine some of the other products produced and sold by DataEase International, Inc. The DataEase Local Area Network (LAN) version will be discussed to show how it differs from a single user version. The DataEase Connect version will be described, showing how personal computers can access data that is stored on a mainframe or a minicomputer. The DataEase GrafTalk software package is also described. It allows users to generate pie, line, bar, and other types of charts from the DataEase ASCII files, regular ASCII files, or Lotus 1-2-3. The DataEase Developer and Runtime software packages are also covered. These enable consultants, Management Information System staff, and dealers to develop their own applications for distribution to more than one user.

DATAEASE LAN

A Local Area Network (LAN) is a way of sharing information among several users. If, as the owner of your simulated computer store, you decided to have a personal computer in each department linked together to share data, then you would use a LAN. The process of linking several personal computers together to share a database is an example of a LAN. Connecting several personal computers requires on-line communications between two or more of them. This linking of computers enables them to share not only software but hardware as well. Printers and hard disks can be shared by several users to reduce costs. If you link computers together, the data can be centrally located, but you have added problems of security, performance, and integrity. DataEase's database can be employed in a multi-user environment.

DataEase provides seven levels of security. With several people accessing the database with the same security levels, there is a need for more control over who can do what to the data in the system. This security must be finely tuned as to who can access certain fields, reports, forms, and databases. A single person who assumes responsibility for the security of the whole system should be appointed. This person has the title of database administrator. It is his/her responsibility to make sure that the system is being accessed by people with the proper security levels.

Performance suffers when several of the users access the information at the same time. This can happen during peak periods of data entry and report generation.

Integrity can be compromised if several people with the same security level access the same information simultaneously. Who is responsible if the data is lost or erroneously changed?

To have a LAN, you must have three things: software, hardware, and an arrangement of network hardware. The DataEase LAN manual covers each of these in depth. In hardware you must look at the individual workstations, communications media, and the computer that serves or stores the programs.

The arrangement of the hardware, or network arrangement, is the configuration of the personal computers in relation to one another. Different network arrangements with their separate advantages and disadvantages are discussed in the DataEase LAN manual.

The last item is the DataEase LAN software itself. Each individual personal computer possesses part of the DataEase operating system that enables it to operate separately or as part of the multi-user environment. DataEase LAN allows several users to share the same database. Problems can arise when two or more users want to update the same piece of data. The database administrator can decide who has a higher priority through the use of security levels and the locking feature of DataEase's LAN.

DataEase LAN has different user levels: the casual or everyday user, the database administrator, and the expert user.

The casual or everyday user does not know or care about the intricacies of a local area network. In terms of networking, they have to know how to log on, what to do if the system breaks down, or how to interpret DataEase LAN error messages. In logging on, the user must specify the network drive where DataEase data files reside. All drives and search paths can be established by the database administrator who sets each user of the LAN on the system. For example,

>**d:** followed by pressing the RETURN key

`>DEASE d:`

Where **d** is the drive where the data files reside.

In almost all cases, users should contact their database administrator if there is a problem that they don't understand. The menus of DataEase for a single or multi-use environment are basically the same to avoid confusion in learning a new system. Always refer any problems to the database administrator if you can't log on, if you lose power in the middle of an operation, or if you do not understand a LAN error message.

In the DataEase Maintenance Menu, there are two new selections that apply only to the database administrator. As a user you are to ignore them. They appear as:

```
5. Lock Database
6. Unlock Database
```

Locking a database prevents more than one user from accessing a piece of data to perform a transaction to update the database. Locking the database keeps all other users out—not just from accessing one piece of data but from accessing anything in the database. Only one user can update a record at one time. All the other users are locked out or prevented from accessing that piece of data. Several users can read the same record if there is no updating of data. The records that are being read are locked for shared access.

All data needed by a transaction is locked at the beginning of a transaction and turned off at the end of the transaction. This is to preserve the integrity of the database.

Records can be locked on an individual basis or the whole file can be locked when a single record is updated. This depends, in part, on the procedures set up by the database administrator. When a form or file definition is being changed, the whole file is locked automatically.

DataEase LAN can also import and export data and file formats from Lotus 1-2-3 and other popular software packages. The imported or exported data will appear as though they belonged to the DataEase database.

As you can see, there are many benefits in using a DataEase LAN. It is a shared database management system that can utilize file and record locking. The data can be available to all users of the database without jeopardizing the security of the whole database. All the data is kept current for all users and can be easily accessed by all users who have the proper security level. It has the same menus or interface that a single user has so he will not get confused or overwhelmed in using a shared system. This makes it easy for the user to adapt to a LAN.

DATAEASE CONNECT

DataEase LAN allows several single users to access a shared data management system through the use of personal computers. DataEase Connect allows the personal computer user to access an IBM mainframe or minicomputer for database information. This is done to utilize the efficiency of mainframe storage. All this is performed through the familiar menu system or interface of DataEase. All the user has to know is the data that he wishes to view or use. There is no need to worry about the operating system of the mainframe computer. DataEase can support the formats of DB2 and SQL/DS databases, IDMS, VSAM files, and ADABAS. DataEase handles all the security and transmission of data without the user caring how it is done. DataEase will handle all security, reporting, and query assignments that the personal computer will ask of the mainframe.

All the data stays in the original format of the mainframe. There is no import or export procedure required of the personal computer user. The user never needs to concern himself with the format of the data or the location of the data in the mainframe.

As you can see, there are many benefits in using DataEase Connect. All mainframe databases can be accessed as if they were local databases. The mainframe data can be accessed by using the simple menu system or interface of DataEase. There is no need to learn the complex operating system of a mainframe, although the database administrator must learn more. The user of a local database need not know or care about the way the data is stored in the mainframe. The importing of the data is done automatically without the need to worry about its format. All data in the system is kept current.

The user needs little help or special training with the sytem. The security of both the mainframe and the personal computers using the database are maintained.

The use of DataEase Connect allows personal computers to be connected to mainframes so that they appear to be one database application.

DATAEASE GRAFTALK

DataEase GraftTalk enables the user to generate charts without learning the intricacies of the computer system itself. It requires an IBM PC, PC/XT, PC/AT, or a 100% compatible computer with at least 256 RAM and at least two floppy disk drives. A hard disk is recommended. GrafTalk supports numerous plotters and printers. It possesses the same type of menu mode as DataEase. GrafTalk can generate pie, line, bar, step, symbol, high-low-close, bubble, smooth line, area, and fill-between charts.

GrafTalk can also take the data from DataEase ASCII files, Lotus 1-2-3, and ASCII formats to produce table charts, logarithmic charts, regression analysis, arithmetic and mathematical functions, text charts with multiple fonts, composite charts, custom designed charts, and has a slide show facility. Data can also be entered or changed right from the keyboard.

Text charts can be used to draw shapes and drawings to create organizational charts. Different types of charts can be placed on a single page.

The documentation is comprised of one manual with three sections. Just as in DataEase, there is a Help facility available at any place in the menu system.

The GrafTalk command language gives the user the availability to construct command files that can be stored and executed like a BASIC program. Multiple charts can be produced through the use of a batch processing mode. GrafTalk is a programmable graphics language that can be embedded in other applications to add graphics to label and explain reports. It can be used to design custom menus.

DATAEASE DEVELOPER

The DataEase Developer is a software package that enables the value-added reseller, consultants, dealers, and Management Information Systems staff of large corporations to develop and distribute applications to users. It simplifies the tasks of distribution, maintenance, and support.

The DataEase Developer contains a copy of DataEase LAN with a special main menu. It automatically creates a user manual. A standard manual is produced as you start creating your application. DataEase creates the user's and systems manual in a special file as the application is being created. Whenever the application is revised, the manuals are automatically revised. All changes in the application are kept in a single file so they can be included in the documentation. All the standard material that is included in any manual is included in the DataEase manual. You can change the standard manual or include your own documentation or changes in any section that you wish.

When you wish to print the documents, there is a documentation function that creates a user's guide or a systems guide. The User Guide includes the cover sheets, table of contents, introduction, a getting started section, chapters organized according to the User Menus, and an index. The User Guide is the result of the merger of three files: an application definition file which is user specific, a DataEase Developer file which contains all the standard documentation, and a file created by the application developer or the user that contains additions or deletions to the standard document. The resulting document may be edited by a word processor and typeset by one of many typesetting programs.

The System Guide consists of the database dictionary, all the form definitions, all dictionary cross-references, all lookup cross-references, all relationships, all report definitions, all cross-references of reports and forms, all import definitions, and all menus.

The DataEase Developer can create a self-running demo of your application that can demonstrate your demo from beginning to end, one screen at a time, or one keystroke at a time. You can also create help or explanation screens which could be useful for in-house training or salespersons in computer stores. This Slide-Show Demonstration Facility will let you create a mini "slide show" demonstration of the application.

If the potential user likes the demo but would like to test drive the program, you can create a test-drive demo that contains a test-drive installation disk with a test-drive version of DataEase. This test-drive disk would only be used for a limited number of records and for a limited time period. It is discussed below as DataEase Runtime. It is not part of the Developer's package.

The Developer will also create an installation disk where all the user has to do is make a choice from the DataEase menu. The application program will instantly be run.

The Developer will encrypt some or all of your forms or reports so that you can protect the time put into your investment. The user needs the applications disk to run these forms and reports. The user can create and modify his own forms and reports but can only use the forms and reports that are encrypted. This prevents the user from modifying the forms and reports without your knowledge.

The DataEase Developer will also assign a serial number to each application disk, which is clearly visible when the program is in use. This will help you keep track of legal and illegal copies.

Field definitions can easily be changed by making changes to the data dictionary. All possible fields that are likely to be changed are placed in this dictionary. All forms and reports that utilize this field will automatically be updated.

As DataEase is upgraded so too will all the applications programs that are generated by the DataEase Developer. All data, forms, reports, and relationships will be upgraded to the new version.

There will always be complete compatibility with other DataEase products such as GrafTalk, LAN, and Connect. Data can always be exchanged with Lotus 1-2-3 and other software packages.

DATAEASE RUNTIME

If you are making a turnkey system or one where the user will make no modifications, then a cheaper run-time version of DataEase can be included. The user cannot make any changes to the application or add anything to it. All the user can do is run your applications code. The user may define and run quick reports but may not save them. This run-time version can also include a limited number of records in an application. The version can be sent out to prospective users as a demonstration.

SUMMARY OF COMMANDS

DEFINITIONS

TERM	DEFINITION
FIELD	Data name where information is entered. For example, First Name, Last Name, Age.
FORM	A set of fields where data is entered.
RECORDS	Forms that have data filled in them.
FILES	A group of forms.
RELATIONSHIPS	Fields that relate different files.
REPORTS	Information that is organized, sorted, or summarized.
DATABASE	A group of files.
EXPORT	Data transferred from DataEase to other programs
IMPORT	Data transferred from other programs into DataEase.
MENUS	Choices that organize an application.

FIGURE 14.1

DEFINE FUNCTIONS KEYS USED IN EDITING

KEY NAME	USE IN EDITING
F2 ENTER	Save Form and Exit.
F3 CUT	Cut a Block of Text.
F4 EXIT	Cancel the Form and Exit.
F5 COPY	Copy a Block of Text.
F6 PASTE	Paste a Block of Text.
F7 DELETE	Delete a Line of Text.
F8 INSERT	Insert a Line of Text.
F9 REPORT	Print the Report Definition.
F1Ø DEFINE	Define a Field.

FIGURE 14.2

FUNCTION KEYS USED IN RECORD ENTRY

KEY NAME	USE IN RECORD ENTRY
F1 MORE	Scroll Menus.
ALT-F1	Gives help on current entry.
ALT-F3 CONTINUE VIEW	Continue view of records.
ALT-F5 UNCHECKED	Unchecked data-entry mode.
F2 ENTER	Saves the data that is entered.
F3 VIEW	Views the records.
F4 EXIT	Exits the data-entry.
F5 FORM CLEAR	Clears all fields on the form.
F6 FIELD CLEAR	Clears the field the cursor is on.
F7 DELETE	Deletes the record on the screen.
F8 MODIFY	Modify the record on screen. NOTE: If there was a deleted record on the screen, it will un-delete that record.
F9 REPORT	Quick Report Menu.
F10 MULTI	Goes to a related file.
SHIFT-F2 ENTER DEFAULT	Enters a default record.
SHIFT-F3 VIEW PREVIOUS	Views the previous record.
SHIFT-F5 DEFAULT FORM	Get default for form.
SHIFT-F6 DEFAULT FIELD	Get default for field.
SHIFT-F7 DELETE DEFAULT	Delete default record.
SHIFT-F9 PRINT	Print the record.

FIGURE 14.3

CURSOR AND EDITING KEYS IN FORM EDITING

KEY NAME	USE IN FORM EDITING
↑ UP	Go to Previous Line
↓ DOWN	Go to Next Line
← LEFT	Go to Previous Cursor
→ RIGHT	Go to Next Character
Home	Go to Top of Form
End	Go to Bottom of Form
PgUp PREVIOUS PAGE	Go to Top of Page
PgDn NEXT PAGE	Go to Bottom of Page
← BACKSPACE	Delete Previous Character
↵ RETURN	Go to Next Line
→ TAB	Go to Next Tab
← BACKTAB	Go to Previous Tab
CTRL- ← START OF LINE	Go to Start of Line
CTRL- → END OF LINE	Go to End of Line
Ins INSERT	Insert Mode On/Off
Del DELETE	Delete Character Cursor is on

FIGURE 14.4

CURSOR AND EDITING KEYS IN RECORD EDITING

KEY NAME		USE IN FORM EDITING
↑	UP	Go to Field Above
↓	DOWN	Go to Field Below
←	LEFT	Go to Previous Cursor
→	RIGHT	Go to Next Character
Home		Go to First Field in Form
End		Go to Last Field in Form
PgUp	PREVIOUS PAGE	Go to First Field on Page
PgDn	NEXT PAGE	Go to First Field on Next Page
←	BACKSPACE	Delete Previous Character
↵	RETURN	Go to Next Field
→	TAB	Go to Next Field
←	BACKTAB	Go to Previous Field
Ins	INSERT	Insert Mode On/Off
Del	DELETE	Delete Character Cursor is on

FIGURE 14.5

FORMS DEFINITION

KEY NAME	USE
UP, DOWN, LEFT RIGHT, HOME, END PREV PAGE, NEXT PAGE RETURN, TAB	Move Cursor
F2 ENTER	Save the Form
F3 CUT	Delete block of text
F4 EXIT	Cancel the Form
F5 COPY	
1: Copy block	Copy block of text
2: Copy Form	Copy selected forms
3: Copy Dictionary Form	Copy Dictionary Form
F6 PASTE	Insert Text
F7 DELETE LINE	Edit Text
F8 INSERT LINE, DEL, INS	Edit Text
F1Ø FIELD	Define a Field

FIGURE 14.6

FIELD TYPES

FIELD TYPES	LIMITATIONS
Text	All characters allowed up to 255 characters long
Numeric String	No Calculations Involved
Unformatted	255 Digits
Soc. Sec. No.	111-11-1111
Phone No.	(111)-111-1111
Formatted	4Ø Characters
Number	14 Digits Accuracy
Integers	Commas Automatically Inserted
Fixed Point/Dollar	Commas Automatically Inserted
Floating Point	--
Date	Ø1/Ø1/ØØ to 12/31/99
Time	ØØ:Ø0:ØØ to 23:59:59
Choice	99 Choices up to 6Ø characters each
Yes or No	--

SEQUENCED FIELDS

FIELD TYPE	EXAMPLE
Numeric String	Sequence from ØØØØØ1
Text	Sequence from "BB-ØØ1"

FIGURE 14.7

CHOICE	NAME	USE IF FUNCTION NAME IS ENTERED	USE IF NO FUNCTION NAME IS ENTERED
1	MAIN MENU	Calls DataEase Main Menu (Function Name is ignored).	Same
2	User Menu	Calls the user menu listed here	Invalid
3	Record Entry	Lets the user enter, change, or view data in the form listed here	Invalid
4	Query	Displays the report menu and the user to view or run any report, but NOT modify; also, lets the user create and run a new report but not save it. (Function name is ignored).	Same
5	Run Report	Runs the report listed here.	Displays the report menu & allows the user to view or run any report, but NOT modify; also, run a report but not save it (Same as Query)
6	Status	Displays status of the database (Function name is ignored).	Same
7	Backup	Backups the database (Function name is ignored).	Same
8	Restore	Restores the database (Function name is ignored).	Same
9	Utilities	Displays Utilities menu (Function name is ignored).	Same
1Ø	Import	Runs the Import listed here (Function name is ignored).	Allows the user to define & run a 1-time import.
11	Program Call	Calls the DOS program	Allows the user to enter a DOS program call.
12	Form Reorg.	Reorganizes form listed here.	Invalid

FIGURE 14.8

RECORD ENTRY

FUNCTION	PROCEDURE
Entering Data Into Field	Type in information. Press RETURN to go to next field if field is not filled.
Choice	Type the choice number or the first few characters of choice.
Date/Time	Type in the digits and not the "/". Leading zeros automatically entered.
Numeric String	Type in the digits without leading zeroes.
Number	Minus sign, if needed, is typed before number.
Integer	Type the digits.
Fixed Point/Dollar	Type digits to the left of the decimal point with decimal point and digits to the right of the decimal point, if needed.
Floating Point	Type the digits with decimal point, if needed.
Fill Field With Default Value	Press RETURN on blank field.
Move Cursor	UP, DOWN, LEFT, RIGHT Arrows; HOME, END, PREV PAGE, NEXT PAGE RETURN, TAB Keys
Edit the Field	BACKSPACE, INS, DEL, F6 FIELD CLEAR F5 FORM CLEAR Keys
Enter New Record	Press F2 ENTER key.
View Records	
View First Record	Press F5 FORM CLEAR, then F3 VIEW.
View Last Record	Press F5 FORM CLEAR, then SHIFT-F3.
View Next Record	Press F3 VIEW.
View Previous Record	Press SHIFT-F3.
Modify Record	Press F8 MODIFY.
Delete Record	Press F7 DELETE and answer Y for YES.
Go to Related File	Press F10 MULTI. Select file to view.
Produce Reports	Press F9 REPORTS for QUICK REPORTS.
Enter Default Record	Press F5 FORM CLEAR. Fill default values. Press SHIFT F2.
Get Defaults for Field	Press SHIFT F6.
Get Defaults for Form	Press SHIFT F5.

FIGURE 14.9

QUICK REPORTS

Record Selection

Operator	Meaning
=	is equal to
>	is greater than
<	is less than
>=	is greater than or equal to
<=	is less than or equal to
between...to...	Between and including the two values
not	opposite of what follows

Defining List Fields

Operation	Meaning
Group	Group by Field
Mean	Average
Min	Find lowest or minimum value
Max	Find highest or maximum value
Order	Sorting in Ascending Order
Reverse	Sorting in Descending Order
Std.Dev.	Standard Deviation
Std.Err.	Standard Error
Sum	Sum or Total of Values

Defining Report Format

Format	Use
Columnar	Row and Column Reports.
Field Per Line	Prints one field per line.
Record Entry	Same as the Record Entry Form.
Template	Report in Predefined Template Format.
Export	Export to other programs.
Lotus 1-2-3	Export to Lotus 1-2-3 in WKS format.
ASCII Fixed Length	Export to Main-Frame Computers.
ASCII Variable Length	General Export Format.
Mail-Merge	Export to Mail-Merge program.
Multimate	Export to Multimate word processor.
DIF	Export to spreadsheet and graphics programs.

FIGURE 14.10

FUNCTIONS

Function	Parameter	Description
DATE		
Month	Date	Month of the Year: 1..12
Day	Date	Day of the Month: 1..31
Year	Date	Year: 1..99
Weekday	Date	Day of the week: 1..7
Yearday	Date	Day of the year: 1..366
Yearweek	Date	Week of year: 1..52
TIME		
hour	Time	Hour of the day: Ø..23
minutes	Time	Minute of the hour: Ø..59
seconds	Time	Seconds: Ø..59
ampm	Time	Text value AM or PM
timeampm	Time	Time with AM/PM, e.g. 1:23:45 PM
SPELL		
spellmonth	month	Spelled out Month: January.. December
spellweekday	day of week	Spelled out day: Monday.. Sunday
spelldate	date	Spelled date: e.g. March 29, 1987
spellnumber	number<999 trillion	Spell out number: e.g. Three Thousand One Hundred and Fifty
spellcurrency	amount<999 trillion	Spell out amount: e.g. Three Hundred and Fifty Dollars and Forty Five Cents
TEXT		
firstc	Text, # of Characters	First few characters of text
lastc	Text, # of Characters	last few characters of text
midc	Text Starting Character # of characters	Characters from the middle of text
firstw	Text No. of words	First few words of text
lastw	Text No. of words	Last few words of text
midw	Text Starting Word No. of Words	Words in the middle of text
jointext	Text, Text	Join two texts together
length	Text	Length of the text
LastFirst	Name: First Last	Place the last name first
FirstLast	Name: Last First	Place the last name first

FIGURE 14.11

```
                          FUNCTIONS

Function         Parameter            Description
--------------------------------------------------------------
FINANCIAL
==============================================================
PresentValue     Future Value,        Calculate present value
                 Installment,
                 Rate, Periods
FutureValue      Present Value,       Calculate future value
                 Installment,
                 Rate, Periods
Installment      Present Value,       Calculate installment
                 Future Value,
                 Rate, Periods
Rate             Present Value,       Calculate Rate of Return
                 Future Value
                 Installment, Periods
Periods          Present Value,       Calculate term of loan
                 Future Value,
                 Installment, Rate

SCIENTIFIC
==============================================================
exp              Number               e**Number
log              Number               Logarithm of the number
                                      with base e
log10            Number               Logarithm of the number
                                      with base 10
power            Number1, Number2     Number1**Number2
sqrt             Number               Square root of the number
abs              Number               Absolute value of the
                                      number
ceil             Number               Smallest integer larger
                                      than the number
floor            Number               Largest integer smaller
                                      than the number
mod              Number, Base         Remainder when the Number
                         Number       is divided by the Base
                                      Number
random                                generates a random number
sin              Angle in Radians     Sine of the Angle
cos              Angle in Radians     Cosine of the Angle
tan              Angle in Radians     Tangent of the Angle
asin             Sine Value           Angle in Radians
acos             Cosine Value         Angle in Radians
atan             Tangent Value        Angle in Radians
sinh             argument             Hyperbolic sine
cosh             argument             Hyperbolic cosine
tanh             argument             Hyperbolic tangent
```

FIGURE 14.12

GLOSSARY

.end the DataEase report formatting command which determines the endpoint for items when printing.

.footer the DataEase report formatting command that causes information to be printed at the bottom of each page.

.group header the DataEase report formatting command used to indicate, at the beginning of each group, data common to all items in the group.

.group trailer the DataEase report formatting command that causes additional information to print below the last item in a group. The Group Trailer may contain summary information, a list of values common to the group, or merely be a way to end each group in a distinctive manner.

.header the DataEase report formatting command that causes information to print at the top of a page; only one header may appear per report. Any text following this command will print on each page.

.items the DataEase report formatting command which determines where the field values for each record will begin printing.

.page the DataEase report formatting command that causes data to print on a new page.

ASCII American Standard Code for Information Exchange. The standard code for representing characters in your computer.

Abbreviated Field Definition a brief description of the characteristics that have been defined for a field. This description will appear on the prompt line during Field Definition, if you place the cursor on the chosen field and press the SPACEBAR.

Ad-Hoc Relationship a relationship defined as part of a report query, valid only for that query.

all in DQL, the relationship operator which finds every related record that matches the selection criteria. This operator is used to list fields from these related records.

All Fields Transfer transferring every record in a file (in sequential order) during a DataEase Import.

and in DQL, the logical operator indicating that both of two conditions must be met to satisfy the criteria.

any in DQL, the relational operator which finds a single related record that matches the criteria in a related file. This operator is used in many-to-one or referenced relationships. If there is more than one matching record, there is no predicting which one will be selected.

Arithmetic Operators the four symbols used in calculation formulas to indicate the different arithmetic operations: + for addition; – for subtraction; * for multiplication; / for division.

Ascending Order in order from the lowest value to the highest. In DQL, the phrase "in order" means in ascending order.

Backup a DataEase copy of all files in an entire database, which can be used to recreate a database in case the original is damaged or accidentally altered. A backup is used to reorganize the database files for greater efficiency when a large number of record modifications or deletions have been performed.

Backup Database with this option, on the Database Maintenance Menu, you can make a backup copy of your database on floppy diskettes, or to another hard disk.

Backup Error any error which may occur due to inconsistencies in your DOS files or your database while you are backing up your database.

Batch Update using DQL to modify a number of records in a file.

between in DQL, the comparison operator indicating all values within a specified upper and lower limit, inclusive.

Blank Field a field without a value, as distinguished from a field with a value of zero.

Calculated Field a field whose value is derived by an arithmetic calculation using other fields.

Cancel/Exit in DataEase, to abort the current function and return to the previous menu; press the F4 EXIT key.

Chain Menu a user-defined menu which links a number of functions in such a way that a single selection will perform them all.

Character any letter, number, symbol, punctuation mark, or blank space.

Characters Per Inch a specification to the printer of the type pitch for a report. The default value is 10; for condensed type, the figure is higher.

Choice the field type which specifies that the field value must be one of a number of user-defined "multiple choice" answers. You can define up to ninety-nine multiple choice answers, each with a length up to sixty characters.

Clear Field to remove the characters in the field where the cursor rests in order to enter new characters; for this function, press the F6 FIELD CLEAR key.

Columnar Format a standard report format, showing data arranged in rows and columns.

Command a report formatting instruction that begins with a **.** as **.end**, **.footer**, **.group header**, **.group trailer**, **. header**, **.items**, **.page**.

Condition in DQL, a record selection criterion.

Condition Statistics in DQL, the values used to report which records in a file have satisfied a condition, what percentage of the records in the file, and how many.

Constant a fixed value.

Count in DQL, the condition statistic that gives the total number of records that satisfy a condition.
Count of in DQL, a relational operator that gives the total number of related records that satisfy the relationship criteria.

Country Customization the second page of the Define Configuration option on the System Administration Menu. Use this option to indicate date and currency formats.

Current Date today's date as recorded by your computer.

Current Time the correct time as recorded by your computer.

Cursor Position Indicator the combination of letters and numbers in the upper middle of the screen that reports at all times the position of the cursor during form and record layout. For example, R5 C6 reports that the cursor is in Row 5 and Column 6 on the screen.

DIF Format Date Interchange Format. One of the standard formats in which DataEase will accept data from another program in a DataEase Import, or send data to another program in a DataEase Export.

DOS Format Command the DOS command used to prepare program and data disks for use on your personal computer.

Data Import Facility an option on the Utilities Menu. Choose it when you want to transfer data from another program to DataEase.

Data Entry Fields those fields in a record where data may be entered.

Data Entry Form in DataEase, the optional form which can be used to enter information when the report is run. Can be used as the transaction input form, when the report is a transaction.

Data Base Maintenance one of the options on the DataEase Main Menu. It is used to backup, restore, display or print information about a database. It can also perform DOS functions.

DataEase Query Language (DQL) the English-like language used to ask DataEase for the precise combination of information you may need from your database.

Database a collection of related files.

Database Name the unique, one-character name (chosen from the twenty-six letters of the alphabet) used to distinguish one database from another.

Database Status this option, from the Date Base Maintenance Menu, gives you a summary of the information about your database.

Data Base Utilities one of the seven Primary Functions on the DataEase Main Menu. Use it to import data, install forms and reports, transfer data, or remove a database.

Date the field type which specifies that the field value must be a date in the form mm/dd/yy.

Date Calculation determining the resulting date when adding a number of days to a date, or the number of days when one date is subtracted from the other.

Date Functions a set of functions for manipulating date fields.

Default Record a record containing default values which you set for selected fields; to fill selected fields in a record with default values, press the SHIFT and FORM CLEAR keys; to fill a single field with a default value, press the SHIFT and FIELD CLEAR keys.

Default Value a value automatically supplied by DataEase.

Define a Form lets you design a record entry form and determine the characteristics of the data to be entered in its fields.

Defined Import an Import you may want to run more than once.

Defined Report a report you may want to run more than once.

Derived Field a field whose value is determined by a formula. DataEase has four kinds of derived fields: calculated, lookup, sequenced, and default.

Descending Order in order from the highest to the lowest. In DQL, "in reverse" means in descending order.

Destination Form Name the name of the DataEase Record Entry Form to which data will be imported from another program.

Dollar the field type which specifies that the field value must be in dollars and cents. Dollar fields may also be defined as fixed point number fields. DataEase automatically places commas and decimals in the right positions.

Duplicate Record a record whose unique fields match that of an existing record in the file.

Edit Mode the mode in which you write or edit the query without the interactive menus. It is used in editing the query. To enter the edit mode move the cursor to the left in the interactive mode.

Export Data the predefined report formats that report the data selected in the report into a form compatible with other programs, such as Lotus 1-2-3, Multimate, Wordstar, DIF, or ASCII.

Field Characteristics the attributes of the data that will be stored in a field, defined during Field Definition.

Field Definition While in the Form Definition option, press the F10 FIELD key. Type in the characteristics of the field that you just created.

Field Format the field characteristics, including an indication of whether to retain or remove leading and trailing spaces.

Field Name the unique name you give a field. The field name must begin with a letter, and may be up to twenty characters long.

Field Position where a field appears on the screen, indicated by row and column.

Field Separator a character that you select during Variable Length ASCII Import specification, to separate the fields in the import file.

Field Size the maximum number of characters that can fit in a given field.

Field Type the kind of data a field may contain. The eight types of fields are: Text, Numeric String, Number, Date, Dollar, Yes or No, and Choice.

Field Value the data in a field.

Field the smallest complete unit of information in a database. A record is made up of fields. A file is made up of records. A database is made up of files.

Field-Per-Line Format the report format which specifies that each field print on a separate line.

File a collection of records.

Fixed Length Format an Import or Export file format in which each field and each record occupies a fixed number of bytes.

Fixed Point Field a number field type with a constant number of digits after the decimal point.

Floating Point Field a number field type with a variable number of digits after the decimal point.

Foreground and Background colors the colors used for characters (foreground) and the screen (background) on a color monitor. The Screen Styles form is accessed from the System Administration.

Form where information is entered into. A Record Entry form is used to enter records in a file which is defined using the Form Definition Menu.

Form Name unique name for a form definition which can have a maximum of twenty characters.

Formatted Numeric String a Numeric string that contains formatting characters to facilitate data entry such as phone numbers and social security numbers.

Full Reports a way of producing comprehensive reports in DataEase. It requires more learning than Quick Reports but allows any kind of report or transaction to be defined. It can be accessed from the DataEase Main Menu and by pressing the F9 FULL key from the Quick Reports Menu.

Function Keys the two columns of keys on the left-hand side of the keyboard labelled F1 through F10.

Function a built-in data manipulation operation. Examples include date, time, text, name, financial, exponential, power, and trigonometric.

group in Quick Reports when Defining List Fields, the word used in a list field to indicate that records should be grouped by the field.

Group Header a report format area that specifies what will appear at the beginning of each group.

Group Trailer a report format area that specifies what will appear at the end of each group.

Grouping arranging data in a report so that records that have the same List field value are grouped together.

High Level Query this option allows use of some advanced features in the query.

High Security Level the security level with the greatest amount of authority to make changes to the database such as assign users, passwords, and security levels to other users.

Highest of the relationship summary operator that selects the highest value of a field across a set of related records from a related file.

Import Format the layout of the data in an external file that is to be imported into a DataEase file.

Import Menu menu to import data from other files.

Import Name the name of the Import specification that specifies how data will be imported into DataEase. The name can be up to eight characters.

Import Specification File file created by DataEase when an Import specification is defined.

in the report query word that precedes the name of a file into which a report will enter records.

in groups in DQL, the phrase that tells DataEase to group a report by the field that it follows.

in groups with group totals in DQL, the phrase that tells DataEase to group report output according to the field that it follows, and to provide summary statistics by group.

in order in DQL, to sort in ascending order, from the lowest value to the highest.

in reverse in DQL, to sort in descending order, from the highest value to the lowest.

Indexed Field field characteristic that significantly improves the speed of sorting, selecting, or relationship matching against the field.

Insert Mode mode that adds characters to text. Press INS key and notice the INSERT indicator in the middle of the top of the screen.

Install adding an external DataEase form or report to the current database.

Integer Field a number field type that can contain only whole numbers.

Interactive Mode mode in which DataEase will assist the user in the definition or modification of a Report Query. Acceptable words or phrases are displayed on the choice selection line when in this mode. To enter this mode press F1 INTERACTIVE.

Item in DQL, the word that indicates that in addition to statistics on a field, the field value itself should be included in the report.

Leading and Trailing Spaces you can specify that DataEase suppress printing of leading and trailing spaces on a text field. This is especially useful to accommodate varying length of addressees' names, when preparing form letters.

Level the Function Key (F9) moves you between the Low Level and the High Level in the Interactive Mode of Report Query Definition.

List Records in DQL, the phrase that instructs DataEase to print the contents of records from a file in a report.

Lookup Field a field whose value is DERIVED by looking for the value on a matching record in a related file.

Lowest of in DQL, the Relationship Operator that instructs DataEase to use the lowest value of the set of all values of the matching field across all records in the related file.

Mail-Merge an Export format that produces a file compatible with the Mail-Merge facility in the Wordstar program and other programs using that same format.

Max the summary statistic that instructs DataEase to print the highest value for a particular field across all the records selected for the report.

Mean the summary statistic that instructs DataEase to print the arithmetic mean for a particular field across all the records selected for the report.

Menu Name the name assigned to a custom menu in DataEase. It is the name by which DataEase knows the menu and is not the name that appears on the screen.

Menus and Relationships used to define a new menu or change an existing one, to define a new relationship, use or change an existing one.

Message Area the area on the upper right-hand side of the screen that displays system status messages.

Modify Field the routine that allows you to change the field name or characteristics for a previously defined field. It is accessed by pressing the F8 MODIFY key.

Modify Records in DQL, the Report Query phrase that instructs DataEase in the course of a report to change the values of fields in the selected records of a file or all the values of a file if there is no selection.

Multi-Page Form a Form Definition that extends over more than one screen. It can consist of a maximum of sixteen screens.

Nested Condition a record selection that contains multiple conditions and contains both **and** and **or** as connecting operators. The use of parentheses is required to make things clearer.

Next Record the record following the current record in the order the records are stored.

not in DQL, the comparison operator which can be used to reverse the meaning of any of the other operators.

Number the field type which specifies that the field value must be a quantity. There are three kinds of numbered fields: integer, fixed point, and floating point. Number fields can be used in calculations.

Numeric String the field type which specifies that the field value is a sequence of digits. Numeric strings may be formatted or non-formatted. Sample numeric strings are phone numbers and social security numbers.

or in DQL, the operator indicating that either of two conditions must be met to satisfy the test criteria.

order in Quick Reports when Defining List fields, the word used in a list field to indicate that records should be ordered by the field.

Page Footer information that prints at the bottom of each page of a report.

Page Header information that prints at the top of a report page.

Password the unique password assigned to each user. The password is required by the Sign-On Screen for each user granted access to database. It may be up to eight characters long.

Print Key the PRINT function key that prints a copy of a record in the Record Entry option, the structure of a form in the Form Definition Screen, or the report definition in the report format option.

Print Style Form the Print Style Specification screen that contains the print device control instructions.

Prompt Line the second line from the top on the DataEase screen used to display single-line menus, provide in-progress status, and ask questions requiring a yes/no response.

Query an English-like sentence in the DataEase Query Language (DQL), requesting any of the following operations: collect data, select records, list fields, perform calculations and statistical operations, sort and group data to any number of levels.

Quick Reports a way of producing reports by using a query-by-example method which requires little training or effort.

Record a group of fields containing related information.

Referenced Relationship a many-to-one relationship. For example, if all records in File C are related to a single record in File A.

Related File the other file from which records will be selected when a relationship is used. The first file is the primary file.

Relationship a relationship exists between two files when records in one file are related to the records in the other file. The relationship is based on the value of a field in one exactly matching the value of a field in the other. The match field is known as the linking field.

Relationship Form the screen on which the linking fields that define the relationship between two files are specified.

Report Query the sentence or sentences written in DataEase Query Language that tells DataEase what data is to be generated in the report or how the data in the database is to be manipulated.

Required Field a field that must have a value placed in this field during Record Entry for the record to be entered into the file.

Required Field Check scan of record on the screen for blank required fields.

Restore Utility allows a backup database to be made current, compresses a database by removing records marked for deletion, and restores destroyed databases to usable status.

Reverse the word used in a list field to indicate that records should be sorted in reverse order by the field.

Screen Style Form used to customize screen display for an IBM machine only.

Security Level indication of a user's ability to access DataEase functions. There are seven different security levels.

Selection Criteria one or more user-specified conditions which records must satisfy in order to be included in the desired subset.

Selection Fields a field used as a Selection Criterion in a DataEase Report Query or Quick Report.

Sequenced Field a derived field that increments the field value by one each time a record is entered into the file. Only Text and Numeric String fields may be derived using sequencing.

Statistical Function in DQL, the phrase that indicates that a database function should be generated across the records selected for the report for a particular field. The Statistical Functions that are available are: item (prints each field value), sum (sums the values), mean (calculates the average of values), max (determines the highest value), min (determines the lowest value), variance (calculates the statistical variance of the values), std. dev. (calculates the standard deviation of the values), and std. err. (calculates the standard error of the values).

Status Line the bottom line of the DataEase screen. This line indicates the database name, the program drive, the data drive, the current date, the current time, and the assignment keys for the current function.

Sum see Statistical Function.

Sum of the Relationship Summary Operator that calculates the sum of the values found in a field in a related file.

Title Line the second line from the top of the DataEase screen. This line indicates at all times the name of the function you are performing, and the position of the cursor on the screen.

Transfer Data copy data from one DataEase file to another.

Unformatted Number String a numeric string that has no fixed format.

Unique Field a field whose value should not appear in any record in a file. For example, social security number.

User Menu a custom-designed menu that replaces or supplements the regular DataEase menus.

User Name the unique name assigned to each user of the system. It may be up to fifteen characters long.

Value the data in a field.

Variable Length Format Report Format that facilitates the export of data from a report to mainframe databases.

View to display the next record in sequential order. Press the F3 VIEW key.

Wildcard Character either of two special characters (* and ?) that may be used in searches based on partial match criteria.

Work Area the main area of the screen where your current work is displayed.

Yes or No the field type which specifies that the field value must be either "Yes" or "No."

INDEX